THE USAF AT WAR

Other books by the same author:

B-24 Liberator, 1939–45
Castles in the Air
Classic Fighter Aircraft
Eighth Air Force at War
Famous Bomber Aircraft
Fields of Little America
Flying to Glory
Four Miles High
Great American Air Battles of World War Two
Home By Christmas?
Modern Military Aircraft
Spirits in the Sky (with Patrick Bunce)
The Bedford Triangle
The Encyclopedia of American Military
   Aircraft
The World's Fastest Aircraft
Thunder in the Heavens (with Patrick Bunce)
Wellington: The Geodetic Giant
The Men Who Flew the Mosquito
Low Level from Swanton

As part of our ongoing market research, we are always pleased to receive comments about our books, suggestions for new titles, or requests for catalogues. Please write to: The Editorial Director, Patrick Stephens Limited, Sparkford, Near Yeovil, Somerset, BA22 7JJ.

THE USAF AT WAR

From Pearl Harbor to the present day

Martin W Bowman

Patrick Stephens Limited

First published in 1995

British Cataloguing-in-Publication Data:
A catalogue record for this book is available
from the British Library

ISBN 1 85260 487 5

Library of Congress catalog card no. 95-78122

Patrick Stephens Limited is an imprint of
Haynes Publishing, Sparkford,
Nr Yeovil, Somerset BA22 7JJ

Typeset by G&M,
Raunds, Northamptonshire
Printed and bound in Great Britain by
Butler & Tanner Ltd, London and Frome

Contents

Acknowledgements

I would like to thank the following for their valuable contributions of time and energy and for providing me with much sought-after information, photos and encouragement: Steve Adams; Mike Bailey; the late Roy W. Baker; Col William R. Cameron, USAF (Retd); SrA Stuart J. Camp USAF; George M. Collar; Philip G. Day; Forrest T. Clark; Capt Ray D. Cornelius III, Director, PIO, Rhein-Main; D. L. Dick, Media Relations, RAF Mildenhall; Jack Dupont; Maj Don Eaton, WOC Mombasa Public Affairs; Patricia Everson; John W. Fields; Kenneth Fields; Harry Gann, McDonnell Douglas; Joe Gualano; Larry Goldstein; Ed Grotfelty; Steven Jefferson; Jack Kings; Joseph Z. Krajewski; Lois Lovisolo, Grumman Corporation; Will Lundy; Ped G. Magness; Ian McLachlan; John W. McClane; Robert T. Marshall; Gus Mencow; Robert L. Miller; Sqdn Ldr Hugh Milroy, RAF; Col William C. Odell USAF (Retd); Stephen A. Oliphant; YN1 'Chuck' C. Perkins, USN; Norman Pickstone; Bill Rose; George Stebbings; Max Stout; John L. Susan; Robert H. Tays; SrA Christopher C. Thomas, USAF; Office of Public Affairs, 435th Airlift Wing; Col Paul Tibbets; Elmer Vogel; Truett Woodhall; T/Sgt Marion J. Woods, 100th ARW Historian, RAF Mildenhall.

Biographies on airmen lost in South-East Asia were kindly provided by Margaret Nevin and H. W. Hoffman of Homecoming II, and Ted Sampley; all of whom worked tirelessly at the *US Veteran News and Report* on behalf of Vietnam War MIAs. Thanks too go to Phyliss Dubois and her team at the 2nd Air Division Memorial Library in Norwich for help with books and volumes on USAAF and USAF history; and S/Sgt Philip L. Guerrero, Chief, Media Relations Division at RAF Lakenheath, USAF (Retd) for cheerfully providing me with information and transparencies and arranging interviews on the 'Fighting 48th'.

Glossary

AAA	anti-aircraft artillery	HARM	AGM-88 high speed anti-radiation missile
AAF	Army Air Force; also Army Air Field	HAS	hardened aircraft shelter
AB	Air Base (prior to 1948)	JTF	Joint Task Force
ACC	Air Combat Command	KIA	killed in action
AEW	airborne early warning	LANTIRN	low altitude navigation & targeting infrared for night
AF	Air Force		
AFB	Air Force Base (after 1948)	LGB	laser-guided bomb
AFRes	Air Force Reserve	MAC	Military Airlift Command
ALG	Airlift Group	MATS	Military Air Transport Service
ALS	Airlift Squadron	NVNAF	North Vietnam Air Force
ALW	Airlift Wing	Pave Tack	Ford Aerospace AVQ-26 infrared target acquisition and laser designating pod
AMC	Air Mobility Command		
ANG	Air National Guard		
APC	armoured personnel carrier	Paveway	laser-guided bomb
ARVN	Army of the Republic of Vietnam	Raven	EF-111A, an ECM aircraft/flyer in the *Steve Canyon* Programme in Vietnam
AWACS	airborne warning and control system		
		SAC	Strategic Air Command
BG	Bomb Group	SAM	surface-to-air missile
BW	Bomb Wing	SANDY	Douglas Skyraider
CENTCOM	HQ US Central Command	SAR	search and rescue
CIS	Confederation of Independent States	Shrike	AGM-45 radar-homing air-to-surface missile
Combat Talon	Special Operations MC-130E Hercules	Sidewinder	AIM-9 air-to-air missile
		SOS	Special Operations Squadron
Compass Call	C-130 command, control & communications countermeasures platform	SOW	Special Operations Wing
		Sparrow	AIM-7 radar-homing air-to-air missile
ECM	electronic counter-measures	Spectre	Lockheed AC-130 gunship
ETO	European theatre of operations	TDY	temporary duty
FAC	forward air control	TFR	terrain following radar
FIS	Fighter Interceptor Squadron	TFS	Tactical Fighter Squadron
FIW	Fighter Interceptor Wing	TFW	Tactical Fighter Wing
FLIR	forward looking infrared	TRW	Tactical Reconnaissance Wing

USAFE	United States Air Force Europe		missiles for operations against SAM sites
USMC	United States Marine Corps		
Wild Weasel	Tactical aircraft fitted with RHAW and anti-radiation	WSO	weapons systems officer (also known as wizzo)

Chapter One

Training for War

On 21 April 1940 Capt Robert M. Losey, Army Air Corps Weather Service officer, was the first American officer killed by enemy action in the service of the United States in WW2 when he was the victim of a German air raid on Norway where he was acting as a US military observer. Adventurers or soldiers of fortune—call them what you will—evaded America's strict 1939 neutrality laws and crossed to China to fly and fight in the war against Japanese invaders, and to Canada where they enlisted in the RCAF before venturing to Europe to fly in France and in the RAF. Between 13 April and 10 May 1940, 32 American pilots, helped by Col Charles Sweeny, arrived in France, where 26 years earlier American volunteer airmen had fought in the Lafayette Escadrille. Before the fall of France four had been killed, 11 taken prisoner, and five had escaped to England.

W. M. L. 'Billy' Fiske from Chicago, who had spent his student years at Cambridge and much of his young life in Europe before marrying famous English beauty, the former Countess of Warwick, returned to England from New York in 1937 and joined 601 (City of London) Squadron at Tangmere on 15 July 1940. Fiske was one of seven American pilots to fight in the Battle of Britain. On 17 August he became the first American volunteer pilot to lose his life defending Britain when he died of his wounds sustained on 16 August while landing his burning Hurricane at Tangmere during a Luftwaffe strafing attack.

By September 1940, quite a number of American volunteers had arrived in Britain to fight with the RAF, and these were put into 71 Squadron, known as the Eagle Squadron, at Church Fenton. After training on Miles Masters, their first aircraft were three Brewster Buffaloes but in November the Eagles received Hawker Hurricane Is. On 5 February 1941, 71 Squadron flew its first operation. Before its transfer to the USAAF, 71 Squadron suffered 34 American casualties. The second Eagle squadron, 121 Squadron, re-formed on 14 May 1941, and the third and final squadron, 133, formed at the end of July 1941. Altogether, 244 American pilots served in the Eagle squadrons. In 18 months of combat they destroyed over 70 aircraft. On 29 September 1942, Nos 71, 121 and 133 Squadrons were disbanded and incorporated into the USAAC at Debden as Nos 334, 335, and 336 (Pursuit) Squadrons respectively. Men like Don J. Blakeslee, Don Gentile, James A. Goodson, and Chesley G. Peterson—the first American to command the Eagles in combat—were to become even more famous in the 8th AF Fighter Command.

Americans also served in RAF Bomber Command. In 1939, Stephen A. Oliphant was in Canada when war broke out. Late in 1940, he headed toward San Diego, California via Vancouver, British Columbia, with the intention of joining the US Navy. In Calgary, Alberta, all his money was taken by a thief. Oliphant recalls:

That left me no place to go as I needed train fare to cross the mountains as it was too cold by this time to hit the rods [riding freight trains] without proper clothing. Managed to eke out a living over winter on one meal a day—the days of being young and tough. So come Spring of '41, I went to an RCAF recruiting office with the grand idea of applying for pilot training. Turned down cold; they wanted two years of college. I'll never figure out why I went back a month later and this time all they wanted was senior matriculation. Told them I had it; then went out on the street to do some questioning and find out what senior matriculation meant. Discovered it meant a high school graduate and that I wasn't, as I lacked four months of getting my diploma. Since I had nothing to lose I decided to bluff it. Sent back to Iowa for a transcript of my attendance and grades. Received them; took them to the recruiter who had so much trouble trying to interpolate from American to Canadian systems that he finally gave up and said, 'Oh Hell! You're in!' And I was.

Oliphant got his wings in February 1942. Four

Americans also served in RAF Bomber Command. Stephen A. Oliphant got his wings in February 1942 and on 13 October 1942 he went from Sgt Pilot RCAF to 2/Lt USAAF. (Stephen Oliphant)

other Americans were in his graduating class. Then he went on leave. 'While back home, the Alburnett, Iowa High School Board met and voted to give me my diploma. Their reasoning was that my pilot training more than compensated for the four months I have missed.' In England, he eventually ended up at No. 12 Advanced Flying Unit at Grantham: 'Sixty hours on Oxfords (found out later my group almost got in on the first 1,000-bomber raid on Germany).'

Sgt Harris B. Goldberg, born in Boston, had trained as an air gunner in the RCAF and in October 1941 had arrived in Scotland. He also missed the 30 May 1942 Cologne raid. However, he and his crew of a Wellington flew the 1/2 June *Millennium* raid on Essen, and 25/26 June raid on Bremen which was attacked by 1,006 RAF aircraft. Goldberg wrote:

That was bad. We lost 52 on that raid. Went in at 12,000 ft, got hit and damn near fell to pieces. Went down to 2,000 ft and sort of stumbled home at about 90 mph. Don't really know how we got home. All my crew were English. We used to have some pretty wild arguments about the States staying out of the war. After that night over Bremen, we argued but we never really got mad any more. Going through something like that brings you pretty close.

After flying 273 operational hours in the RAF, and surviving a crash in a 'Wimpy' in the Sinai desert in November 1942, Goldberg was transferred to the 8th AF. Oliphant, too, was destined for the USAAC. Just before he was due to be posted to Malta with a Wellington torpedo squadron, Oliphant used a three-day pass to go the Air Ministry in London and request a termination of RAF duty for the purpose of signing up with the USAAC. 'And talk about the Gods smiling! In less than two weeks I was long gone. Six other Americans in my squadron had been trying to effect a transfer ever since Pearl Harbor but were unsuccessful up to that point. So on 13 October 1942 it was Sgt-Pilot, RCAF to 2/Lieutenant, USAAF.'

Twenty-eight-year old James H. Howard, a Navy pilot who had been born in China, joined Col Claire L. Chennault's American Volunteer Group in China hoping to see combat. Chennault had been a captain in the Army Air Corps in 1937 when he resigned and went to China at the invitation of Madam Chiang Kai-shek to train Chinese airmen under the Nationalistic government of her husband Gen Chiang Kai-shek. Chennault had no sooner arrived when China was invaded by the Japanese. He returned to the United States in 1940 and obtained 100 outdated Curtiss P-40s, which were diverted from a consignment earmarked for Britain. In April 1941, President Roosevelt issued an executive order permitting American servicemen to resign their commissions, go to China to fight for a year, and then return and resume their rank and service in the AAC and US Navy. James Howard was one of 33 pilots in the first of 123 American volunteers in the AVG, which arrived in Rangoon in September 1941.

The American Volunteer Group was established at an RAF base at Kyedow airfield near Toungoo in Burma. Pilots would be paid salaries of $750 a month, plus $500 for every Japanese aircraft destroyed. On 10 December, the Burma campaign began, when 21 P-40s of an AVG squadron reinforced the RAF contingent at Rangoon. On 20 December, the AVG, or Flying Tigers as they became known, went into combat in their shark-nosed P-40s for the first time, shooting down nine bombers. On 23 December, the Japanese made a massive air assault on Rangoon and 16 AVG P-40s and 20 RAF Buffalo fighters went into action. Ten Japanese bombers were shot down but five Buffaloes and four P-40s were lost. After the fall of Rangoon the AVG retreated to China. Of the 318 AVG men originally recruited, 253 still remained on

A C-46 Commando comes into land at a Chinese airfield where a Curtiss P-40 Warhawk awaits the next mission. On 10 December 1941, the Burma campaign began, when 21 P-40s of an AVG squadron reinforced the RAF contingent at Rangoon. On 20 December, the AVG, or Flying Tigers as they became known, went into combat in their shark-nosed P-40s for the first time, shooting down nine bombers. (USAF)

Aviation Student (A/S) Day at College Training Detachment, West Texas State Teachers College, Canyon, Texas. First flight in single-engined, 65 hp, high-wing, tandem monoplanes. They would not solo but would be evaluated for further flight (pilot) training. (Philip G. Day)

the roster on 4 July 1942 when the Flying Tigers were incorporated into the 10th AF. Their score stood at 297 victories and 153 probables for the loss of only 10 P-40s. James Howard, who scored 6.5 kills, became a squadron commander in the new 9th AF in Europe. Chennault was promoted Brigadier General and assumed command of the new China Air Task Force, later the 14th AF.

Training airmen to fly was begun in earnest in the USA during 1941. With the expansion of the

Pilot Training Program for the AAF in late 1941, the primary training phase of flight instruction was placed with civilian-operated schools where all services and facilities, except the aircraft, were furnished by the operator but with AAF control of the methods and manner of instruction. Philip G. Day, Aviation Cadet, recalls:

There were as many as 40 of these schools scattered across the Southern United States, from California to Georgia. This method was first proposed by Gen Arnold, Chief of Staff, AAC, in 1939 when he called in operators of civilian flying schools and asked them to prepare to train 12,000 pilots per month. His plan was that the civilian schools, at a fixed amount per graduated primary pilot trainee, a lesser amount for a wash-out, would furnish the primary flight training phase of pilot training. There were an average of 600 potential pilots at each school for the required nine weeks of instruction, 300 in each the upper and lower classes of four and a half weeks each. The three primary trainers in use at the time were the Stearman PT-17, Fairchild PT-19 Cornell and the Ryan PT-22.

The Ryan was of all-metal, monocoque construction with open tandem cockpits. The wings and tail assembly were fabric covered, and it sat on fixed gear with very rugged struts. There were wire braces from upper wing to fuselage, and lower wing to wheel struts that vibrated and sang as you flew. You could estimate air speed by their hum. We learned later that those below the wing were 'flying wires'. They kept the wing from coming up in flight, and those above were 'landing wires' to keep the wing from dropping down while on the ground. The engine was a 160 hp Kinner R-540-1, five-cylinder, air-cooled radial, one cylinder directly in the centre of the line of vision with open pushrods that let lubricating oil escape into the slipstream, and onto us, causing dirty windscreens, goggles, helmets, and clothing. It had a fixed-pitch wooden propeller and would cruise at about 105 mph, was red-lined (do not exceed) at 180 mph and supposedly had a range of 250 miles or about two and a half hours' flying time.

I flew it on occasion to as high as 12,000 ft. Empty, it weighed only 1,000 lb; with fuel and two pilots, 1,600 lb. The wing span was just over 30 ft, and from prop spinner to rudder, 21 ft. Students flew from the rear cockpit whether solo or dual, the instructor in the front cockpit. The fuselage was natural metal finish with a large black ship number on each side. The wings and tail section were painted

Top Ryan PT-22, the type flown by cadet Philip Day and his contemporaries in Primary Training. The 160 hp Kinner R-540-1, five-cylinder, air-cooled radial had one cylinder directly in the centre of the line of vision with open pushrods that let lubricating oil escape into the slipstream, and onto the pilots. It had a fixed-pitch wooden propeller and would cruise at about 105 mph. (Author)

Above PT-17 Stearman primary trainer for the USAAF. (Author)

Below Fairchild PT-19 Cornell, one of three primary trainer types in use with the USAAF. (Author)

yellow. Some had 13 alternating red and white stripes on the rudder. It was not hard to fly, in fact was a lot of fun, a 'forgiving' airplane of our mistakes, bad landings and such.

We thought classification and pre-flight were tough. We now found out the meaning of the word. The second Big Day, we met our instructor and one by one were taken up for a 40-minute ride by Mr Miller, who did a few acrobatics (tried to make us air sick), were shown the limits of our authorized flying area and the two auxiliary fields we would practice from, and then a very little time of instruction. Accidents happened. A student bailed out of a solo ship when he could not recover from an acrobatic manoeuvre. He returned to the field with his parachute rip cord which earned him a bottle of beer from the parachute rigger but he owed the rigger a fifth of whiskey, and his life. An embarrassed lieutenant pilot of the staff nosed over and tore up a propeller after braking too hard. He had forgotten he was not in the BT-13 basic trainer he normally flew.

I had 40 minutes of dual with three landings at the auxiliary field, then Mr Miller had me taxi off to one side of the field and said something through the Gosport like: 'Well you're ready.' He got out of the plane and stood by my cockpit to tell me to take off, fly the pattern, land and taxi back over to him. 'Good luck.' I taxied away feeling mighty lonesome. I hesitated an instant on take-off but then I eased the throttle open and went down the runway gathering speed until a little forward pressure on the control stick brought the tail up to flying altitude, then more speed building until the plane was light on the landing-gear, then just slight back pressure and it came off the ground. I was soloing! Reduce the RPMs now and climb out at 80 mph straight ahead to 400 ft, now a right turn, stick and rudder co-ordinated just so, straighten out now still climbing to 500 ft, now level off at 105 mph on the downwind leg of the traffic pattern, flying parallel to the runway. There's my instructor down there, looking up at me, looking awfully small. On past the end of the field, judging when to turn again to the right to enter the base leg. Now turn. Straight and level. Decide when to throttle back to make the final right-hand turn into the wind to start my descent to landing. Now turn, start descending, line up with runway. Good! Got a green light. Everything is just right. Pull on the flap lever and put down half flaps, going right on down toward the landing end of the runway, lined up real good.

Now the ground seems to be rushing up, ease back on the stick and flare out from the descent and hold the plane off the ground by more back pressure on the stick, try to make the two main wheels and the tail wheels touch at the same time, keep the plane straight with the runway. The tyres squeal slightly. I'm down, now the tail wheel a little late. Keep the plane straight, now to the end of the runway, turn off onto the taxi-way, pull up the flaps, taxi over to Mr Miller. I HAVE SOLOED! He shook my hand and offered his congratulations and told me to do it again. We had to have 50 landings to get the 'skunk stripe', a piece of white adhesive tape, off of our helmets signifying a 'full' solo student. I had 12 more to go.

Cadet John Wallace Fields completed Primary Training on the Stearman.

It looked tremendous compared to the Taylorcraft and sure looked big to me when you saw all those extra instruments in it. In the PT-13, the instructor pilot flew in the front seat and the cadet flew in the back, and the instructor had some instruments, namely, an air speed indicator, cylinder head temperature, RPM, and pitch control. In the back seat we had just a very few of these and did not have an air speed indicator. The way that we were taught to gauge our speed for landing was by listening to the wind that came whistling through the struts of the two wings, and the faster you went, well, the greater the vibration; the slower you went, the less vibration; therefore you knew you were slowing down and you could gauge your speed accordingly and adjust your speed for landing and take off.

My instructor pilot in Primary Training was Mr. Graham. He had been a crop-duster and he had been hired as an instructor pilot. Graham let us know that he was a top pilot; he showed us some techniques that we weren't supposed to do, but things you could do in an airplane. Then, our check pilot, Mr Townsend, gave us a check ride and he and Maj Dearing, who was our Air Commandant, had the final say on whether or not we stayed in the Cadet Corps or whether we got into the 'washing machine' and eventually were separated and had the opportunity to go into navigator's school or bombardier's school. About 52 per cent of us made it through Primary, which left us 48 per cent casualty.

George M. Collar was one of the 'casualties'. Having made it through pilot training at Maxwell Field, Alabama but washed out on check rides in Primary at Carlstrom Field in Arcadia, Florida.

I was sent to Ellington Field, Texas for bombardier

pre-flight school. Ellington Field is situated about half way between Houston and Galveston, at Webster, Texas, and in addition to being a pre-flight school for bombardiers, it was also a twin-engine advanced school for pilots. We were in class 43-18 and stayed at Ellington for 12 weeks. The Commandant of Cadets was Capt Roscoe Ates, who had been a stuttering comic in western films. He was a re-tread from WW1, and in real life did not stutter. The food at Ellington was excellent, the best I ever had in the army.

From Ellington, we proceeded to Laredo Air Base for six weeks of aerial gunnery training. Even though it was very hot, and the food was terrible, it was a lot of fun. We shot a lot of skeet and moving base trap. We studied turrets and fired thousands of rounds using everything from machine BB guns to .50-cal Brownings. We studied the three rad. lead system, and fired at clay pigeons from a Martin turret mounted on the back of a truck and equipped with shotguns. At the end of our six weeks, we were presented with gunner's wings, and sent back to Big Spring, Texas for 12 weeks of advanced bombardier training. We had excellent training at Big Spring. The senior ground school instructor was Lt L. K. Bowen who taught us the theory of bombing and the M series bomb-sight. He was a fine teacher, and could have made a dummy understand.

Lt E. J. 'Dashpot' Johnson taught us all about the automatic pilot and also the Sperry bomb-sight. Big Spring was one of the few bombardier schools which taught both Norden and Sperry bomb-sights and this probably accounts for the fact that so many Big Spring graduates ended up in B-24s in the 2nd Division of the 8th AF (B-24s had mostly Sperry bomb-sights, while the B-17s had Norden).

My flight instructor was Lt Elliot and my bombing partner was Louis Celantano of Minong, Wisconsin. We flew in AT-11s and dropped 100 lb practice bombs, which contained 10 lb of black powder, with the balance being sand. It was amazing how accurate you could be with the correct training. In order to graduate we had to have less than 210 ft average circular error for 100 bombs dropped. While you were dropping, your partner took aerial photos of the strikes, and accurate records were kept.

George Collar graduated as a bombardier and was commissioned second lieutenant. He joined a B-24 crew and was posted to the 8th AF in England.

Robert T. Marshall also washed out of pilot training, and was posted to radio school at Scott Field where he learned to send Morse, before being sent to AAF Gunnery School at Kingman,

Vultee BT-13 Valiant, better known to cadets like Philip G. Day, Robert H. Tays and John Wallace Fields, as the 'Vibrator'. (Charles Nicholas)

Arizona. Despite a fear of flying—the first experience in crawling into the belly turret of the B-17 shot his nerves—Marshall completed practice aerial gunnery in a B-17, firing .30s out of the waist at a sleeve towed by a pilot in a trainer over the desert and earned his combat crew gunner's wings. Marshall wrote:

Eleven weeks of Kingman. The place hasn't changed; dust, space, more dust and flying. I am a borderline crewman. I haven't whipped my demon. What will I do when I join a crew? I am on a conveyor belt, unable to get off. I have no time to worry about the future. My fate is set; nothing short of death is going to get me off this conveyor belt. I am not going to quit.

For cadet pilots who completed Primary the next stage was Basic Flight Training School. John Wallace Fields recalls:

We were the first class to fly the Vultee BT-13 Valiant in Basic Training. It was so bad it was called the 'Vibrator.' It was an all metal (except for the ailerons, elevators and rudder, which were fabric covered), low-wing, two-seat monoplane that sat on conventional landing-gear, two main non-retractable wheels and a tail wheel. The engine was a 450 hp Pratt & Whitney R-985-25 nine-cylinder radial, cowl enclosed, driving a two-position (fine and coarse pitch) Hamilton Standard propeller. The BT-13 had a lot more instruments than we had in a PT-13 and was a fine aircraft to fly but it was one that you couldn't be foolish with and if you were, you could get into trouble. We lost several pilots and the airplane was grounded right at the end of my class and for a couple of classes until they found some of the aerodynamic problems.

It would spin like a dream. It just didn't want to come out of it. Near the end of my time flying BT-13s they just turned us loose and let us fly and do what we wanted to do. The only thing we had to do was put in the hours, so I thought I'd run an experiment. I put it into a good diving speed and pulled it up on its prop, kind of straight up position and kicked it into vertical, climbing spin. When it came out of that it was really wound up. It fell off on one wing and spun for 10,000 ft before I ever got out of it. I didn't try that anymore.

Cadet Philip G. Day completed Basic Flying Training in the Vultee BT-13 and 13A Valiant at Minter Field, California.

When I first saw a 'Vibrator' up close, I could think only that it was as big as a Republic P-47, the 'hottest' fighter airplane of that time. Its wingspan was slightly less than 41 ft while from prop hub to rudder it was over 36 ft; a big airplane. When you climbed up and across the wing to be seated in the front cockpit, your eye-level was nearly 11 ft above the ground, when you put your seat up to its maximum height, as you did for taxiing, you were king of all you surveyed. The engine exhaust was on the right at 3 o'clock to the engine. It chuckled, burbled and roared like that of no other.

Aviation Cadet Robert H. Tays flew the BT-13 at Cochran AAF, Macon, Georgia, after completing Primary Training on the Stearman.

The BT-13 was the aircraft to be mastered—all metal, much more horsepower, radios, flight instruments, and navigation equipment. Runways, as opposed to an open grass-covered field, added that extra precision. We lost more cadets in Basic to crashes and other mishaps than during the other two phases. One night I was shooting touch-and-go landing on an auxiliary field when upon taking off, my craft wouldn't climb. My landing lights were still on when I saw this huge haystack coming toward me. I knew something was wrong so I quickly—yes quickly—went through the check list of things to do for take off and remembered I had forgotten to roll up half flaps. Needless to say, I did hurriedly and climbed over the haystack. Check lists are so important was the lesson and has been ever since. Check rides continued and the washing-out procedure was ever prevalent. By the time we finished Basic, almost half of the original class was gone. It was wartime and the luxury of pampering and extra effort for slow learners just did not exist.

Our military status grew at this field. As Aviation Cadets, we were not enlisted personnel and we weren't officers, but we were accorded many officer privileges to help us get ready for that great day when we were to be commissioned and awarded our silver wings. Upon completion of Basic, a decision was made by military instructors as to whether each of us should continue in the single-engine programme and go to combat in fighters or to multi-engine training for combat bomber training. Roughly, the short ones went to fighters and the tall ones to bombers. Flying proficiency was given consideration.

The next stage for pilots was Advanced Flight School Training. Cadet Philip G. Day, did his

Advanced Pilot Training at Douglas AAF, Arizona.

The training planes were the Curtiss AT-9 'Jeep', twin-engine pilot transition trainer, the fabric-covered Cessna AT-17 and the UC-78 Bobcat, disparagingly called the 'Bamboo Bomber' or the 'Twin-Breasted Cub'. The AT-17 had fixed-pitch propellers and was limited to two crewmen. The Bobcat was the same plane but with two-position metal propellers that could carry up to five, but mostly three, crewmen. They were a light-weight (3,500 lb empty), conventional-geared (main wheels retractable), twin-engined nothing. The engines were Jacob R-755-9s, nine-cylinder radials of 245 hp each. It taxied poorly but it flew practically by itself. I called it 'nothing' back there but really it was an excellent plane for its intended use and I did enjoy flying it.

Principally in Advanced we learned two-engine airplane operations and concentrated on formation flying, both day and night, and on instruments and on cross-country flying. We flew our longest cross-country, to Tucson to Phoenix, to Nogalas and to Hereford; something over 450 miles. Also, we had a so-called 'five hundred foot' cross-country from place to place at sagebrush height, below the hill and mountain tops, dodging power lines and windmills. Lots of fun and excitement. We also flew cross-country at night, to Cochise, to Benson, to Tucson and back, over Fort Huachuca, down to Bisbee. We also flew at Hereford night formation flights, droning around in the sky, not knowing where you were, not caring really, just wanting it over with so we could go home to bed.

On a night-training mission Lt Sloper and I were first to an auxiliary field to act as landing and take-off control for the rest of the squadron. The field had a dirt runway shaped like an 'L', and was used as an emergency landing field. The dust we raised landing hung in the air and the first several planes landing after us added to it. It got so dusty that we finally could not see the planes in the air or on the ground and Lt Sloper called the whole exercise off when one plane took out a string of landing lights and another landed with its wheels retracted. The planes in the air were sent back to Hereford. Two landed out of gasoline, their engines quitting on the final approach. Two collided in the traffic pattern, all four cadets bailed out and another taxied into a parked airplane. In trying to get the few planes off of the auxiliary field, one taxied into another, the first losing a propeller, the second its tail, a plane ground looped on take-

On Advance Flight School Training, at Douglas AAF, Arizona Cadet Philip G. Day did his Advanced Pilot Training in the Curtiss AT-9 'Jeep' twin-engined pilot transition trainer, the fabric covered Cessna AT-17 (pictured) and the UC-78 Bobcat, disparagingly called the 'Bamboo Bomber' or the 'Twin-Breasted Cub'. (Cessna)

off—virtually an impossibility. It was a wild, terrible, night.

Cadet John Wallace Fields recalls:

On graduation from Moffett we went to Stockton Air Force Training Centre on the West Coast where we flew AT-6 Texans. The Texan was a single-engine monoplane, two seats, with retractable gear and was really well equipped with instruments and landing lights and all the things that go with flying a nice airplane. It would have been an ideal airplane for peacetime, just to go cross-country and tooling

Cadet John Wallace Fields (front row, right) pictured during pilot training. He completed Primary Training on the Stearman and after flying the BT-13A 'Vibrator', moved on to the AT-6 Texan at Mather Field, an old grass-covered WW1 bombing range. Fields graduated from flying school on April 25 1941. (John Wallace Fields)

around in for personal pleasure. We completed AT-6 training at Mather Field, which was an old grass-covered WW1 bombing range and graduated from flying school on April 25, 1941.

Following the completion of their training, fully fledged bomber pilots, gunners, engineers, navigators and bombardiers began flight crew training. Philip G. Day was assigned as a copilot on B-24s. He recalls:

I was most unhappy with this assignment because I knew that I would be 'the best' twin-engine bombardment pilot that there could be and had my heart set on flying the B-25 Mitchell twin-engined bomber. Most of the pilots had been through transition school together, the majority of the copilots were from Douglas, in general the navigators, bombardiers, engineers, radio operators, armour gunners and gunners, were from the same graduating class and school so that we all knew someone in the shipment.

We had B-24Ds, Es, Hs and Js at Tonapah (the worst place in the world to be assigned, or as we said at the time 'if you wanted to give the world an enema, this is where you would put it in'). I had 33 flights in B-24s at Tonapah and logged 99.35 hours. We also attended ground school classes or went to simulations, link or celestial navigation trainers. We first flew single-ship missions including aerial gunnery with sleeve targets towed by Martin B-26s and ground gunnery against fixed targets on the dry lake beds, practice-bombing missions with 100 lb sand-filled bombs. My recollections were that we thought we were going to the South Pacific as we were issued light- and medium-weight flying clothing and all other gear required for over-water flight. The light and medium flying gear could have been for a southern crossing of the Atlantic to England, or Italy, however we turned all this clothing and gear and were told we would ship out by rail. We were on our way to England and the 8th AF.

Cadet John Wallace Fields recalls:

A person who was very articulate and demanded perfect discipline of himself and followed instruction perfectly, was wanted for instructors. Command-type people, good pilots, who could think for themselves, who had quite a bit of mental depth and ability to think and fly, who were secure in their aircraft and followed instruction well, were suggested for heavy bombardment. The people who were not particularly strong in piloting, and were not the fighter pilot type,

Norman Pickstone, a flight engineer, and Philip G. Day who was assigned as a copilot on B-24s, trained on the Consolidated B-24 Liberator. These B-24Ds are pictured 'on the line' in Utah.

they put in observation. Those that just didn't care whether school kept or not, kind of the daredevil, carefree, kind of people, who don't care whether they live or die, they put in fighter planes. Quite fortunately for me, when I asked for heavy bombardment in the Midwest, I was assigned to Fort Douglas, Utah, to the 7th BG in Salt Lake City. This put me about as close to my home in Shamrock, Texas, as I could get, and still be in heavy bombardment.

Norman Pickstone, a B-24 flight engineer recalls:

Our flight crew training at Walla Walla, Washington was a transitional training which included 223 hours of flying in a little over two months. This was the last of our formal military training before the final shift to combat status. The training period was a very busy time. We had to be prepared to fly day or night. We had not only flight training but also specialized ground training in our individual positions. Time off was kept to a minimum. At first, many felt that much of the training was designed to just occupy one's time. Later in combat, it was realized how vital it had all been. From Walla Walla the crew was sent to Hamilton Field, California. Trained on B-24s, we had always felt that we were slated for the Pacific Theatre. Little did we know that our fate would be quite different. We soon found ourselves on a troop train bound for the East Coast and for Europe.

Chapter Two

The Arsenal of Democracy

America was thrust headlong into WW2 by the Japanese air attack on Pearl Harbor on 7 December 1941, and the following day, Germany declared war on the USA. John Wallace Fields, now a lieutenant and B-17E pilot in the 19th BG at Hamilton Field, California, recalls:

We were awakened on the morning of 7 December 1941, about 11 o'clock by the then squadron commander, Maj Kenneth D. Hobson, woke me up and said 'Pearl Harbor's been attacked'. He told us that Hickam Field in Hawaii had been attacked; that we were to get our planes in the air and take them to Muroc Lake. Muroc is what is now known as Edwards Air Force Base, and is just a big salt-flat lake bed where you could land in any direction at any time for miles and miles. We went down from our little barrack's beds to the other fellows' beds and woke them up, and we all immediately began to get

The Japanese attack on Pearl Harbor on 7 December 1941 and Germany's declaration of war on the US the next day meant America was faced with a war on two vast fronts. Even before America's involvement, plans had already been laid for US bombers, like these B-17 Flying Fortresses, to be sent to England to begin raids on German targets. (Boeing)

our stuff packed and out to the airplanes, and got them off the ground as soon as we could.

I was surprised. I had no depth of thought toward what this thing really meant. I was really, totally surprised and I couldn't help but think about the guys that were already in the midst of it at Hickam Field. I flew as copilot with Maj Hobson, with a crew chief, to Muroc Field. We didn't have a navigator or any gunners. I was squadron armaments officer, and they immediately told us to take our bomb-bay tanks out and load the ship with bombs, because they were fearful that a Jap fleet was steaming in to the West Coast; that they were going to move in on the West Coast and take it. We dropped our bomb-bay tanks and loaded up with bombs, and about this time we'd get loaded with bombs, they'd change their orders again, and we'd take the bombs out and put the bomb-bay tanks in. That went on for about seven days. During this time we were chasing imaginary flyers up and down the West Coast, flying out of Muroc. We kept expecting at any moment to have orders to send us for Hawaii until 16 December. During this time we would occasionally get airborne and go out searching for a Jap fleet, and imagine that we saw them, and then we'd realize that it wasn't a Jap fleet, and we'd come back in and unload our bombs and load our gas tanks again.

When we were having our briefing and preparing for our take-off for Hickam Field from Hamilton Field on 16 December, we were told by the airline pilots there that we would have good weather and favourable winds, and that we should arrive at Hickam Field in Hawaii within about 15 hours. We flew and flew with a heavily loaded plane, and 14 hours came and went; 14$\frac{1}{2}$ hours, and no land in sight. Fifteen hours came with no land in sight, and finally, after 16 hours and 10 minutes, we arrived at Hickam Field. Both Jack Carlson and I had been taking celestial shots and realized that we were not making as good time as we thought we were supposed to. This did alarm us somewhat, because neither of us had ever flown into Hawaii before, and we thought that there was a chance that we could have missed the chain of islands, but we were consistent with our shots and checks that we made on each other, and felt like we were staying within the ballpark on our position. We were of course concerned about our fuel consumption, as a B-17 with bomb-bay tanks loaded had 2,400 gallons of fuel and it was also approximately 2,400 nautical miles from Hamilton Field in California to Hickam Field in Hawaii, which meant that we had to go a mile per gallon. A B-17 would use within the neighbourhood

of 150 to 180 gallons of fuel an hour, depending on the load and depending on what speed you're flying, and your altitude, so 16 hours and 10 minutes after take-off, we landed at Hickam Field, and, probably, had 100 gallons or less of fuel when we landed there.

As for Hickam itself, the runways had been cleared off, but many of the buildings had been bombed and there were still burned aircraft visible along the side of the runways. Of course, Hickam is adjacent to Pearl Harbor, and the entrance to Pearl Harbor was right by the officers club at Hickam, and the officers quarters. There was still smoke from burning vessels in Pearl Harbor and an oil slick all over the water. It was really a mess. Ships, those that weren't burning, had been damaged, and the *Arizona*, of course, was sunk. There were many of them that were damaged, including those which had been dry-docked and bombed. The dry docks were also damaged, the ships in them being wrecked while they were at their mooring in dry dock.

The barracks buildings had been strafed and bombed, and the kitchen had been blown up. It was just a mess. There was a 20 mm gun emplacement just outside the officers barracks and they told me that it was five days after the Pearl Harbor attack before they got any ammunition for their gun, so they felt pretty low. They were just not equipped for an attack on Pearl Harbor or Hickam Field.

The Hawaiian Department countermanded our orders, which had been to go to the island of Mindanao, confiscated our airplanes; impounded our equipment, and put us to work flying patrol missions out of Hawaii. Finally, Maj Hobson, J. R. Dubose and Jack Hughes departed for Mindanao, but they never got there, although they did make it to Java, where they met the 19th BG, which had evacuated from the Philippines. They came out with the 19th from Java and the Philippines to regroup in Australia. [On 10 December 1941 the first AAF mission of WW2 was flown by five B-17s of the 93rd Squadron, 19th BG, led by Maj Cecil Coombs, flying from Clark Field, and attacked Japanese ships near Vigan in the Philippines.]

Americans of all denominations and from all walks of life presented themselves for service in the USAAF. The story of 41-year-old Fred Meisel, barely five feet tall and weighing about 120 lb, is one of the most astonishing of the war. Meisel was born in Minsk, Russia on 7 November 1905, to a Russian mother and a German father. He was moved to Berlin at an early age. His parents separated and Fred was left with an uncle while his mother went to medical school in Switzerland, where she became a dermatologist. Fred attended school in Berlin and in 1917 he and his entire high school class of 200 boys enlisted in the German army, despite the fact that most of them were in their teens. He recalls: 'Boys in that period were born soldiers. It was their life. We were schooled under army commands.' Six weeks later, the boys were fighting in the last battle on the Russian front. Fred, a machine-gunner, and his comrades marched through Poland and on to the Western front, to confront the British and French armies. Out of Meisel's class of 200, only five made it to France. The others were buried all the way from the Carpathian Mountains to the Western Front. He recalled: 'We were starving. The Germans had no food. Bandages were made of paper, and bread of sawdust and flour. We wanted to meet the Americans because they had white bread and food. Everyone knew Americans threw out white bread and corned beef.'

Fred was awarded the Iron Cross, 1st and 2nd Class. After WW1, Fred stayed in the army, and in 1922, when he was discharged from the German Army, he emigrated legally to the USA. He worked as a truck driver, brick layer, and contractor. A staunch union man (as a boy, Fred had watched the rise of German trade unions and in his youth had seen them destroyed by Hitler), he became a union organizer. Fired in 1937 by one anti-union employer, Fred organized all the workers in the place and picketed for two months alone until the employer signed a union contract.

Craving combat, Meisel tried to enlist in tanks, mechanized cavalry or any 'fighting outfit'. The Draft Board looked dubious so Fred lied about his age. He was inducted into the US Army on 29 December 1941 at Fort McArthur and placed in chemical warfare service. After constant badgering and pleading, Meisel got transferred to the infantry and ended up at Ft. Worth, Texas, before going overseas. He saw active service in the 138th Infantry Regiment in the campaign to drive the Japanese out of Dutch Harbor in the Aleutians. Fred recalled: 'We went without milk and sometimes had very little food.

Fred Meisel, born in Minsk in Russia on 7 November 1905, to a Russian mother and a German father. In 1917 he fought in the German Army on the Russian Front and was awarded the Iron Cross, 1st and 2nd Class. After WW1, Fred stayed in the army and in 1922, when he was discharged from the German army, he emigrated legally to the USA. (via Jack Dupont)

It is the dreariest place on earth. There is nothing there but fog, mists, and 100 mph winds.'

The ground fighting over, Fred got tired of the inactivity and started hanging around the Air Corps' operations headquarters. Finally, he ran into a colonel who would listen to his constant harping for active service and got transferred to the Air Corps permanently. On the same day he was transferred, Fred talked himself into the tail turret of a B-24 bomber and wound up doing missions over the frozen wastes of Alaska and the Aleutian Islands. The small 11th AF in Alaska, with its advance base on Umnak Island, 2,400 miles from Anchorage, defended the vast Alaskan wastes and the Aleutian island chain in the Bering Sea. The Japanese held the other end of the Aleutians, at Attu and Kiska to prevent any proposed American invasion of Japan through the Aleutian chain and the Kuriles.

Late in 1942, the 36th and the 21st Bomb Squadrons of the 11th AF were joined by the

Right *Fred Meisel pictured in the gun turret of a B-24 Liberator bomber. Inducted into the Army on 29 December 1941 at Fort McArthur, Meisel saw active service in the campaign to drive the Japanese out of Dutch Harbor, later seeing action on missions from Alaska in the 11th AF. (via Jack Dupont)*

Below *Late in 1942 the 404th Squadron, known as the 'Pink Elephants' because its B-24Ds were painted desert pink, arrived in Alaska. The 404th was very successful, flying 39 patrols over the Bering Sea without losing a single plane, but between June and October 1942 the 11th AF lost 72 aircraft. Only nine of these were combat losses.*

404th Squadron, equipped with B-24s and known as the Pink Elephants because its B-24Ds were painted desert pink. They had originally been intended for North Africa! The 404th was very successful, flying 39 patrols over the Bering Sea without losing a single plane, but between June and October 1942 the 11th AF lost 72 aircraft. An indication of the kind of weather experienced in this theatre, is that only nine of these were combat losses.

Maj Wilbur Miller, fighter squadron commander in the Aleutians, briefing his pilots for a raid on Kiska in December 1942, wrote:

You fellows with the P-40s will go with a bomber that's to look over Gertrude Cove on the south side of Kiska. Somebody thought they saw a couple of subs in there this morning. If you don't find anything, you can come over and join us. There's a little valley that runs from Gertrude Cove almost over to the harbor, but be careful you don't get tangled up with us. You'd better wait until the bombers have finished and you'll only have Joe and me to watch out for in case we have to come back for another shot at those float planes just north of the dummies. Any questions now?

The mission went something like this:

'Look out Bill, there's one above you.'

'Take that one Ed, I'll cover.'

They drew closer to the radio to try to make out the voices . . . A few minutes of breathless, unseen action and then out of a welter of calls, answers and hurried warnings, a strange voice was heard clearly.

'Where are you going now Eddie?'

The Jap radio operator on Kiska even had the name right as he tried to draw out the raiders' next move . . . A torrent of profanity drowned out the static . . . 'Come back here you American —. You die.'

'We'll come back, don't you worry. With more bombs' . . . Then a sharp call for the PBY rescue ship. 'P-39 down just west of Little Kiska,'

'Drop a life raft somebody.'

'Where is it? Where is it? Can't see it from here.' All the B-24s returned; all the peashooters but one came back.

'I saw him get out of his ship,' said a pilot. 'He was floating on his back waving me on but I don't know whether the PBY found him or not. It was pretty close to those guns of Little Kiska.'

'Maybe the Japs picked him up,' added another. 'He came down just outside the harbor.' Lt A. T. Rice,

who got two of the five Jap float planes bagged that day, swore softly to himself, 'I'd trade the two I got in a minute for the one that knocked him down,' he said.

Air Force magazine in December 1942 ran this story of the Alaskan Offensive:

A . . . pursuit pilot turned over in his fingers a bullet he had fished out of the ammunition compartment in front of the cockpit and whistled softly to himself, 'I wonder where that one came from?' A slap on the back jarred him.

'Well Jack, I'll tell you. It came from the late Tom Tojo, or maybe he was Sam Saki, pilot of one Zero float plane just fresh deceased. He's now fish food in Kiska harbor, thanks to your very fine work as a decoy.'

'Decoy hell. I never even saw him. All I saw was tracer bullets whizzing by both sides of the cockpit and I sure pulled in my elbows. 'Where did he come from?'

'Search me. All of a sudden he just appeared out of nowhere into the here, as my Dad used to say to me. He flew right into my sights practically. One burst did it.'

'Thanks Pal, I owe you three beers. Those Zeros sure can climb like hell and turn on a dime but I wouldn't trade this old battlewagon for one of them. Those Zeros can't take it.'

Throughout 1943, 11th AF pounded Japanese shipping and positions in the Aleutians from its new base at Adak, only 250 miles from Kiska. Amchitka was successfully invaded on 5 January, and on 18 July Fred Meisel became one of the first members of the 'I Bombed Japan Club' which was very exclusive at that time, when he participated in the first raid on the Paramishiro and Katoaka Naval Bases in the Japanese Kurile Islands, a 1,700 mile round trip involving $11^{1}/_{2}$ hours flying time. All participants were volunteers and the mission established a new record for distance at that time. Fred recalled: 'We really caught those Japs by surprise. We came in from the west and found them flat-footed.' It was one of the toughest missions he ever flew. No man left his position on the entire $11^{1}/_{2}$-hour round trip in sub-zero weather. 'And if you went down you just gave up. They could never find you in the snow wastes of that country.'

For six months after Pearl Harbor, America and her allies were, for the most part, impotent as the Japanese invaded the Philippines, the East Indies, Guam and Wake. Among the first air units to suffer were the Netherlands East Indies Force, equipped with obsolete Martin B-10s (top) for bombing operations and Brewster Buffalo fighters (bottom). In Britain late in 1940 a number of American volunteers trained on the Buffalo. On 23 December 1941 when the Japanese made a massive air assault on Rangoon, 16 AVG P-40s and 20 RAF Buffalo fighters went into action. Ten Japanese bombers were shot down but five Buffaloes and four P-40s were lost.

A second mission to Paramishiro was flown on 11 August 1943. Four days later, Kiska was invaded and on 11 September a mixed force of seven B-24s and 12 B-25s bombed Paramishiro once again. It was the last mission for a while. Ten aircraft failed to return and the badly depleted 11th AF was reduced to training for raids on the Kuriles later in the New Year. (On 19 June 1945, Liberators of the 11th AF completed a 2,700-mile trip from Shamya to Kruppu. The 11th AF flew its last mission of the war on 13 August 1945 with a raid on Paramishiro in the Kuriles.)

Fred twice turned down commissions to remain on active service. After 58 missions he was sent home for reassignment. For a short time he was a gunnery instructor. He soon tired of this and 'determined to reach my 100 mark' pressed for an air combat assignment.

For six months after Pearl Harbor, America and her allies were, for the most part, impotent as the Japanese invaded the Philippines, the East Indies, Guam and Wake. Among the first air units to suffer were the Netherlands East Indies Force, equipped with obsolete Martin B-10s for bombing operations and Buffalo fighters. Lt Henry Simon, of the Brewster Buffalo squadron, Netherlands East Indies Force, at Bandoeng in January 1942, was to recall:

In our first battle we met a sky full of Zeros right over Gen Wavell's HQ. We were caught by the top cover of Zeros as we dove to attack a group below. Then all of a sudden the sky was empty and I was all alone except for a few planes in the distance. I was disappointed because I don't think we had shot down any Zeros, but the next day our ground patrols found the wrecks of five Japanese planes . . .

In the battle of the Java Sea we flew escort for an American dive-bomber squadron—three dive bombers and 20 fighters—to attack the big Jap transport fleet. We had eight American P-40s, seven Hurricanes flown by Dutchmen and five Brewsters.

That day we saw a sight that none if us will ever forget. Below, the Japanese warships were racing around the edges of the convoy spouting flame and smoke and leaving long white plumes of spray in their wake. In the haze of the setting sun we could see the long rows of transports steaming along in perfect battle order. It was a terrible and a beautiful sight.

The dive bombers sank one transport. When we landed we all looked at each other, everybody thinking what would have happened with 300 dive bombers instead of three. But thinking did not help us any. We took a drink and went home . . .

With the dawn at our backs, we skimmed the water raking the landing barges along the beaches. We could see the soldiers dive over the sides as our bullets hit the barges and silenced the anti-aircraft guns in the stern of each barge.

Within two hours after we landed from that mission, the Americans were ordered to leave Java. Two days later we had only one fighter in shape to fly. The battle of the Indies was over for us.

We had too few planes and what we had lacked performance. But they were sturdy and never fell apart in the air under the heaviest fire. I have seen planes land with 20-inch holes in wings and rudders, with windshield screens shot away, tyres punctured and holes all through the fuselage. It was amazing. All those planes needed to be perfect was a few hundred more horsepower and additional guns.

On 8 December 1941, 53 of the first 56 B-26A Marauders had taken off from Langley Field, Virginia for Australia where they formed the 22nd BG. In April 1942, they saw action for the first time, during attacks on New Guinea. B-25Bs of the 3rd BG in the Philippines were also first used against Japanese targets in April. On 16 January, meanwhile, five Liberators and B-17s of the 7th BG in Java carried out the first Liberator action of the war by USAAF crews with a raid on Japanese shipping and airfields from Singosari, Malang. In February 1942, the 10th AF was activated for action in the China–Burma–India (CBI) theatre and one of the re-possessed LB-30s had joined four B-17s for the first mission by this command on 2 April in an attack on the Andaman Islands. In March 1942, the 10th AF arrived in India with one B-24 group, the 7th. Its motley collection of B-17s and B-24s was streamlined into 35 Liberators late in 1942, and by the end of the year had 32 B-24s on paper. One squadron was still in the Middle East and two others were cadres waiting for aircraft. The 7th BG flew its first offensive mission north of the Yellow River on 21 October 1942 when a flight from the 436th Bomb Squadron bombed the Linhsi mines but with little success.

However, the greatest morale boost of 1942 occurred in the Pacific, on 18 April. Lt Col (later General) James H. Doolittle earned the Congressional Medal of Honor for leading an audacious carrier-borne strike by 16 Mitchell

B-24D Liberator of the 308th BG, 14th AF at Kunming in China takes off over the heads of Chinese wagons and parked C-46s and C-47s. (USAF)

bombers, with crews hand-picked from the 17th BG and the 89th Recon Squadron, in low-level attacks on Tokyo and three other cities. Doolittle had planned to fly the B-25Bs off the deck of the *Hornet* while some 450 miles from his targets but the carrier was spotted while still

On 18 April 1942, Lt Col (later General) James H. Doolittle earned the Congressional Medal of Honor for leading audacious low level attacks on Tokyo and three other Japanese cities using 16 B-25B Mitchell bombers flown from the deck of the carrier Hornet. *Crews were hand-picked from the 17th BG and the 89th Recon Squadron.*

B-25D Mitchell 41-30574, Available. *B-25Ds were delivered to combat theatres from the spring of 1942 to March 1944. In the South-West Pacific the B-25 saw service in the 5th AF and in China it served with the 10th AF. Mitchells also replaced the B-26 Marauder in Alaska. (North American)*

some 823 miles distant. Ten hours earlier than anticipated, the Mitchells were flown off and crews told to land in China as planned. Most aircraft crash-landed in China but several crews were captured and three airmen were executed by the Japanese. Bomb loads were, of necessity, small, but at home news of the 'Tokyo Raiders' had the desired effect. Morale soared while the Japanese were forced to plan counter-attacks on the US Fleet.

Sgt Edward J. Saylor, B-25 engineer/gunner, one of Doolittle's raiders who attacked Kobe, wrote:

We just sighted the outskirts of Kobe. The skies are still vacant, and that scares you a little. It's 1:52 and we're over the edge of the city. We're coming in at 2,000 ft. Lt Sessleris talking over the interphone in his Boston accent which always gives me a hell of a hoot, it sounds so English:

'That's our baby,' the looie is saying. 'I see the target.'

We roar across the city, raising such an almighty racket the noise kind of bounces back, it seems like, and the Japs down there are running back and forth in the streets like so many ants in an ant hill. Buses are running back and forth, but the Japs don't seem to catch on to the fact that the Stars and Stripes Forever are right up there over their heads, equipped with plenty of horsepower and plenty of bombs and that darned old 20-cent bombsight.

There's our target. She's an aircraft factory, a mess of buildings down there, scattered over a block or better. There are the docks. All we got to do now is let go.

Hirohito, the Yanks are coming, sprinkling it along the course.

'Let 'er go, Sess,' Smith yells to the bombardier.

I felt her go when she went. The bombs, I mean. Sweet as you please, that B-25 takes a sudden uplift, a little bit of a lurch, and the minute I feel it I know: Hirohito, the Yanks have arrived.

They had. About 100 B-17Es had been delivered to the US Army Air Corps by the time of Pearl

The P-38 Lightning was supplied to the RAF under Lend-Lease as well as equipping US Air Forces in the Pacific and Europe. On 18 April 1943, P-38G Lightnings of the 339th Fighter Squadron intercepted and shot down Admiral Yamamoto, the architect of the 6 December raid on Pearl Harbor, 550 miles from their base at Guadalcanal.

Harbor and equipped a handful of bomb groups in the Pacific where they fought the Japanese in the Philippines and Java before the survivors retreated to India. In the Battle of the Coral Sea, 6 May 1942, the B-17Es of the 19th BG hit back at the Japanese. John Wallace Fields, a pilot in the 435th 'Kangaroo' Squadron, wrote:

We sighted an aircraft carrier of the Japanese fleet and made a run on it. We had heavy anti-aircraft fire, but not too many fighter planes, because they were all carrier based. Their fighters were too busy with the Navy and the low-level stuff. There was a squadron of B-26s on the mission with us also. We were coming in at about 18,000 ft and could see some planes flying below and diving at low level. We thought that those were the B-26s, so we lined up on the battleship that they were bombing and dropped our bombs on it. It turned out that it was the Australian flagship *Australia*, and the planes that we saw diving were Jap bombers.

During the Battle of Midway 3–5 June 1942, a handful of Marine Corps Grumman TBF-1 Avengers, F4F-3 Wildcats, SBD-2 Dauntless dive-bombers and obsolete F2A-3 Buffaloes and SB2U-3 Vindicators, plus a few AAC B-17E Flying Fortresses and B-26 Marauders defended the island from Japanese attack. On 3 June, 12 Buffaloes and Wildcats intercepted the first strike by 108 aircraft, shooting down four and damaging a few others before the Zeros shot down 24 of the US fighters. Six Avengers and four B-26 Marauders launched their torpedoes against the Japanese carriers but seven aircraft were shot down and three badly damaged. American aviation units lost 85 out of 195 aircraft. However, Japan's loss of her carriers meant she would never again dictate events in the Pacific.

On Sunday 18 April 1943, P-38G Lightnings of the 339th Fighter Squadron, commanded by Maj John W. Mitchell, succeeded in intercept-

The P-38 Lightning destroyed more Japanese aircraft than any other American aircraft and the two leading American aces, Maj Richard Bong and Maj Tom McGuire, 40 and 38 kills respectively, flew P-38s in the Pacific Theatre. Lightnings on display in their honour are at Oshkosh—in the colours of Maj Bong's P-38 Marge—and at McGuire AFB in New Jersey where the memorial displays a P-38 in the colours of McGuire's Pudgy (V). (Author)

ing and shooting down the Mitsubishi transport carrying Admiral Yamamoto, the architect of the 6 December raid on Pearl Harbor. The interception, 550 miles from their base at Guadalcanal, was made possible by the use of long-range drop tanks. (The P-38 went on to destroy more Japanese aircraft than any other American aircraft, and the two leading American aces, Maj Richard Bong and Maj Tom McGuire, 40 and 38 kills respectively, flew P-38s in the Pacific Theatre.) Admiral 'Bull' Halsey, on receiving the news of the shooting down of Admiral Yamamoto, sent the following signal to Henderson Field: 'Congratulations stop. Major Mitchell and his hunters sound as though one of the ducks in their bag was a peacock.' The US Navy was to bear much of the responsibility for regaining air superiority in the Pacific but the part played by the 5th, 7th and 13th Air Forces cannot be overstated, while in China Gen Claire L. Chennault's China Task Force (later the 14th AF), mounted its important offensive.

But although fighting the Japanese in the Pacific was crucial to the outcome of the war, America had to fight on two fronts. In Europe, its air forces helped secure total victory.

Chapter Three

European War

*The RAF was decimated. We were on our knees.
And the Americans suddenly appeared . . .*
George Stebbings,
a 14-year-old Air Training Corps cadet.

Far-reaching decisions had been made in the event that America should become involved in the conflict with Germany. Between 27 January and 27 March 1941 agreements between the USA and Great Britain were made for the provision of naval, ground and air support for the campaign against Germany. Potential bases for US Army Air Force (USAAF) fighter and bomber groups had been reconnoitred. In June

Maj General Henry H. 'Hap' Arnold, Commanding General, 8th AF, seen here inspecting officers of the 389th BG at Hethel in 1943, signed the order activating the 8th AF on 2 January 1942. (USAF)

1941, President Franklin D. Roosevelt had approved the plan for the formation of a new, autonomous army division; the Army Air Forces (AAF), although the Air Corps and Air Force Combat Command were to remain in being until 9 March 1942. Maj Gen Henry H. 'Hap' Arnold was given overall command of the new service. Arnold and his staff formulated a policy (AWPD/1) of relentless air attacks against Germany, strategic defence in the Pacific Theatre and air operations in the defence of the Western hemisphere. First priority was given to Germany's electric power grid, followed in importance by its transportation system of rail, road and canal, then its oil and petroleum industry. It was argued that strategic bombing of these targets, together with the neutralization of the Luftwaffe, submarine and naval facilities might render a land campaign unnecessary. The Boeing B-17 Flying Fortress and the Consolidated B-24 Liberator were to be the prime weapons in the US offensive in Europe and the method would be daylight precision bombing.

On 2 January 1942, the order activating the 8th AF had been signed by Maj Gen Henry Arnold, the Commanding General, AAF. On 22 February at High Wycombe, VIII Bomber Command was formerly activated under the command of Brig Gen Ira C. Eaker. Meanwhile, four B-17E/F and two B-24 heavy bombardment groups were activated for deployment to Britain. The first B-17Es of the 97th BG landed in Britain in July 1942 but were not the first to fly a mission. On 4 July, Independence Day, six American crews from the 15th Bomb Squadron (Light) together with six RAF crews took off from RAF Swanton Morley, Norfolk on a daylight sweep against four German airfields in Holland. It was the first time American airmen had flown in American-built bombers against a

Independence Day, 1942, was chosen for the first official bombing sorties by American crews operating from England. The most successful attack was that carried out against Bergen Alkmaar, two bombs bursting in a hangar outside which is standing a Fw 190. Another bomb can be seen in the air, and a second Boston can be seen coming in at low-level to attack. Inside a covered shelter can be seen a Bf 109F.

German target but although it was important historically, the raid was not an unqualified success. Two of the aircraft manned by Americans were shot down and few bombs hit their targets.

Capt (later Colonel) William C. Odell, who led three Bostons to Haamstaede (the other eight attacked De Kooy and Valkenburg airfields), wrote:

After getting in the air we settled down and flew right on the trees to the coast. Then we went down to the water. Nice ride until the other 'vic' left us. Felt a little uneasy because there was a cloudless sky but no fighters appeared. Found land ahead and could spot the landmark of the lighthouse a long way off. Swung over the edge of the coast even lower than the leader and stayed right on the grass. I opened the bomb doors, yelled to Birleson and then it started. I fired all the guns for all I was worth and Birly dropped the bombs. I saw the hangar but that wasn't my dish. I saw Germans running all over the place but I put most of my shots over their heads. Our bombs were OK. I thought we would crash any moment for I never flew so reckless in my life. The next moment we were flashing past the coast and out to sea—the water behind us boiling from the bullets dropping into it all around. I kicked and pulled and jerked from side to side. I didn't look at the air speed, I was trying to miss the waves. Over the target we were doing 265 but shortly after I opened up a bit. 'Digger' claims he shot his guns into a formation of troops lined up for an inspection—his bombs hit well where they should have. 'Elkie' was a bit behind but he got rid of his load. He got a broken radio antenna and a mashed-in wing edge. I picked up a hole just above the pilot's step and a badly knocked-up bomb door. We zigged and zagged while 8 miles out and then closed up waiting for fighters. None came. We reached the coast and were the first ones home.

All came back except Loehrl, Lynn and a Britisher. Loehrl was hit by a heavy shell and hit the ground right in the middle of the airdrome. 'He flew into a million pieces,' one of the gunners said. And I owed him £1 10s. I feel like a thief! Lynn was following before the flight hit the target, but never came away from it. His wife is to have a baby in November. He really wasn't cut out for this game. At breakfast he was salting his food, trying to hold the salt spoon steady, yet throwing salt over his shoulders! I hope he didn't crash. Henning was shot down by a Me 109 that took off just ahead of him. He tried to get it, but it turned, got behind him and set one motor on fire.

He crashed into the sea. Gen Eaker, Gen Duncan and Beaman were there at the start and finish and didn't look so happy at the finish. They must have thought it was a 'piece of cake' until three turned up shot down—two being American. Thusly, we celebrated Independence Day!

Two days later, the first C-47 arrived in the UK and on 9 July seven P-38s arrived after flying the North Atlantic route. On 14 August, as Lt Elza Shahn was ferrying his P-38 to England, he spotted a Focke-Wulf Kondor flying near Iceland. Shahn shot the Kondor into the sea to become the first active duty American pilot to shoot down a German aircraft in WW2.

On 17 August, 12 B-17Es of the 97th BG, led by the CO, Col Frank Armstrong in *Butcher Shop*, piloted by Major Paul Tibbets, made the first all-USAAF raid with an attack on the marshalling yards at Sotteville (Rouen) in northern France. Eaker flew the mission aboard *Yankee Doodle*. Maj Paul W. Tibbets, recalls:

It was just past mid-afternoon when we lifted off into sunny skies. All the planes were in the air at 15:39 hrs. We started our climb for altitude immediately and had reached 23,000 ft, in attack formation, by the time we left the coast of England and headed south across the Channel. I wondered whether or not all aircraft would make it or whether there would be aborts. However, it was a banner day with no aborts. As we departed the English coast out over the Channel, the RAF escort of Spitfire Vs joined us. Grp Capt (later ACM) Harry Broadhurst was leading the RAF escort fighters and it was an emotional, spine-tingling event—we were off to do battle for real and fighters were there to give us protection and comfort . . . We caught the Germans by surprise. They hadn't expected a daytime attack, so we had clear sailing to the target. Visibility was unlimited and all 12 planes dropped their bomb loads. Our aim was reasonably good but you couldn't describe it as pinpoint bombing. We still had a lot to learn . . . By the time we unloaded our bombs, the enemy came to life. Anti-aircraft fire, erratic and spasmodic at first, zeroed in our formations as we began the return flight. Two B-17s suffered slight damage from flak. Three Me 109s moved in for the attack but were quickly driven off by the Spitfires that accompanied us. The only German planes I saw were out of range and I got the impression they were simply looking us over . . . A feeling of elation took hold of us as we winged back

Maj Paul W. Tibbets pictured in November 1942 at Biskra in North Africa. On 17 August 1942, he flew the lead B-17E of the 97th BG when the USAAF made the first all-USAAF raid with an attack on the marshalling yards at Sotteville (Rouen) in northern France. (Tibbets)

across the Channel. All the tension was gone. We were no longer novices at this terrible game of war. We had braved the enemy in his own skies and were alive to tell about it.

A few bombs landed short but most hit the large target area. Several repair and maintenance workshops were badly damaged. First of the congratulatory messages to arrive came from Air Marshal Sir Arthur Harris, Chief of RAF Bomber Command: 'Congratulations from all ranks of Bomber Command on the highly successful completion of the first all-American raid by the big fellows on German-occupied territory in Europe. Yankee Doodle certainly went to town and can stick yet another well-deserved feather in his cap.'

Eaker sent his few bombers to shipyards and airfields on the continent. On 6 September, two B-17s were shot down; the first US heavy bombers to be lost in the ETO. On 14 September, the 97th and 301st Bomb Groups were assigned to the 12th AF in North Africa but 17 Liberators of the 93rd BG arrived and in

October were joined by the 44th BG. From September to November four new B-17F bomb groups joined the 8th AF and on 9 October Eaker could dispatch 108 bombers to Lille accompanied by P-38 and RAF Spitfires. Only 69 bombers dropped their bombs on the target area.

Lt Col Paul Tibbets when interviewed by DeWitt Mackenzie, of the Associated Press, about the Lille raid, 9 October 1942, said:

We had it hammered into us constantly that in practice we must watch out for the folks beneath us. This reaction persisted during my first three raids. Finally, I got used to the idea but I am cautious. When I look at a 2,000 lb bomb in the bay of my ship, I know a lot of people may get hurt. My anxiety is for the women and kids. You see, I have a three-year-old boy of my own at home. I hate to think of him playing near a bombed factory. That makes me careful.

Lille is the most heavily populated area we have attacked and our target was in the thick of it. As we came above a great circle with a church beside it which was the guide for our target, it came over me that if we missed the target we would hurt a lot of people. I gave the bombardier a heap of mental support to get his target. We don't want to kill French people. We don't want to hit anything but our target.

On 7 November the North African campaign opened and US paratroopers were flown out from England in 47 AAF transports. Ten days later, Brig Gen Asa N. Duncan, first 8th AF Chief of Staff, died when his B-17 crashed at sea. He was part of Maj Gen Carl Spaatz's party who were flying to Gibraltar to talk to Gen Eisenhower about creating a unified air command. Duncan flew in a separate B-17 with a duplicate set of papers. About 75 miles off the French coast, his Fortress experienced engine failure, ditched in rough seas and broke up. On 1 December, Lt Gen Ira C. Eaker assumed command of the 8th AF.

Eaker had many problems to wrestle with as his small force of B-17s and B-24s at first made short bombing runs on U-boat bases in France. Losses in late 1942 were high, bombing accuracy was poor, and differences in performance between the B-17 and B-24 made mission planning difficult. Shortages of replacements did not help his cause either. US bombers were a valuable commodity in Europe and apart from equipping the 8th AF, the 9th in the Mediterranean also had call on the Liberators. On 4 December 1942, the first American raid on the Italian mainland took place when 20 B-24s of the 9th AF attacked Naples.

In England, Col Curtis E. LeMay, the 305th BG CO, pioneered the practice of group bombing using lead bombardiers which called for a straight-and-level bomb run to ensure accuracy. LeMay, writing about the 23 November 1942 raid on St Nazaire said:

I remember distinctly: it was seven minutes from the time we saw the target until the bombs fell off the shackles. Quite a long seven minutes for everybody concerned. Next thing I know I'm talking to my bombardier. 'How did you do? How was the run?'

'It was a good run and we got bombs on the target.'

'You sure of that?'

He said, 'Yes I am sure of it. It was a good run. But I could have done a little better if it hadn't been for those clouds: they kind of got in the way.'

There wasn't a speck of cloud over the target in that hour. The clouds he was talking about were flak bursts.

Just shows what complete tenderfeet we all were. This boy was looking down through the bombsight and he saw those big black clouds drifting by . . . no wonder it bothered him.

LeMay's tactics were tried with some success on 3 January 1943 against St Nazaire when the majority of bombs fell on the submarine pens. On 27 January, 91 B-17s and B-24s were dispatched to Germany for the first time. Bad weather reduced the attacking force to 53 B-17s, which dropped their bombs on the U-boat construction yards at Wilhelmshaven from 25,000 ft. Three bombers were shot down and the bombing was described as 'fair' but the press proclaimed the start of an all-out offensive on Germany. On 4 February, in the deepest penetration into enemy territory so far, 86 bombers hit the marshalling yards at Hamm. Five bombers were shot down. Four more were lost on a follow-up raid on 4 March.

A Liberator pilot who flew missions in the 44th BG from Shipdham at this time was Capt

Col (later Brig Gen) Curtis E. LeMay, the 305th BG CO, pioneered the practice of group bombing using lead bombardiers which called for a straight-and-level bomb run to ensure accuracy. Later, LeMay was equally effective in his deployment of B-29s in the Pacific on low-level raids over Japan. (USAF)

(later Col) Bill Cameron, copilot, *Little Beaver*. On 26 February 1943 he was one of the pilots who flew a follow-up raid on Wilhelmshaven:

There were German fighters all over the place. They flew in so close to us that I could easily see the pilot and not only could I count their guns but I could pretty accurately judge their calibre. Fighters would fly alongside just out of range then turn in towards us. Our crew would fire like mad but just couldn't score a hit. I sat there feeling like a 'bulls eye' in a shooting gallery!

On 27 February we went to Brest. Sixty bombers with RAF fighter escort. I watched in anguish and frustration as our boys began shooting at a Spitfire. We were not used to seeing friendly fighters and those who did the shooting probably thought it was better to shoot first and identify later. By this time they had been well shot up by enemy fighters and were becoming a little quick on the trigger. The Spit' swung away from us. I doubt that he was hit . . . March 8 was also one of those days I am likely to remember. We went against Rouen with 16 B-24s. Spitfires were to cover us over the target for five minutes but due to our poor navigation (or theirs or both) they were not there when we were.

On 4 April 1943, the B-17s went to the Renault Works in Paris. Lt Olan L. Hubbard, a group bombardier, wrote:

As we go out we have just crossed the French coast. It is only a few minutes now until we reach the target outside Paris. I can see the River Seine over to our right as it makes its turns and curves. From here it looks like a silver snake in the sun's reflection. I hope I can follow it all the way because our target lies just in the middle of the second big bend it makes after it enters the suburbs of the city. I already have figured the bombing conditions three times but will do so again. I can't afford to miss today. If I do, I'm sunk.

Okay Bill, turn on the target now . . . back to the left about 5° . . . okay, we're perfect now . . . everything's set . . . good grief! . . . the squadron ahead's tearing hell out of the place . . . Boy! I can see their bombs through my sight . . . Check, check, check and re-check . . . all okay . . . Lammers, stand by the camera . . . level now . . . level . . . just a few seconds and we can turn . . . here they go . . . camera! . . . *bombs away!*

Okay to turn now . . . fighters coming up at 3 o'clock. Boy, those bombs had to be in there because I had it perfectly synchronized . . . fighters at 11 o'clock and at 3 o'clock . . . seem to be attacking the low group. Look, Jim, a B-17 in trouble . . . look at those fighters swarm him. There he goes now. Poor devils in 'chutes going down through that flak! Here come the *Spitfires*! . . . Are they *Spits*, Bill? . . . Do they look like *Spits* to you? . . . Yes . . . Okay, taking no chances.

P-47D Thunderbolt of the 56th FG, 8th AF. On 24 December 1942, the first P-47 Thunderbolt arrived in the UK and joined the 4th FG. On 10 March 1943, P-47s were flown in combat over western Europe for the first time. (Geoff Thomas)

P-47D of the 62nd Fighter Squadron, 56th FG. On 4 May 1943, P-47s flew their first escort mission when the 56th FG, together with six RAF fighter squadrons, escorted 79 B-17s to the Ford and General Motors plant at Antwerp. No bombers were lost. On 5 November 1943, the 56th FG became the first 8th AF fighter group credited with 100 enemy aircraft destroyed. (Bill Cameron)

Look, there's Rouen. Looks like a graveyard . . . no trains . . . no tracks . . . burnt out. Wish I could see the Renault works tomorrow. Bet it looks like Rouen does now.

On 17 April, for the first time, over 100 bombers attacked a single target when 106 bombers attacked the Focke-Wulf plant at Bremen. Sixteen B-17s were lost. In April, four new B-17F groups joined the 8th, and the 92nd BG was removed from training status and resumed bombing operations. Fighter escorts were badly needed. On 24 December 1942, the first P-47 Thunderbolt had arrived in the UK and joined the 4th FG. On 10 March, P-47s were flown in combat over Western Europe for the first time. On 4 May, P-47s flew their first escort mission when the 56th FG, together with six RAF fighter squadrons, escorted 79 B-17s to the Ford and General Motors plant at Antwerp. No bombers were lost. Meanwhile, on May Day, the 8th attacked St Nazaire. In the 306th BG, Lt Lewis P. Johnson's B-17 was hit several times and it caught fire in the radio compartment and in the

tail area. S/Sgt Maynard 'Snuffy' Smith, the ball turret gunner, who was on his first mission, hand-cranked his turret to get it back into the aircraft. He climbed out and discovered that the waist gunners and the radio operator had bailed out. He could have bailed out himself but he elected to remain in the aircraft and fight the fire with a hand extinguisher. The aircraft did not show any signs of leaving formation so Smith assumed the pilots were still aboard and he went to treat Harris B. Goldberg, the badly wounded tail gunner. (Goldberg was by now a veteran of 42 'ops' in RAF bombers and 17 missions on Fortresses). Smith then jettisoned the oxygen bottles and ammunition in the radio compartment, manned the two waist guns during an attack by enemy fighters, stopping to dampen down the fires and treat the tail gunner. Johnson managed to bring the bomber home and put down at Predannack near Lands End after Smith had thrown out all the equipment that was not nailed down. For his actions this day 'Snuffy' Smith received the Congressional Medal of Honor from Secretary of War, Mr Stimpson. He was the first and only enlisted man in the 8th AF to receive the Congressional Medal of Honor.

On 14 May, Eaker sent out over 200 bombers for the first time when 224 B-17s and B-24s and B-26 Marauders attacked targets in Holland, Germany and France. Altogether, the four targets cost the Americans 11 aircraft. Six were Liberators in the 44th BG, which were lost bombing Kiel. T/Sgt John L. Susan, radio operator in *Miss Delores*, one of the 67th Squadron losses, wrote:

We took a hit and started to fall behind as one of left-side engines was knocked out. Sgt Gib Wandtke was operating the top turret but the flak burst had also hit Gib, taking some metal in his knee, and he came tumbling down out of the turret. He motioned to me that I should get into the turret—and I did. Unknown to me flak bursts had also knocked out the intercom! Everyone, therefore, was on his own . . . We were already a sitting duck as we were falling behind the formation due to the lost engine. For some reason my guns would not fire between the two vertical stabilizers. I kept cussing as I would bring the guns down to shoot at the six or more following Jerries who were taking pot shots at us from the rear. I don't know if our tail turret guns were functioning or not but soon our left wing started on fire—it was time to start getting out.

T/Sgt Michael J. Denny, Engineer in *Little Beaver*, another in the 67th Squadron which failed to return, wrote:

We were hit after we left the target. Two bursts in the back end, knocked out one engine; then a burst in back of navigator, Tom Bartmess. The whole inside of the flight deck was a mass of flames. It must have hit accumulators. We went into a flat spin—had a hell of a time standing on my feet and putting on my parachute. Tried to put out the fire, but impossible. Could not get out the doors so I walked back to the waist windows to get out. Bailed out at about 800 ft. Was last one to leave plane. Saw ship crash and burn . . .

The Marauders' first mission, to a generating plant at Ijmuiden in Holland, had gone well. Early in 1943 in North Africa, the USAAF had stopped using Marauders on low level raids after suffering high losses during low-level strafing and bombing raids. Marauders had begun equipping the 3rd Bomb Wing of the 8th AF in the spring of 1943 for low-level operations. On 17 May, all 10 attacking B-26s were shot down. Marauders were quickly allocated bases in Essex to place them nearer the continent and within range of escort fighters and that summer were switched to a high-level bombing role. Success

Early in 1943 the USAAF stopped using B-26 Marauders on low-level raids in North Africa after high losses on low-level strafing and bombing raids but Marauders began equipping the 3rd Bomb Wing of the 8th AF in England in the spring of 1943 for low-level operations. (Bill Cameron)

The oilfields at Ploesti, Romania under attack by B-24D Liberators on 1 August 1943. (Earl Zimmerman)

was only finally achieved, late in 1943, when all B-26 groups were transferred to the 9th AF for tactical missions in support of the Allied build-up to the invasion of Europe. By May 1944, the 9th AF commanded eight Marauder groups and a pathfinder squadron.

In the Mediterranean on 14 July, Comiso airfield in Sicily became the first airfield captured after the invasion of the island, and on 19 July Rome was bombed for the first time. Seven hundred American bombers dropped 800 tons of bombs. In November 1942, IX Bomber Command had been activated under the command of Gen Lewis Brereton. Early in June 1943, Brereton was informed that the three 8th AF Liberator groups (the 44th, 93rd and 389th) would join his 98th and 376th BGs (also equipped with the B-24D) in North Africa for a second attack on the oilfields at Ploesti in Romania (12 B-24s of the HALPRO

Detachment, led by Col Harry A. Halverson, flying from Fayid, Egypt, had bombed the oil refineries on 12 June 1942 in the first AAF bombing mission against a European target). B-17s were ruled out because they did not possess the required low-level range but the B-24D could make the trip to the target, some 1,350 miles, and back again. Ploesti lies on the Romanian plains 50 miles north of Bucharest. In WW2 it was the greatest single source of fuel for the German war machine in all Europe and in 1941 refined a large portion of the 2.1 million tons of Romanian oil supplied to the Third Reich. After flying missions in support of the Allied invasion of Sicily and some raids on Italy, the mission went ahead on Sunday 1 August. A total of 177 B-24Ds were dispatched but malfunctions and accidents en route reduced the effectiveness of the force. Navigational errors caused severe problems in the target area forcing

Col (later Brig General) Leon W. Johnson, CO of 44th BG, one of the five men to receive the Congressional Medal of Honor for the low-level raid by B-24D Liberators on Ploesti on 1 August 1943. (Bill Cameron)

some groups to bomb each other's assigned targets. In all, 45 Liberators were lost and eight crews interned in Turkey. Of the 88 that returned to North Africa, 55 were damaged. All five groups received Presidential Unit Citations, while five Congressional Medals of Honor (three posthumously) were awarded. The plants were repaired and operating at pre-mission capacity within a month.

Col (later Brig General) Leon W. Johnson, CO, 44th BG, one of the five men to receive the Congressional Medal of Honor, when interviewed by Andrew A. Rooney of *Stars & Stripes*, said:

As we passed through the flames the plane on our left wing blew 1,500 ft in the air and the ship on our right went down burning. I personally think our losses would have been greater if we had been forced to fly through the fire of the other groups' bombing. While we were under cover of the smoke and fire we were comparatively safe from flak. It was after we got clear of that that the ground fire became intense . . . right after we passed the target area my pilot, Maj Bill Brandon, turned to me, grinned, and yelled 'all we have to do to get a medal now is get home.' I didn't think much about not getting back because I had a feeling that I would get back. Of course a lot of men had that feeling and it didn't do them any good.

I scare about as easily as anyone and I don't know as I'd want to do it again, but it is easier to take a few minutes like we did in the target area than hours of fighter opposition. The whole show was over in 15 minutes at Ploesti, although we were in the air for 14 hours. Sgt Ray, our waist gunner on the trip, was on his first raid that day, and I had to assure him when we got back that they weren't all like that.

The two 9th AF groups, the 98th and 376th, were transferred to the 12th AF after Ploesti. Meanwhile in England on 13 June, the Fortresses bombed Bremen and Kiel. A total of 26 B-17s were lost. When on 22 June, 235 B-17s went to Huls, 16 Fortresses were lost and another 170 damaged, but 183 B-17s bombed the plant and put it out of full production for six months. On 17 July, a new milestone was reached when a record 332 bombers went to Hannover. On 24 July, Eaker launched *Blitz Week*, an all-out air offensive on enemy targets throughout Europe. Some 324 B-17s flew a 1,900-mile round trip to Norway and bombed the nitrate works at Heroya and shipping at Trondheim. On 25 July, Kiel, Hamburg and Warnemünde were bombed and 19 B-17s were shot down. Next day, over 300 bombers attacked Hannover and Hamburg. On 28 July, 182 bombers hit the Fieseler Werke aircraft factory at Kassel, escorted by P-47 Thunderbolts of the 56th and 78th Fighter Groups, carrying unpressurized 200-gallon ferry tanks below the centre fuselage for the first time. Fifteen B-17s were lost on the raid by 120 Fortresses on the Focke-Wulf 190 factory at Oschersleben but production was stopped for a month. On 29 July, the shipyards at Kiel and the Heinkel assembly plant at Warnemünde were hit.

On 30 July, 186 Fortresses escorted almost to

the target and back again by Thunderbolts, hit aircraft factories at Kassel for the loss of 12 Fortresses. Maj Eugene Roberts, pilot of 78th FG P-47, *Spokane Chief*, made the first hat trick of kills, to become the first US pilot to score a triple victory in Europe. He wrote:

When we sighted the bombers off to our left we made a 90° turn and picked them up near Winterswijk. One straggling bomber was observed flying below the main formation in a dive, trailing black smoke and being attacked by about five E/A. I peeled my flight down and to the rear of the straggler. This would be about 1,000 ft below the main formation at about 21,000 ft. All E/A sighted us and took evasive action to the extent that I was unable to close, although I did fire a burst with improper deflection. The E/A was in a diving attack from the rear on this straggler. I initiated my attack from the port side rear of the fighters, swinging in behind them to the right and broke sharply downward to the rear. I followed them in the climb, attempting to get a deflection shot. When he broke downward I found I was directly beneath the bombers and saw a number of ball turret gunners firing at my flight. I broke down and to the rear, and pulled up to starboard side of the bombers about 1,000 yards out and at about their level.

Looking up, I observed six E/A flying parallel to the bombers and about 1,000 feet directly above me. They failed to see us and did not take any action, so after they passed I made a climbing turn to the left to come up to their level and behind them. At this point I missed my second element and found myself alone with my wingman. In our pull up we missed the original six E/A sighted but sighted a single E/A ahead on same level at about 1,500 yards. I dived slightly below, opened full throttle, and closed to about 400 yards. I pulled up directly behind the E/A and opened fire. Several strikes were observed on E/A, his wheels dropped and he spun down trailing a large volume of dark smoke and flame.

I continued parallel to the bombers and sighted two more E/A about 2,000 yards ahead. I used the same tactics, closing to 400 yards astern, pulled up and opened fire on port aircraft. Observed strike reports and E/A billowed smoke and flame, rolled over and went down. I was closing so fast that I had to pull up to avoid hitting him. I observed my wingman, F/O Koontz, firing at the second aircraft but did not see the results. Both of these aircraft were Fw 190s.

After this second engagement, we were about two miles ahead of the bombers still well out to their star-

board side. About this time I observed one E/A, an Me 109, peeled to starboard to attack the bombers head-on, and I followed closing to 500 yards before opening fire. Two bursts were behind but the third burst caught him and he spun down, trailing smoke and flame, some 1,500 yards ahead of the bombers.

Blitz Week cost Eaker almost 100 aircraft and 90 combat crews. Losses were made good but when, on 12 August, 330 bombers bombed targets in the Ruhr, 25 bombers failed to return. On 15 August, VIII Bomber Command took part in the *Starkey* deception plan which was created to make the Germans believe that an invasion of the French coast was imminent. More raids on enemy airfields in France and the Low Countries were carried out on 16 August, then on 17 August, in the anniversary mission of the 8th AF, 376 Fortresses bombed the aircraft plants at Regensburg and the ball-bearing plant at Schweinfurt. Sixty B-17s were shot down; almost three times as high as the previous highest, on 13 June, when 26 bombers were lost. Twenty-seven B-17s in the First Division were so badly damaged that they never flew again while 60 Fortresses of the 4th Wing, which flew on to bases in North Africa, had to be left behind for repairs. Bill Rose, a pilot in the 92nd BG, wrote:

It was indescribable. This was the first time I had any thoughts that we were in for a fight. I will always remember the tail gunner reporting formations of B-17s flying into positions behind to protect our rear. We thought we weren't going to have the attacks on the tail like we had been getting on our last two missions. Then all of a sudden, 'Oh my God!' the Germans were letting go air-to-air rockets, straight into our group. I was fortunate in that one went right past my window. The rocket landed right in the wing of the lead plane right by a gas tank. I watched it burn and it wasn't long before the entire wing was on fire. The pilot dropped back and the stricken crew bailed out. Eventually, the B-17 blew up. It was a terrible sight to see.

My crew and I were now 10 nervous wrecks and we didn't sleep much that night. In fact we slept fitfully for about the next year. Nightmares continued most nights until 1945. The battle has affected everyone, myself included, morally and in other ways, for the rest of our lives. Like the terrible battles of WW1, when 24,000 men could be, and were, lost on a single day, the nightmare would not and never will go away.

The next big loss occurred on 6 September when P-47s escorted 388 B-17s on the mission to the aircraft components factories at Stuttgart. Forty-five bombers were shot down. On 13 September, VIII Bomber Command was officially divided into three bomb divisions, with the B-17 equipping the 1st and 3rd, and the 2nd being wholly equipped with the Liberator. On 27 September, P-47s escorted the bombers for over 600 miles but there were still not enough escorts to deter the German defences.

During 8–10 October, the 8th AF lost 88 bombers on raids on Germany, including 33 (and 102 damaged) on the 10th, when 313 bombers went to Münster. The 100th BG lost 12 B-17s, bringing its losses to 19 in three days. Other 13th Wing Groups did not escape the carnage either and were badly mauled at Münster. Gus Mencow, lead navigator, 520th Squadron, 390th BG, wrote:

This was the most frightening of all the missions I flew. I still get scared and have weird dreams about that day. We did not have complete air supremacy and our fighters did not yet have long-range belly tanks. They could not follow us on long-range missions. We lost eight out of 19 aircraft. The flak was unbelievable and the Luftwaffe must have had every one of their planes attacking us. The loss of so many friends was overwhelming. I got a 109 and it went down smoking and burning.

Capt Gordon-Forbes, in the 390th BG, adds:

We caught the brunt of the first attack. 2/Lt George Starnes was hit at the middle of his ship by a rocket, and the plane started to break in half. It nosed up and crashed into another, just above in the formation. Both planes fell away and went down in a column of smoke. A ship on our right blew up with a great red flash. I saw the right waist gunner come out of his

On 17 August, the 8th AF lost 60 Fortresses on the double strike against the aircraft plants at Regensburg and the ball-bearing plant at Schweinfurt. Gus Mencow (right), lead navigator of 520th Squadron, 390th BG was one who took part and who also flew the 10 October mission to Münster when the 390th lost eight out of 19 aircraft. (Gus Mencow)

On 9 October, the 8th AF bombed the Fw 190 factory at Marienburg, which Eaker called 'a classic example of precision bombing'. Sixty per cent of the bombs dropped by the 96 Fortresses exploded within 1,000 ft of the mean point of impact (MPI) and 83 per cent fell within 2,000 ft. (USAF)

window in a grotesque swan dive. His chest was shot away . . . All the weariness of battle seemed to drain every ounce of strength I had. I felt like yelling and praying at the same time.

On 14 October, the 8th dispatched 291 bombers to the ball-bearing plants at Schweinfurt again. The fighter escorts were overwhelmed and 60 bombers, or 19 per cent of its force, were lost and 142 were damaged.

Obviously something had to be done, and fast. The B-17G version of the Fortress with a chin turret was developed in response to the head-on attacks by the Luftwaffe, while more immediately, on 15 October, the 55th FG, equipped with the P-38H Lightning, entered combat. The 55th,

and the 20th FG, which was also equipped with the P-38H, had arrived in England during August and September respectively. In November the North American P-51B Mustang entered theatre operations as a tactical fighter assigned to three groups of the tactical 9th AF, which on 16 October had transferred from North Africa and was re-organized in England as a tactical arm of the USAAF in the ETO. Bomber crews in the 8th AF were desperate for a long-range fighter but they continued flying unescorted missions deep into Germany while the politics were sorted out.

In the Mediterranean, on 24 October, 12th AF B-17s and B-24s bombed the aircraft factories at Wiener Neustadt in the first US attack on

On 15 October and 28 December 1943, the 55th and 20th P-38H Lightning Fighter Groups respectively entered combat. The Fighter Collection's P-38J-10-LO Lightning is painted in the colours of California Cutie *of the 55th Squadron, 20th FG flown by 1/Lt Richard O. Loehnert at King's Cliffe, Northamptonshire. The mission symbols include top hats and canes for top cover missions, umbrellas are escorts, and the broomsticks represent fighter sweeps, while the bombs are for fighter-bomber missions. (Author)*

Austria from Italian bases. On 31 October, after 10 days of bombing operations against U-boat pens in France, Gen Carl Spaatz informed Gen Henry H. Arnold that missions were too costly for the results obtained. While the general mulled over the ramifications of achieving a

In November 1943, the North American P-51B Mustang entered theatre operations as a tactical fighter assigned to three groups of the tactical 9th AF. On 1 December 1943, P-51Bs of the 354th FG flew their first mission, a sweep over Belgium. The first Mustang fighter-escort mission for the bombers was flown on 5 December 1943.

higher degree of accuracy by bombing the pens from just 4,000 ft, his plan to split the 12th AF in two to create a Strategic Air Force in the Mediterranean, was realized. On 1 November, the 15th AF was officially activated at Tunis, Tunisia under the command of Maj Gen Jimmy Doolittle with a strength of 90 aircraft in two B-24 groups and four B-17 groups transferred from the 12th AF. (The 12th also lost four fighter groups and a recon group to the new air force, and three more fighter groups followed in May 1944. For the rest of the war the 12th, using A-20s, B-26s, B-25s, and P-47 fighter-bombers, supported the armies in Italy.) The 15th flew its first strategic mission on 2 November with a raid on Wiener Neustadt. Germany was under attack from all sides. On 3 November, the 8th dispatched over 500 bombers for the first time, when 539 aircraft blasted Wilhelmshaven. Two days later, the 56th FG became the first 8th AF fighter groups credited with 100 enemy aircraft destroyed.

That same day, 5 November 1943, Forrest S. Clark, a gunner in the 67th Squadron, 44th BG, flew to Münster on his first mission:

We had just passed over the Dutch coast. I had never seen the sky so steely blue and such good visibility. I was flying in the tail gun turret and could see for many miles to the rear. We were in one of the lead groups and I could see spread out behind us most of the entire formations of the 8th AF. What a sight. What am I getting into? Wow. I never saw so many

aircraft, I said to myself as I swivelled the turret about to coast as we passed over, a thin line edging a blue sea, the North Sea. We were bound for Germany and the target was the industrial city of Münster. It was an important war-production centre and believed to be one of the key targets of the bomber offensive. The RAF had gone there a few weeks before and been severely attacked and suffered considerable losses. However, this day looked serene and deceptively beautiful. Below me the dykes of the Zuider Zee stood out clear and straight. I could see sunlight glinting off the surfaces of the bombers in the sky behind us, elements stacked up high and low, covering a large segment of sky. We were at bombing altitude by this time and I could see the small farms, little villages and canals of Holland below.

It was getting cold in the turret and my feet were stuck so I worried if I could get out in time should there be a bailout.

We were on oxygen, having exceeded the 10,000–12,000 ft altitude. I could smell the rubber of the oxygen face mask and the faintly sweet odour of pure oxygen. It gave me a little high, a kind of euphoria of the heights. Had I remembered to check everything? Would the guns work when called on to do so if there was an attack? I checked the .50-calibre cartridge belts many times. The air was smooth and there was little or no turbulence. We were making our way inland over Nazi occupied Europe now and yet no enemy fighters were in sight. I thought this might be a milk run and began thinking of life back at the base.

Next thing I saw were small clouds drifting by the tail section. I thought, 'That's strange, we must be getting into some cloud formations; perhaps a slight

The B-17G Fortress, whose most distinctive feature was a chin turret containing two .50-calibre machine guns to counter head-on attacks by Fw 190s and Bf 109s, was developed late in 1943 and was used almost exclusively in the ETO. (Boeing)

overcast.' I didn't think much about that at first but as these clouds continued and increased in numbers I thought it best to push on the intercom button and report to the pilot and copilot. Just as I was going to do so the voice of the copilot came over the intercom asking the tail gunner to report in. I had neglected to report as required of all crew members. I pushed the intercom button and said, 'Everything okay back here, except for a few small black clouds.'

'Black clouds?' came back the voice at the other end of the intercom. 'They look black to me,' I replied. 'Damn it. That's flak!' shouted the copilot.

I looked out at the small clouds, closer now, fearing I was really in trouble with the pilot and copilot for not being more alert. I noticed now that the clouds were closer to us and each had in the heart of them, a red core, which flashed and then disappeared as the cloud drifted off to the rear. 'They're shooting at us,' I called out, not realizing I had the intercom button still depressed.

'How did you know?' came the reply. 'Who do you think they're shooting at?' Just then a violent vibration shook the plane and it seemed to rear up in the front, dipping the tail section downward. 'We've been hit,' came the call over the intercom.

'Check for damages. Any reports. All report in.' Again and again the plane rocked from side to side. From then on all hell broke loose. I saw planes going down, flaming wreckage as planes exploded and others spiralling down leaving a trail of smoke.

Suddenly, I had more respect for the small black clouds. I realized that the war had begun for me and that the enemy was actually after us; after me! I began to sweat through my heated suit and nervously pressed the face mask to my face. This was my baptism under fire, in a tiny, cramped turret 25,000 ft over Germany on the way to Münster with a load of 500-pounders.

We were lucky that day and got back to the base. The copilot took me aside and said he was recommending I take a refresher aircraft identification course. 'After all,' he said, 'If I couldn't see flak, how could I see enemy fighters?' I decided, 'If I see anything with a wing and a propeller and it points its nose at us—I shoot!'

On 14 November, Bulgaria was attacked for the first time when 91 B-25s of the 12th AF bombed Sofia. In December, this air force came under the control of MAAF (Mediterranean Air Forces) and Lt Gen John K. Cannon assumed command. On 1 December, 15th AF HQ moved to Bari, Italy where it would remain for the remainder of the war, Maj Gen Nathan F. Twining succeeding Gen Doolittle as Commanding General on 3 January 1944.

In England, another milestone was reached on 1 December when P-51Bs of the 354th FG flew their first mission, a sweep over Belgium. The

On 1 November 1943, the 15th AF was officially activated with a strength of 90 aircraft in two B-24 groups and four B-17 groups transferred from the 12th AF. For the rest of the war the 12th, using medium bombers such as the B-25, pictured here in the North African Desert, and P-47 fighter-bombers, supported the armies in Italy. (Bill Cameron)

first Mustang fighter-escort mission for the bombers was not flown until 5 December. In a record flight on 13 December, when 649 bombers bombed Bremen, Hamburg and Kiel, P-51s escorting the heavies reached the limit of their escort range for the first time. Bomber crews were quick to praise good fighter cover. T/Sgt Jack Kings, a B-17 waist gunner in the 388th BG, which on 31 December, went to Paris, wrote:

We were to do some of the first really pin-point bombing if you could call it that. Hitting just and 'only' an airfield and nothing around it was touchy. Due to spots of thick clouds scattered about, we as a group, had to circle the city several times to make certain the target was fully visible. Our fighter cover made sure no enemy aircraft would bother us. We really had deep respect for those fighter pilots.

On 11 January 1944, Maj James H. Howard, ex-Flying Tigers pilot in China, now CO of 356th Squadron, 354th FG, 9th AF, displayed 'conspicuous gallantry and intrepidity above and beyond the call of duty in action with the enemy near Oschersleben, Germany' when he came to the rescue of some 8th AF Fortresses. The Mustang was still a well-kept secret and the 354th was the pioneer Mustang group in the ETO. Howard was flying his usual mount, *Ding Hao!* (Chinese for 'very good') when the 354th provided support for a formation of B-17 Flying Fortresses on a long-range mission deep into enemy territory. As the P-51s met the bombers in the target area the bomber force was attacked by numerous rocket-firing Bf 110 *Zestörer* fighters. The 354th engaged and Howard destroyed one of the Messerschmitt 110s but in the fight lost contact with the rest of his group. He immediately returned to the level of the bomber formation and saw that the B-17s of the 401st BG were being heavily attacked by German fighters and that no 'little friends' were on hand. Howard dived into the formation of more than 30 German fighters and for 30 minutes single-handedly pressed home a series of determined attacks. He shot down three fighters and probably destroyed and damaged others. Toward the end of his action, Howard continued to fight on with one remaining machine-gun and his fuel supply dangerously low. Maj Howard's brave single-handed action undoubtedly saved the formation. He was awarded the Congressional Medal of Honor.

The VIII Fighter Command had dire need for the long-range escort fighter which could fly as far on its internal fuel as the P-47 could with drop tanks, but the first 8th AF unit to receive the P-51B was the 357th FG, stationed at Raydon, Essex. It did not fly its first escort mission until 11 February 1944. However, the weapon the 8th had needed so badly ultimately equipped all but the 56th FG in the command and literally proved a war winner.

Chapter Four

The US Strategic Air Force

On 4 January 1944, heavy bombers flew their last mission under the command of the 8th AF. The 8th AF, and the 15th AF, which in December 1943–January 1944 received six additional B-24H/J Liberator groups, were merged into a new headquarters called, US Strategic Air Forces, Europe, (USSTAF—the overall USAAF command organization in Europe) at Bushey Hall, Teddington, Middlesex, previously Headquarters, the 8th AF. Gen Carl 'Tooey' Spaatz returned to England to command the new organization while Maj Gen Jimmy Doolittle took command of the 8th AF; its head-quarters moving to High Wycombe. Lt Gen Ira

C. Eaker was transferred to the Mediterranean theatre to take command of the new Mediterranean Allied Air Forces.

Spaatz and Doolittle planned to use as soon as possible the US Strategic Air Forces in a series of co-ordinated raids, code-named Operation *Argument*, supported by RAF night bombing, against the German aircraft industry. Bad weather postponed the start of the offensive but on 29 January, the 8th dispatched 763 heavy bombers to Frankfurt am Main. It was the first time that more than 700 bombers had attacked a target. When *Big Week*, as the offensive became known, finally went ahead on 20 February, the 15th AF was already committed to supporting the Anzio operation and could not participate. Roy W. Baker, engineer/gunner in B-17G *Mr Lucky*, 347th Bomb Squadron, 99th BG, 15th AF, flew what he thought would be a milk run, on 17 February, over the Anzio beachhead.

B-24 Liberators of the 15th AF come under heavy attack on a mission from Italy in 1944. In December 1943–January 1944 the 15th AF received six new B-24H/J groups. (USAF)

Everything seemed OK mechanically. We had to feather one engine due to flak on the way to the target area. Of course, the enemy saw we were hurt and the flak was aimed right at us and was so thick you could nearly walk on it. They got [number] three engine and the prop ran away so we only had two engines left and we started losing altitude fast. We passed near Cisterna at about 14,000 ft and they were throwing everything at us by now. The pilot called for me over the intercom and I opened the door to the bomb-bay. Wham! A burst of flak blew the catwalk away right in front of me. I shut the door and tried to help Jerry by intercom. I looked out of the waist window at [number] four engine which received a hit and was throwing oil very badly, so to avoid fire we had to feather it. I've flown in 17s that could fly on one engine and even manoeuvre a little but *Mr Lucky* was a log wagon and could not. King, the other waist gunner, called out, 'Two Fws on our tail!' They were Spitfires covering our descent, so back to the business at hand. We threw out every last thing in the plane except three life rafts. [Number] one was pulling 60" of mercury and we could maintain controllable air speed of about 90 mph by going down at about a 45° angle. It was one of those 'wing and a prayer' situations. We five men in the rear of the plane sat in bob-sled fashion. Jerry made a beautiful landing in the water about 12 miles off the Anzio beachhead . . . Our flight surgeon decided we needed a rest and sent us to the Isle of Capri for R & R.

Big Week began on 20 February when the 8th AF dispatched 1,028 bombers escorted by 832 fighters with 16 RAF squadrons of Mustangs and Spitfires to 12 aircraft factories in Germany. German aircraft production was cut by 20 per cent as a result of effective bombing but 25 bombers and four fighters were shot down. Three Congressional Medals of Honor (two

posthumously) were awarded to B-17 crewmen. Next day, 924 bombers escorted by 679 fighters bombed aircraft factories and other targets for the loss of 19 bombers and 5 fighters. On 22 February, the 15th AF, which had been grounded by bad weather, sent its bombers to Regensburg, escorted by 185 fighters. One hundred and eighteen B-24s wrecked the Obertraubling assembly plant but 14 B-24s were shot down. Most of the 8th AF bombers aborted their missions because of bad weather over England and 41 bombers were shot down. Next day, the 8th AF was grounded because of bad weather but 102 B-24s of the 15th AF hit the Steyr ball-bearing works in Austria and destroyed 20 per cent of the plant. Seventeen Liberators were shot down. On 24 February 867 bombers of the 8th AF bombed targets in Germany and Poland. Eleven B-17s and 28 Liberators were lost. The 15th AF dispatched its B-17s to Steyr again. Sixteen Fortresses were shot down.

On the final day, 25 February, 754 8th AF and 400 15th AF bombers, escorted by 1,000 fight-

P-38J Lightning 42-68008 showing the distinctive chin radiators beneath the V-1710-89/91 engines. Late Js had their fuel tank capacity increased to over 1,000 gallons to enable them to escort the heavy bombers on deep-penetration raids over the Reich. (Lockheed)

ers, bombed industrial targets in Germany. Second Lieutenant Robert V. McCalmont, B-17 bombardier in the 390th BG, 8th AF, saw a gallant Fortress pilot on the mission to Regensburg, which was the target for 176 bombers:

I watched this guy do everything but a snap roll to shake off four Germans who were out with everything they had to get him. He dived, climbed and banked, and one time went so close to the ground that plane and shadow seemed to converge [sic]. He headed back up again with one fighter still hugging his tail and levelled off below us. His last message came through our earphones: 'That's all brother, you're looking at my last engine!' The ship's nose pitched forward and a minute later it crashed and burned.

The 8th AF lost 31 bombers and the 15th AF, 39. Total losses during *Big Week* amounted to 226 bombers.

On 4 March, a few B-17s dropped the first American bombs on Berlin when 31 B-17s released bombs on the Kleinmachnow area

S/Sgt Forrest S. Clark, radio-operator/gunner in Lt Rocky Griffith's crew, 44th BG, 8th AF. (Forrest S. Clark)

south-west of the German capital. On 6 March, the 8th dispatched 730 heavies and almost 800 escort fighters to Berlin: 'Big-B'. The 672 bombers dropped 1,600 tons of bombs on the city and gunners claimed over 170 German fighters destroyed but the 8th lost 75 bombers. On 8 March, 623 bombers escorted by 891 fighters hit Berlin again. The leading Third Division lost 37 Fortresses. Next day, nine more bombers were shot down by flak as the 8th tried to bomb Berlin through thick cloud. On 27 March, after a break in missions against the capital, Spaatz sent his bombers to Berlin again. Altogether, the 8th AF dropped 4,800 tons of high explosive on Berlin during five raids in March 1944.

Heavy bombing raids continued to be made on targets in Germany. On 30 March, the 15th AF flew its first 1,000-ton raid, striking targets in Italy. On 3 April, 375 B-17s and B-24s made the first heavy raid on Budapest. Two days later, attacks by 542 bombers of the 8th AF on industrial targets in Poland, escorted by 719 fighters of VIII and IX Fighter Commands, resulted in the loss of 42 bombers.

Most crews were fatalistic. Some missions were regarded with superstition. S/Sgt Forrest S. Clark (radio operator/gunner in Lt Rocky Griffith's crew, in 44th BG, 8th AF) was superstitious and feared flying a mission on 13 April.

I would have preferred another date but I and the crew had no choice. As we prepared for take-off I said, 'Why me on the 13th?' Anyway, it proved to be quite a mission among many I had flown to that date. It was a long haul by air, a deep penetration, as they called it. I can still see that clear, steely sky over Germany, the farm lands and the small villages shining in the sunlight, looking so peaceful, yet so deadly. We knew that to come down in that part of Nazi Germany would likely mean being beaten by a hostile civilian population because we had been warned of such incidents by our officers at previous briefings.

The decisions we made that day shaped the rest of my life and my survival in WW2. We were at about 20,000 ft over Lechfeld, a strategic Nazi airfield in southern Germany, when all hell broke loose. Flak came up at us from all sides and we scrambled to get out of the target area after 'bombs away.' I saw them go, fishtailing down on the runways, and saw the Nazi planes parked on the dispersal areas go up in a thousand splinters of steel and flames. Later, we learned the bomb pattern was 'excellent' and we had bombed what was a key German jet fighter base of the dreaded Me 262 and others of the once famous Luftwaffe.

We found we were losing fuel at a rapid rate and falling inexorably behind the rest of our formation. It was impossible for us to maintain air speed.

'Can we make it back?' came the question over the intercom. 'Back to our base?'

My hands got quite sweaty as I peered out of the small window by the radio compartment to get glimpses of the formation now disappearing to the west. The pilot asked me for a heading to Lake Constance which formed the border between Nazi Germany and neutral Switzerland. By this time, there were enemy fighters coming up to our altitude to pursue us.

There is no feeling so helpless, so fearful, as being in the vast sky all alone with enemy fighters about. I gripped the dial of the radio transmitter but I could not hear anything except static on the earphones. Finally, the decision came from the cockpit that we were to break off and make a desperate dash to the Swiss border, a manoeuvre that required the utmost daring and on which all our lives depended.

Later, the pilot called over the intercom for me to fire off flares as the navigator hastily checked the charts for a heading to Swiss territory. Just as we neared the border our aircraft was hit by four loud bursts of flak, wounding one of the waist gunners, Sgt Jack Harmon, and rocking the plane from nose to tail. One piece came up through the radio compartment and others narrowly missed the bomb-bay and apparently hit in the waist area.

Flak had ripped through the plane in several places and one piece had hit our waist gunner in the hand as he gripped the waist guns. The flight engineer, Sgt Earl Parrish, checked the fuel gauges and found he had lost so much fuel it was impossible for us to make it back across enemy territory. We would have to either crash, a very risky business, or if successful, land and be taken prisoners of the Germans. The other possibility was to fall into the hands of a cruel crowd of pro-Nazis. We barely had enough fuel to make the Swiss border.

Adding to our woes there suddenly appeared Me 109s following us as if waiting for the kill. We learned later that some of these aircraft were Swiss Air Force 109s.

I thought we would never make it until, finally, I heard a cry over the intercom, 'Freedom! We made it!' It was at that very moment when the four flak bursts hit us. I believed it was German flak but some of the crew thought it was from Swiss AA gunners on the border with itchy trigger fingers who were retaliating for the US bombing a few days earlier of Schauffhausen, a Swiss border town. Some even went so far to joke that Sgt Harmon was going to be the only airman wounded by flak from a neutral country.

I saw the lake slide beneath us. Then the shoreline and a very close view of the snow covered Alps gleaming in the sunlight. We managed to limp the crippled bomber to the Swiss Air Force base at Dubendorf near Zurich. I activated the explosive device to prevent any classified material from falling into the hands of the Swiss or Germans.

As I got out of the plane through the bomb-bay, the first thing I saw was a ring of men with automatic rifles surrounding the plane and pointing weapons at me. They were dressed as German soldiers and for a moment I was sure we had miscalculated and landed at a German base. I started walking away from the aircraft, fearing it might explode, and as I got a few yards away, I felt a soldier behind me and the sharp

American aircrews not only met BF 109s of the Luftwaffe. Sometimes they belonged to the Swiss AF, as Lt Rocky Griffith's crew in the 44th BG, 8th AF discovered on 13 April 1944 when they were forced to seek refuge in Switzerland following flak damage to their Liberator over Germany. (via Forrest S. Clark)

end of his automatic weapon in the small of my back. I knew then I wasn't going any farther and I stopped, raising my hands. I had my .45 sidearm but didn't dare reach for it.

Our navigator, Lt Ralph Jackson, got out and the first thing he did was hang his parachute harness over the rifle of one of the dozen soldiers. He said he was so disgusted because he had lost his original crew and had flown before, but only three missions with us.

The soldiers closed in around us and soon a Swiss colonel in full dress uniform stepped out of a car and told us we were in neutral Switzerland. This was our welcome to a neutral country in the midst of WW2, a not totally friendly welcome party. I had a sense of elation, yet sadness, because I had wished to finish my tour of duty and return to the US. Now my future was in doubt because no one knew then how long the war in Europe would last. [In December 1944, Forrest Clark escaped from Switzerland with the aid of the US agents in Berne and the French Resistance, making his way to Lyons, France, just before Christmas 1944 during the Battle of the Ardennes.]

Meanwhile, in April the 15th AF began bombing oil and transportation targets in the vicinity of the Ploesti oilfields in Romania. One of the airmen who was sent to Italy, eventually winding up at Cerignola near Foggia, flying B-24s in the 456th BG in the 304th Bomb Wing, was Fred Meisel who had last served in the Aleutians. One of his first missions was on 21 April 1944 when he flew as tail gunner. John L. 'Jack' Dupont, his copilot, recalls:

We set out for Bucharest to bomb the railroad marshalling yards. We were carrying 500 lb demolition bombs. The weather was bad and we could not see to bomb Bucharest. We tried secondary targets of Turnu Severins and Belgrade with no success. With no fighter escort, we encountered a heavy fighter attack and our plane was badly damaged. We salvoed our bombs, and with two engines out, we started across the Adriatic Sea. About halfway across and still losing altitude, we called to the crew to prepare to ditch. The response was a frantic call from Sgt Miller, the radio operator, telling us that Sgt Kenny Mayberry, our ball turret gunner, could not align his turret to get out.

Our total concentration was now on Sgt

1/Lt Rex Wilkinson's crew, 456th BG, 304th Bomb Wing, 15th AF in Italy 1944. Back row, left to right: 1/Lt Rex Wilkinson, pilot; 1/Lt Jack L. Dupont, copilot; 2/Lt Bill Jenkins, bombardier; 2/Lt Jim McIntosh, navigator. Front row, left to right: Sgt Charles Miller, radioman; Sgt Alvernon Boltis, upper turret gunner; Sgt Aaron Saloven, nose turret gunner; Sgt Boyce Duncan, flight engineer; Sgt Fred Meisel, tail gunner; Sgt Kenneth Mayberry, ball gunner. (via Jack Dupont)

Mayberry's predicament as we continued to lose altitude. We were now below 500 ft elevation above the water and gradually losing more. Sgt Duncan, our flight engineer, called: they had tried everything and could not get the ball door to align with the ship to release Kenny. In desperation, I headed back into the waist section carrying my .45 automatic and the fire axe. I was determined to somehow get the turret to rotate. To my amazement when I reached the waist, there stood Kenny, looking more composed than anyone else. I could see the top of someone's head in the ball turret, and Kenny told me it was Sgt Fred Meisel, our tail gunner, who had climbed down in the turret to retrieve Kenny's gloves! We immediately jerked him up out of the ball. Kenny assured us he was all right and 'it wasn't any big deal' but we observed that he had totalled his wrist watch in trying to free himself.

We managed to maintain our altitude at a little over 200 ft, and after making an emergency landing at a field near the Adriatic coast for repair and refuelling, we finally reached our base at Cerignola. Our pilot, Rex Wilkinson, was awarded the DFC for this mission. Our plane never flew again due to extensive structural damage, and Kenny Mayberry had a very frightening ride across the Adriatic Sea, one that he will never forget. Nor will I.

Up until May 1944, railway junctions, airfields, ports and bridges in northern France and the Atlantic coastline were bombed in the run-up to the invasion of Normandy. May Day marked the opening of a series of all-out attacks from England on the enemy's rail network in support of the *Pointblank* directive, when 1,328 8th AF bombers struck at targets in France and Belgium. On 7 May, 1,000 American heavies were dispatched for the first time and next day the 8th AF began all-out attacks on French and Belgian airfields. On 9 May, 772 bombers attacked transportation targets. Three days later, 973 bombers targeted marshalling yards in Germany and the Low Countries. On 11/12 May, 1944 Exercise *Eagle*, a full-scale invasion practice was carried out by IX Troop Carrier Command in England. It was the culmination of three command and 38 wing exercises in the run-up to *Overlord*. On 21 May, Operation *Chattanooga Choo Choo*, the systematic air attack on trains in Germany and France, began.

By June 1944 the 15th AF was bombing railway networks in south-east Europe in support of Russian military operations in Romania.

C-46D Commandos of the 47th TCS, 313th TCG, 9th AF await their next troop carrier drop. On 11/12 May 1944, Exercise Eagle *took place, the last full-scale invasion practice by IX Troop Carrier Command in the run-up to Operation* Overlord.

B-24 Liberators of the 15th AF coming off the target at the Concordia Vega oil refinery at Ploesti on 31 May 1944 (altogether the 15th AF attacked Ploesti on 20 occasions). By June 1944, the 15th AF was bombing railway networks in south-east Europe in support of Russian military operations in Romania. Throughout the summer of 1944, Austrian aircraft manufacturing centres at Wiener Neustadt were bombed and oil-producing centres were also attacked. (USAF)

Throughout the summer of 1944, Austrian aircraft-manufacturing centres at Wiener Neustadt were bombed and oil-producing centres too, were attacked. On 2 June, the 15th

AF flew the first shuttle mission when 130 B-17s and P-51 escorts landed in Russia after a raid on Hungary.

Early on the morning of D-Day 6 June, the 14 troop carrier groups of IX Troop Carrier Command, led by 19 pathfinder C-47s, dropped paratroops on drop zones around Ste Mère Église on the Cotentin Peninsular, the western flank of the invasion area. In 821 sorties on D-Day, 16 TCC transports were lost to enemy action. At 15 minutes after midnight on 6 June 1944, Capt Frank Lillyman led his team of 101st

Early Douglas C-47A in flight. C-47s served in every theatre of war. In 821 sorties on D-Day, 6 June 1944, 16 Troop Carrier Command transports were lost to enemy action. Later that day the C-47s again flew over the Normandy beachhead, this time towing 48 Horsa gliders carrying field artillery reinforcements to the area around Ste. Mère Église. (Douglas)

The 78th FG P-47s (pictured) were not unique in flying several missions (0330–2300 hours) on 6 June 1944. (Via Andy Height)

Airborne Division Pathfinders out of the door of a C-47 transport and parachuted into occupied France. Behind them came 6,000 'Screaming Eagles', the paratroopers of the 101st Airborne, in C-47s of the IX Troop Carrier Command. It was planned to drop 13,000 paratroopers from the US 82nd and 101st Airborne Divisions using 882 aircraft on six drop zones, all within a few miles of Ste Mère Église. Returning to England after their early D-Day mission, the C-47s once more flew over the Normandy beachhead, this time towing 48 Horsa gliders carrying field artillery reinforcements to the area around Ste Mère Église.

In the early hours of D-Day, the 82nd Airborne Division, the All Americans, was dropped by parachute and flown in by glider to positions astride the Merderet River. Glider-borne infantrymen played an important role during the Normandy operations. As counter-parts of the parachute infantrymen, they delivered weapons, equipment, personnel and vehicles to both airborne divisions. The first daylight glider operation occurred on the morning of 7 June. By D-Day + 6, the 82nd had secured the area north of Ste Mère Église after fierce fighting.

Some 1,361 bombers were dispatched on the first of the four missions flown on D-Day. Coastal installations were bombed by 1,015 heavies, while 47 hit transportation choke points in Caen, and 21 more hit alternative targets. Altogether, 2,362 bomber sorties involving 1,729 B-17s and B-24s were flown on D-Day, dropping 3,596 tons of bombs. The VIII Fighter Command flew 1,880 sorties and claimed 28 enemy fighters shot down. A total of 742 B-26 sorties were flown in support of Operation

By May 1944, the 9th AF commanded eight Marauder groups and a pathfinder squadron for tactical missions in support of the Allied build-up to the invasion of Europe. A total of 742 B-26 sorties were flown in support of Operation Overlord by the 9th AF. (USAF)

Overlord by the 9th AF. Three bombers—a 487th BG Liberator, and two B-24s in the 493rd BG, 8th AF (flying its first mission) which collided—were the day's only losses. Lt J. Cooper's B-24 in the 863rd BS struck the tail of Lt D. Russell's B-24 in the 862nd BS and both Liberators were seen to disintegrate and disappear into the overcast over the Channel. Dan Dufphey in the 860th BS, who saw the collision from his top turret, recalls: 'All who witnessed the crash were dumbfounded and shaken.' Lt Joe Gualano, a pilot in the 860th Squadron, 493rd BG, adds: 'It was said that Lord Haw Haw, that evening, announced that Germany had nothing to fear from the new Group with the "X" tail markings as they were killing themselves.'

A B-24 in the 44th BG from Shipdham almost came to grief also. John W. McClane, the 21-year-old navigator aboard one of the B-24s, who flew two missions on D-Day with two different crews, recalls:

All was going well. We were climbing on course through very dense clouds. Visibility was at best only 50–100 ft. Suddenly, a loud and confusing shout of voices filled my earphones and about the same time I felt the tail of our aircraft go down sharply, perhaps as much as 30°, then almost as rapidly level out again. The babble of voices continued until the pilot calmed them down enough to find out what had happened. The men in the rear were almost in shock. A British bomber had hit the right twin rudder of our plane! I mark it up to the SNAFU that goes with the best of planning.

On 11 June, in a shuttle raid between the USSR and Italy, 15th AF aircraft bombed the Romanian airfield at Foscani and 10 days later the 8th flew its first shuttle mission, bombing Berlin and landing at Poltava, Russia. Following the mission, 43 B-17s and several P-51s were destroyed in an audacious attack carried out by the Luftwaffe. The 8th AF also continued with missions to France to help the armies fighting in Normandy. Edward R. Glotfelty, B-24 pilot, 863rd Squadron, 493rd BG, recalls the 25 June mission to France:

After we dropped our bombs we had a runaway prop on [number] two engine. I tried to feather but was unable to control it. The vibration was tremendous, shaking the whole plane. The noise was deafening. We lost speed and dropped out of the formation.

The shortest return route took me over the Normandy beaches. My interest at the time was to hold altitude as much as possible but we were going down because of the great drag on the plane caused by the runaway prop. I started having trouble with the [number] four engine, the rpm surging, engine cutting out, and the plane yawing because of the loss of power on the outboard engine. We were now down to 12,000 ft and arriving over Normandy. I marvelled at the panorama of ships and barrage balloons. With the second engine in trouble I didn't think we could make it back to England and I saw two airfields below me, one obviously new, one-runway fighter strip carved out of the countryside, and one paved, mature field that was farther from the beaches. I decided to go down and chose the field closer to the coast.

I circled over the field, saw fighters on the strip, guessed at the wind direction and had another engine lose power! We were out of position, no power, and dropping like a rock. I ordered wheels up and decided to land on the wide dirt strip alongside of the runway. We hit perfectly. The left wing tip hit [a] second after the fuselage seemed to help cushion the crash. The fuselage split on the right side and the crew was able to get out through the crack. No one was injured, though Gene Cromer, the engineer, had some radio equipment fall on him. The force of the landing was so great that the number one engine was torn off completely and the plane was a totally destroyed. The last I saw of the plane, a large crane was trying to drag the wreck out of the way so they could continue the war!

We were checked out by a Canadian doctor, loaded on a truck going to the beach, put on a British LST, and by the next day [were] back in England. The funny thing was that the only clothes we had were electric-heated flying suits. We spent the night in London and were treated like Poles or some foreign air force.

In July, the 15th AF lost 318 heavy bombers as it began softening up targets in southern France in preparation for the invasion of the South of France, code-named *Anvil*. Marseilles, Lyon, Grenoble, and Toulon all shook from the weight of bombs dropped by the B-24s and B-17s. On 2 July, Fred Meisel participated in his forty-eighth mission from Italy on a raid on the marshalling yards at Budapest, Hungary, flying as a volunteer replacement on another crew, and was shot down. Flying in 'trail' formation, the group lost six planes that day. Fred was wounded by shrapnel and the plane was on fire, but he helped two other crew members out of the ship before jumping. He was later awarded a Purple Heart and the DFC for his actions. The five crew members who survived were picked up by peasants 20 miles from Budapest, in what Meisel described as an 'ugly crowd getting uglier by the minute because word was out that we hit a school house'. The Hungarian peasants were about to stone him to death when a German corporal took him prisoner and saved him from the civilians. The German apparently had a brother who was a school teacher in Los Gatos, California!

After 26 days of hospitalization, the crew were taken to Gestapo headquarters in Budapest for questioning. Although they had Fred's service record from WW1 and ordinarily might have shot him as a traitor to Germany, Fred's protestations that he was an American Indian saved the day and he was thrown into solitary confinement for 80 days. Eventually, he was transferred to Stalag Luft IV at Grosstychow in north-eastern Germany. On his return to America Meisel was given a hero's welcome during a parade at Ft. McArthur. M/Sgt Meisel was discharged 6 October 1945 with 138 points but stayed in the active reserve for the next 13 years, before finally retiring in 1965 after nine more in Army Intelligence. Fred passed away on 22 February 1987.

Lt Donald Puckett, a B-24 pilot in 98th BG, brought his aircraft home against incredible odds from Ploesti on 9 July 1944. Just after 'bombs away' flak killed one crew member and severely wounded six others. The control cables were cut, a fire started in the oxygen system, and two engines were put out of action. Puckett handed over control to his copilot while he inspected the aircraft and cared for the wounded. The bombbay was awash with fuel and hydraulic fluid but he managed to hand-crank open the doors and drain the fuel. He threw out the guns and equipment but the B-24 seemed doomed. He ordered the crew to bail out but three refused and Puckett would not leave them. He fought hard to pull the Liberator out of its fatal descent but it crashed into a mountainside and exploded. Puckett was posthumously awarded the Congressional Medal

of Honor; the last of seven awarded to crew members during raids on Ploesti.

On 22 July, the 15th AF made the first all-fighter shuttle raid on Europe, attacking Luftwaffe airfields in Romania and then landing at Russian bases. Operation *Cobra*, the break-out of the American forces from Normandy, began on 25 July. It was heralded by air attacks by 3,000 Allied aircraft. On 9 August, Capt Darrell R. Lindsey led 30 B-26 bombers on a vital mission over Pontoise, France. Hit during the bomb run, the plane's right engine was set on fire. Although knowing the fuel tanks might explode, Lindsey completed the bomb run, gave the order to bail out, and continued to fly the plane so crew members could jump. Refusing to relinquish his post, Lindsey died when the Marauder, exploded, just after the last crew member had jumped. For his heroism, Capt Lindsey was posthumously awarded the Congressional Medal of Honor.

On 11 August, 956 heavy bombers of the 8th AF, escorted by 578 fighters, attacked transportation targets in France. T/Sgt Robert T. Marshall, radio operator/gunner in the 385th BG, who had flown his first mission on 21 June to Berlin, flew his seventh mission this day when the group went to Belfort in southern France.

This was not Channel hopping but it was a milk run. Variety, it's great. We were flying our first mission as the lead plane (in the B Group). Our target was a railroad yard at Belfort, which is in the south-east corner of France, near the Italy–Switzerland area. I studied the briefing map longer than usual. I made sure I knew where Switzerland was and allowed myself knowledge of what direction I would take off in should worse come to worse. I saw no flak on this trip and that defines a no-ball to me. A milk run. How many more like this can we get? I rolled another seven today although in the front of the plane they said they saw flak in the distance.

The bombs fell on the target on a beautiful summer day. We were at 14,000 ft, low by our standard. The bombardier said he saw boxcars sail into space when the bombs exploded down there. I watched through the camera-well because there was no indication enemy fighters were in the area. First I saw a deserted little city come into view, picturesque, beautiful. It glistened in the sun, a peaceful scene that

T/Sgt Robert T. Marshall, radio operator/gunner in the 385th BG, who flew his first mission on 21 June which was to Berlin. He flew his seventh mission on 11 August when 956 heavy bombers of the 8th AF escorted by 578 fighters attacked transportation targets in France.

made me wonder if we were close to the Mediterranean. Roofs sparkled in the sun. Everything looked clean and was painted bright, pastel shades. It was 11:55, almost high noon, when we sailed over and the bombs fell. It was a hellish sight. Eruption after eruption tore up the railyard as I watched. I did not want to see a stray bomb fall into that pretty town and none did while I watched.

I continued to gawk through the camera-well after we pulled off and headed home. It wasn't long before I saw signs of war in Europe. As we moved into the general area of Paris I saw intersection after intersection where bombings and artillery shellings, apparently, left rubble. I saw bridges that were pulverized. Villages were rubble piles. We had P-51 escorts. I watched them dive down and strafe a train. It blew up

as I watched. The train was all that I saw moving on the ground and soon it did not move.

A wood came into my view and smoke wafted out of it, perhaps a sign our fighter planes earlier had paid a call. It was simple to imagine German troops and tanks were in the woods. The smoke I saw was not like the smoke earlier over the target. At Belfort the smoke was created by the Germans. I saw their smudge pots burning around the field. The smoke was no more than a poor token. When our bomber stream went over the railyard it was completely uncovered: the smoke wafted away from a railyard.

We were aloft 8 hours and 30 minutes and on oxygen for 5 hours. After we landed Brackett told me we had come within 10 miles of the Swiss border, after I asked. He and Benton got Charlie into more hot water today. The command pilot overheard their discussion on the bomb run and told Charlie afterward they seemed to be more concerned about a bet with friends for a bottle of Scotch (whose bombing would be more accurate: keep the bombs in the railyard) than they were about bombing the target.

Soldiering is a strange business. Maybe business is not the word for what I saw today. Nothing seemed heroic about it and I don't see heroic figures on this base, other than the Colonel. Epic characters, where are you? These are ordinary people doing war work, like dropping bombs on a beautiful city on a bright summer day. War is not noble.

On 18 August T/Sgt Terry Parsons (radio operator/gunner, 862nd Squadron, 493rd BG, 8th AF) went to an airfield in France, near Amiens—Rue de Balcourt, or something like that. Rough!!! Wooee! those ack-ack gunners have really been checked out. We lost two planes and the 34th BG, three. Their first shot blew our leader's tail off clean. He just went straight down—poor devils didn't have a chance. Washington got it too but I guess they all got out. Hansen was really scared, I guess, but so were we all. Our formation just split from hell to breakfast. 'A' Group didn't get much flak at all.

This same day, 2/Lt Philip G. Day flew his first mission, as copilot in the 467th BG, which bombed an aircraft engine plant at Woippy, near Metz. Day recorded: 'No flak—no fighters— Excellent results . . . The 100-mission party of the Group was on 19 August, and it was a wild, glorious, all night drunk out time. The Group had been stood down for 20 August; I am sure no one was fit or able to fly.' On 20 August 1944, the 20th Wing Liberators were converted

Bombs dropped from 8th AF Liberators explode at an important rail junction at Angers, France on 6 August 1944. (USAF)

for 'trucking' fuel and supplies to the Allied ground forces in France. On 25 August, Paris was liberated. The following day, 956 bombers escorted by 897 fighters attacked targets in France, Belgium, Holland and Germany. Thirteen bombers and 13 fighters were lost, and 148 bombers and 15 fighters were damaged.

On 27 August, Robert H. Tays flew his first mission with the 392nd BG, 8th AF, to Hannover. He wrote:

Aircraft are everywhere for the entire 8th AF is out this day . . . Upon arrival at the IP . . . a flak burst hit our No. 3 engine. It stopped running almost immediately with just enough time to feather the prop. I added power to the remaining engines, stayed with the formation in position . . . Then it was bombs away. The sky was dark with flak bursts,

some bursts close enough to hear over the roar of the engines and see the little orange flame in the centre of the bursts.

Tays made the decision to drop out of formation and make it home alone. They landed 30 minutes behind the rest of the group.

On 3 September, T/Sgt Robert T. Marshall flew his tenth mission, when the 8th went to Brest, France.

Briefing was 02:30 this morning. I readied myself for a long haul, maybe to East Prussia. S-2 raised the curtain that covers the map and the route ribbon was short. Brest! Again! A coastal-battery target! S-2 said 19,000 Nazis are holed up at Brest and thereabout.

'Take-off was at 05:15, a night take-off. Up we went into the dark for assembly. The whole 8th Air Force seemed to be up and milling around. My anticipation made the sweating-it-out begin early. Light, when it came, was eerie. A kind of golden light, not strong, not bright, just gold daylight. And then I witnessed something that made man, the bombers, the war, insignificant. It was an apparition bathed in soft, golden light. It was a peek into the unknown with the Supreme Being exposed. It was holy, majestic, awesome; and it took me away from preparing myself to go into battle.

On one side of the sky in half light, a beautiful full moon set. At my left I saw a beautiful sun rising over the English Channel. Rays of color fired from the sun. In that light the sun, the moon, and the shoreline were parts of an awesome painting. The rays gave the painting an effect that made me think of the times when I was a kid looking at pictures in the Bible: angels wearing halos, the sky ablaze as it was when John baptized Jesus, like the picture when the dove flew in radiating light over Noah's Ark, like the scene when the angels sang above the manger in Bethlehem. Celestial, refracted light. It was all there with the sun and the moon. I watched and watched it. I had been searching the sky anxiously moments before, anticipating airplanes on a collision course as we went round and round assembling. Then this; a perfect full moon going down, awesome in itself in golden light, golden light giving the sun a supernatural appearance making it shout the power of the Creator.

Daylight slowly increased in intensity. The shoreline below us—I suspect it was England—slowly etched into a hardness as it came out of the shadow. The mysticism of the scene disappeared too quickly. Routine of assembly returned. We flew on, a mission unfolding, and I pushed the moments out of my mind and returned to looking for enemy fighters. We flew toward Brest at 10,000 ft and we were at that altitude when we went over the target at 09:38, some 4 hours after take-off. 'Bombs away!' I watched through the camera-well, looking between my boots. I saw the bombs fall, the explosions. I heard the sound above the noise of the engines. The sequence of noise sounded like an ammunition dump might be exploding. The target was well camouflaged, one of many pillboxes back of the beach. Wrecked equipment littered the beach. I thought I could see barbed wire entanglements down there from 10,000 ft. Later, Benton said his accuracy was excellent. The mission took 7 hours and 35 minutes to dump 38 100-pounders. It was a milk run except for the apparition.

On 10 September, over 1,000 8th AF heavy bombers, escorted by several hundred fighters, attacked targets in Germany. Next day, the 8th began its last shuttle raid, when 139 aircraft attacked an armaments factory at Chemnitz and flew on to bases in Russia. On 13 September, the force bombed the Diosgyoer steel works in Hungary. On 16 September, fighter groups of the 8th AF, four carrying bombs, strafed the Hannover–Bremen–Osnabrück areas and bombed Alhorn airfield and the Mannheim and Kaiserlautern areas. The noose was tightening around Germany's neck. When the Allies launched Operation *Market Garden* using American and British airborne divisions to take the Eindhoven, Nijmegen and Arnhem bridges in mid-September, the B-24s were once again called upon to supplement the troop carriers. Altogether, 252 supply-carrying B-24s flew to France on the first full divisional 'trucking' mission on 18 September, including six specially modified 458th BG Liberators which delivered over 9,000 gallons of fuel to Gen Patton's forces.

On 22 September, the last shuttle mission ended when 84 B-17s and 51 P-51s returned to England from Italy. On 27 September, 315 B-24s were dispatched to the Henschel engine and vehicle assembly plants at Kassel in central Germany. The 445th BG lost 25 B-24s in fierce fighter attacks. Second Lieutenant George M. Collar, a bombardier in the 445th BG, had by now flown 28 missions, and he filled in on 2/Lt

James W. Schaen's ship. He describes the sad demise.

A wolf-pack of Fw 190s . . . came out of the high clouds behind us, and hit us so fast that our tail gunner never got to call them. He and the two waist gunners must have been hit almost immediately. I was in the front turret and was helpless as the Fw 190 streaked past. He couldn't have cleared us by more than 6 ft . . . At this time I heard the bail-out bell ringing, so I got out of the turret and found Corman Bean, the navigator, putting on his 'chute. The whole nose compartment looked like a sieve. By this time we were nosing down and the whole left wing was on fire. We opened the nose wheel door and bailed out. Unfortunately, Jim Schaen never made it. He left a wife and baby. [Collar was among five of the crew who were captured.]

The losses of 15th AF in Italy also continued to rise. T/Sgt Joseph Z. Krajewski (B-24 engineer, 778th BS, 464th BG, 15th AF) based at Cerignola, Italy, flew 13 missions. On 4 October 1944, he flew his last:

Our last mission was Munich in ship *Brown Nose*. We were hit by four ack-ack strikes—three engines cut out at 22,000 ft, dropped to 14,000 ft—two engines cut back in and we recovered. Three buddies and myself were wounded. Gas leaked into bomb-bay—blown around. Bomb-bay doors buckled. No intercom. Had to release (10) 500 lb bombs with screwdriver. Kept losing altitude. Headed for France. Two Me 109 fighters (Swiss markings) intercepted us and we crash landed at Dubendorf airfield, Zurich.

On 24 October, 415 P-47s and P-51s of the 8th AF carried out fighter-bomber raids in the Hannover–Kassel area. Nine aircraft were lost. On 16 November, the largest air and ground co-operative effort to date occurred when over 4,000 Allied aircraft dropped more than 10,000 tons of bombs on enemy targets. Two days later, the 15th AF dispatched over 680 aircraft to oil refineries in Austria and to airfields in Italy, protected by an umbrella of 86 P-51s. On 25 November, the 491st BG lost 16 B-24s in almost as many minutes during a mission to oil refineries at Misburg. Attacks on oil targets had assumed top priority by the autumn of 1944 but the refineries were dispersed throughout the four

Smiling faces of the ground crew of P-51D Heat Wave *of the 359th FG, 8th AF at East Wretham, Norfolk in 1944. On 24 October 1944, 415 P-47s and P-51s of the 8th AF carried out fighter-bomber raids in the Hannover–Kassel area. Nine aircraft were lost.*

corners of the Reich so a concentrated and effective offensive proved difficult. Nevertheless, vast aerial fleets of 8th AF and 15th AF B-24s and B-17s escorted by P-51s and P-38s, bombed oil refineries in Germany, Czechoslovakia and Romania during late 1944–early 1945. Total air superiority meant that the USSTAF could roam far and wide throughout the Greater Reich, hitting targets as far afield as Ploesti in Romania, Brux in Czechoslovakia, Budapest, Komorom, Gyor and Petfurdo in Hungary, Belgrade and other cities in Yugoslavia, and Trieste in north-eastern Italy. By the end of 1944, only three out of 91 German refineries were still working normally; 29 were partly operational and the remainder were out of action for months.

On 16 December, German panzer divisions punched a hole, or 'bulge' in the American lines in the Ardennes. The Allied air forces were grounded by fog. Robert Tays in the 392nd BG recorded: 'We were briefed almost every morning for a mission and then after going through the total procedure of getting ready for take-off,

the missions were scrubbed. Much icing during this time of foul weather. Much effort put forth and a bit of despondency prevailed.' On Christmas Eve a record 2,034 8th AF bombers and 500 RAF and 9th AF bombers, took part in

The oil refinery at Lutzkendorf, Germany comes under attack by B-24H Liberators of the 834th 'Zodiacs' Squadron, 486th BG, 3rd AD, 8th AF on 28 May 1944. (USAF)

By the end of 1944, only three out of 91 German refineries were still working normally; 29 were partly operational and the remainder were out of action for months. This reconnaissance photo shows the damage to the oil refinery complex at Politz on 3 March 1945. (USAF)

the largest single strike flown by the Allied Air Forces of the war, against German airfields and lines of communication leading to the Bulge. The weather was still very bad on 27 December when the 8th attempted another mission. Max Stout, a copilot in the 453rd BG, at Old Buckenham, recalls:

We were to be the first plane off. It was an instrument take-off. We were late to taxi and when we arrived, a new crew was lined up to take off. Being a new crew in the 733rd I suppose they were eager to show their mettle. The order of take-off wasn't all that important. Lt Brown hurtled down the salt strewn, slippery runway. The B-24 refused to rise more than a few feet and crashed near the edge of the field. Three gunners scrambled clear before the bomb load exploded in three terrific explosions. The mission was scrubbed with no more planes taking off.

On 1 January, about 850 German fighters attacked 27 airfields in northern France, Belgium and southern Holland in operation *Bodenplatte*. The 4-hour operation cost the Luftwaffe 300 aircraft, most of which were shot down by Allied anti-aircraft guns. Two days later, American and British forces counter-attacked under cover of allied air power. Despite the show of German defiance there was little the Luftwaffe could do to stop the relentless air raids on its homeland. On 3 February, over 1,200 American bombers escorted by 900 fighters made the most concentrated attack on Berlin to date with 2,266 tons of bombs being dropped on the capital. On 21 February, P-47 Thunderbolts attacked Hitler's retreat at Berchtesgaden for the first time, and on 28 February, 1,104 bombers of the 8th AF escorted by 737 fighters, attacked transportation targets in Germany.

On 2 March, when the bombers were dispatched to synthetic oil refineries at Leipzig, Me 262s attacked near Dresden. Eight days later, Trier became operational as the first tactical American airfield in Germany having been over-run by the Third US Army, and a member of the 36th Fighter Squadron landed a P-47 on an airstrip near Aachen, Germany, the first American combat plane to voluntarily land in Germany since the start of the war. On 11 March, 4,738 tons of bombs were dropped on Essen. On 18 March, a record 1,327 bombers went to Berlin. Next day, *Carpetbagger* aircraft dropped 82 agents into Germany. On 21 March, a massive four-day assault on the Luftwaffe began, with 42,000 sorties being made over German airspace. Philip G. Day flew his thirty-fifth and final mission when the 467th BG made a visual bombing of an airfield near Osnabrück. Day wrote:

No flak or fighters. Excellent results. After passing over the target we started a left assembly turn and out of the cloud bank to our right, at our altitude and on collision course, popped a group of B-17s. There was grand confusion, a melee of aircraft and a bunch of fright, but all missed and both groups reformed. And so to Rackheath where I greased the B-24 in for the last time, then to debriefing, to critique and to get drunk. The great adventure was finished.

On 23/24 March, Allied ground forces,

supported by 1,747 bombers of the 8th AF escorted by 570 fighters, crossed the Rhine into Germany. Approximately, 6,000 aircraft took part but ground fire was responsible for most of the 14 supply-carrying B-24s shot down and the 104 B-24s badly damaged. On 24 March, the 15th AF bombed Berlin for the first time when more than 150 B-17s hit the Daimler-Benz tank works in the city. Meanwhile, 271 B-24s finished off the Neuburg jet plant, bombed on 21 March. On 27 March, 12th AF P-47 Thunderbolt fighter-bombers strafed Lechfeld airfield in Bavaria and destroyed large numbers of German jet aircraft.

On 7 April, Robert L. Miller, pilot of B-17 *Son Of A Blitz* in the 863rd Squadron, 493rd BG, was one who went to Gustrow, Czechoslovakia. He wrote:

Got hit by fighters today for the first time. Emo gets a confirmed one who came in on us and damned near rammed us. A Fw 190, r.l.m. Nick Teodosio and Pete Gamoian each got a Me 109. 'Twas a perfect day for it (fighters) and we were only at 15,000 feet. Had about 6/10 cumulus which made it swell for them. Had mighty fine fighter cover and they saved our necks. I saw them shoot down three myself, but not before 4 Me 109s nailed three B-17s from the group ahead of us. I've never felt so sick in my life before as when I saw them blow up. We lost one ship over the target. Seemed under control but they bailed out.

Our P-51 escort was cruising up and down the bomber stream when the alert, 'Red Bandits in the area!' was given. Our whole crew really perked up. I looked out. In the distance was a plane that resembled a P-51. Something was hanging below the wings, like a belly tank. Our fighters had already dropped their belly tanks on the bandit alert! And this plane was flying alone, something our fighters never did. I called the waist gunners to alert them and they had already seen the same thing. This Me 109 turned toward us on a pursuit curve and our right waist gunner opened up. The German flew past our tail where Pete began firing, and he came on around to our left side where Nick got him.

In a short time they got another Me 109 I never saw but which was confirmed. We began to relax a bit when suddenly the engineer's guns behind me started shooting. I looked out my cockpit window to see a Fw 190 shooting at us and the lead plane, just to our right. He appeared to be trying to ram the lead plane if he wasn't successful in shooting him down.

On 2 March 1945, when the bombers were dispatched to synthetic oil refineries at Leipzig, Me 262s attacked near Dresden. On 10 April, German jet aircraft shot down 10 American bombers but 297 German aircraft were destroyed on the ground and on 16 April over 700 aircraft were destroyed. (USAF)

His wheels fell down and he began to wobble from side to side. Had he wobbled to his right he would have rammed the lead plane and we would have gone too in the explosion but he passed in front of us, wobbling to his left. I could see his head slumped down. I'm sure he must have been dead.

On 8 April, 32 B-17 and B-24 groups of the 8th and 14 Mustang groups hit targets in Germany. On 10 April, German jet aircraft shot down 10 American bombers but 297 German aircraft were destroyed on the ground, and on 16 April, over 700 aircraft were destroyed. The biggest 15th AF operation of all occurred on 15 April when 1,235 bombers were dispatched to Wowser near Bologna. Three days later, 305 B-17s and 906 B-24s plus over 1,200 fighters attacked Berlin. Forty Me 262s shot down 25 bombers in the 8th AF formation.

During the week 18–25 April, missions were briefed and scrubbed almost simultaneously. The end came on 25 April 1945 when the 8th AF flew its last full-scale mission of the war. B-17s bombed the Skoda armaments factory at Pilsen and Liberators hit four rail complexes surrounding Hitler's mountain retreat at Berchtesgaden

VE Day in Europe, and at the 448th BG Liberator base in Norfolk, personnel celebrate by firing rockets and flares into the night sky. Similar scenes were repeated throughout East Anglia. (via Pat Everson)

while the 12th and 15th Air Forces prevented German troops escaping from Italy by bombing lines of communication in Austria and the Brenner Pass. First Lieutenant Raymond Knight piloted a P-47 fighter-bomber in a series of low-level strafing missions in the northern Po Valley in Italy, destroying 14 grounded enemy aircraft and leading attacks that wrecked 10 others during a critical period of the Allied drive into northern Italy. During this final attack, Knight's aircraft was damaged so badly it was virtually inoperable. He attempted to return his shattered aircraft to base but he crashed in the Appennino Mountains and was killed. For his gallant actions and self-sacrifice, Lt Knight was awarded the Congressional Medal of Honor.

On 26 April, fighters of the 8th AF destroyed a record 747 German fighters on the ground in one day. During April, 8th AF fighters attacked over 40 Luftwaffe installations in Germany and Czechoslovakia. The Germans in Italy surrendered on 29 April and Germany surrendered unconditionally to the Allies on 7 May. Victory in Europe Day was 8 May 1945. Victory may have come sooner had the Boeing B-29 been used in Europe but by the end of 1943 it had been decided that all Superfortresses would equip the newly formed XX BC in India for raids on Japanese targets. To these units, and those of the B-25 Mitchell and B-24 Liberator groups, fell the task of delivering the *coup de grâce* in the Pacific.

Chapter Five

Pacific War

You know the movies when you see the Indians are totally surrounding the little group of pioneers and suddenly there's the music and here comes the cavalry? Those Mustangs, they were our cavalry!
Robert Ramer, B-29 pilot

A line of longitude placed the 5th AF on the South-West Pacific side and the 13th AF, activated in December 1942, on the South Pacific side. The 5th AF had fought in the Philippines at the outbreak of the Pacific war and had covered the retreat south to Java, playing a small part in the Battle of the Coral Sea, but it had really come to life late in 1942 when Gen George C. Kenney assumed command. The 5th AF operated the A-20 at masthead height in the Pacific and used the aircraft to excellent effect during the Battle for Dutch New Guinea. Other aircraft were tried in the Pacific, some without success. The B-26 had shown a marked dislike for rough, improvised landing strips and it was found that the Mitchell was better suited to the Pacific island-hopping campaign.

Col Donald P. Hall, CO, recalling a B-25 raid on Boram-Wewak aerodrome, on 17 August 1943, wrote:

We changed to offensive formation—line abreast. I kept expecting trouble. It was too much to ask, it seemed at the time, that we would catch the Japs completely off guard. Yet that is precisely what happened. We moved in unmolested . . . Ahead the scene was peaceful. Even then nobody on the airdrome seemed aware of our presence. We crossed and re-crossed a winding road leading to the airdrome. Several vehicles were moseying along. We

let them have it and they stopped as if paralysed. One turned over in the ditch. Jap soldiers were swimming in the surf, the men in the wing ships reported afterwards. Many were lolling on the beach. A few were playing medicine ball. Our fifties blazed away at

Two P-70 night fighters equipped with airborne interception radar and ventral gun tray. (McDonnell Douglas)

them. Some ran. Some fell. I guess we'll never know how many of them got up again under their own power.

Before we were within effective range, we threw in a few shots to make them duck. We waited a few seconds, and then cut loose again. A Betty bomber blew up on the runway. From then on we held our gun switches down, raking plane after plane . . . Fires were blazing everywhere and broken, twisted planes lined both sides of the runways. The Boram drome looked like two burning powder trains. We hadn't lost a plane.

On 12 October 1943 Col Donald P. Hall, took part in a B-25 raid on Rabaul aerodrome.

Pulling up to get over the ridges surrounding the targets, we could see columns of dust from the dromes. It was apparent that the enemy had not been caught completely off guard. We estimated later that the notice had been about three minutes. As results proved, three minutes is not enough warning for adequate defence. Several Jap airplanes were taking off and four or five were in the air, low and climbing. We tightened our formation. A Sally broke through our formation in attempting to clear the drome, and we gave him a burst. He made no effort to fire or to turn. He went down.

Three more Nip planes headed into us. We fired and so did the P-38s. All three crashed. Another started through us directly in line with my ship. I opened up on him. His right wing exploded, and he dove into the ground. One ship ground-looped trying to take off . . . We were extremely low. We went over in three waves, each in the usual line-abreast formation. The first squadron attacked along the longitudinal axis, the second at an angle to the left, and the third at an angle to the right . . . Along the runway, parked airplanes started burning. Parafrags floated down . . . Indeed, as the boys said, 'We-waked Rabaul.'

Maj Ennis C. Whitehead, deputy commander, 5th AF and tactical commander of the northeastern sector sent the following message to Brig Gen Frederick H. Smith Jr, commander of the 1st Air Task Force, on the night of Monday 1 November 1943: 'UTILIZING MITCHELL ATTACK BOMBERS AND LIGHTNING FIGHTERS, STRIKE JAPANESE SHIPPING IN SIMPSON HARBOUR AT RABAUL FROM MASTHEAD ALTITUDES USING THOU-

SAND POUND BOMBS.'

Lee Van Atta, INS War Correspondent, sent back this report of a raid on Simpson Harbour, Rabaul, 2 November 1943:

Simpson Harbour, in that quick look we had before we dove down at a 60 degree angle to begin our bomb-strafing runs, resembled a small bathtub jammed with toy ships. Only these weren't toys. They were desperately manoeuvering heavy cruisers, light cruisers, light cruisers and destroyers; they were four and six and ten thousand ton merchantmen; there were innumerable coastal vessels. Over the township, a thick smoke arose to cover effectively, the flak-positions while specks which we knew to be our lead B-25s roved in and out of the smoke.

As one, Henebry's lead ships opened fire, selecting their bombing targets with the speed so essential to successful attack bombardment. Henebry himself dove down on a 5,000 ton freighter-transport, dropped a bomb directly down the hatch which we could see explode; Ellis, flying so low his B-25 looked like a speed-boat, roared against a 4,000 tonner, silencing ack-ack posts on the vessel with triphammer blows from his .50-calibre guns.

Up and over he pulled, skipping his thousand-pounder into the merchantman's vulnerable side. He crossed the bows of a Jap heavy cruiser, ignoring salvos from the warship's eight-inch guns, and launched a second run on a two-stack 8,000-ton transport.

Again success was his—direct hit through the forward hold. Wilkins' right wing was almost severed in half by a powerful burst from the heavy cruisers. Wilkins chose to complete his last run. Fighting controls all the way, he engaged a Nipponese destroyer leader, scoring a direct hit on it that spelled doom for the war vessel. Then, barely retaining his grip on his mortally injured Mitchell, Wilkins raced on to level a waterline hit on a medium-sized freighter-transport. He climbed up across that target, too—but then flipped over on his back and crashed into Simpson Harbour.

Range and weight limitations resulted in all Marauders in the Pacific being replaced in February 1944 by the B-25H, which packed a nose-firing 75 mm cannon for anti-shipping strikes in the Pacific where 'masthead' bombing strikes were the norm, but cannons were not successful and the type was withdrawn in August 1944. The B-25J, introduced four .5-inch

Above left *Waist gunner aboard a B-17 during a photo-reconnaissance mission over New Guinea. The B-17 Flying Fortress operated in the Pacific until 1943 when the B-24 Liberator replaced it in the island hopping campaign. (USAF)*

Above right *Range and weight limitations resulted in all Marauders in the Pacific being replaced by the B-25H, which began arriving in the US Far East Air Forces in February 1944 for service with the 498th Squadron. The B-25H was the most heavily armed of all Mitchell bombers, having 14 .50-calibre machine-guns, a 75 mm cannon and eight 5 m 3,000 lb rocket projectiles. It was much more successful in 5th AF anti-shipping strikes than the M-4 cannon-armed B-25G had been, and was also lethal on strafing missions.*

Below *The B-25J was issued to squadrons in the South-West Pacific where it re-equipped B-26 squadrons. The Marauder had shown a marked dislike for rough, improvised landing strips and it was found that the Mitchell was better suited to the Pacific island-hopping campaign. Initially, the B-25J, like this one, 43-3869, was fitted with a glass nose for the bomb-aimer but experience in the Pacific from spring 1944 onwards proved that as missions were mostly at low level, the bomb-aimer was dispensed with. A field modification, later adopted in production, was the fitting of a solid nose with eight .50-calibre machine-guns. It became one of the most effective attack bombers of the war. (North American)*

'blister' guns, two on each side of the fuselage below the cockpit. The majority of USAAF B-25Js fought in the South-West Pacific.

The B-17 Flying Fortress operated in the Pacific until 1943 when the B-24 Liberator replaced it in the island-hopping campaign. Some of the most exciting offensive operations in the Pacific were carried out by B-24s of the 5th and 13th Air Forces, collectively known as the Far East Air Force, which in September 1944, began attacks on the Philippines and supported the island-hopping campaign across the Pacific. Elmer R. Vogel, a ball gunner in the 372nd Squadron, 13th AF, recalls:

When we arrived overseas I was a nose gunner on Lt Paul Kimble's crew. After he had flown our third mission on 16 September 1944, to Miti R/W [railway works], the ball gunner, John Warne, asked me if I would like to trade turrets. He did not like the ball. After clearing this with the pilot we decided to fly our fourth mission in each other's turret. I liked the ball better but since I was 6 ft 1 in tall and weighing 145 lb, I was really cramped. My knees almost touched my chin but I got used to this. From the ball you had quite a view from all over beneath you and sometimes you saw too much as on the Balikpapan raid.

In September 1944, 5th AF in the New Guinea campaign had begun flying missions against the oil refineries at Balikpapan in Borneo. This refinery was known as the Ploesti of the Pacific and only second in production to Palembang in Sumatra. The first raid on the Balikpapan oilfields had been made by B-24s of the 380th BG on 13 August 1943 in a 17-hour sortie from Darwin, Australia. Two further raids were made and, in September 1944, the airfield at Noemfoor in north-west New Guinea became available, reducing the flying time to 14 hours and allowing the B-24s to carry a 2,500 lb bomb load.

On 3 October 1944, Elmer Vogel flew a mission to Balikpapan.

The weather was always a problem and this day was no exception. I lowered the ball and had on my Mae West, harness and my .45-calibre pistol in my shoulder holster. I could not wear the flak jacket in the ball. When I got in we were in some bad weather and

In September 1944, 5th AF in the New Guinea campaign began flying missions against the oil refineries at Balikpapan—the 'Ploesti of the Pacific', and only second in production capacity to Palembang in Sumatra. The first raid on the Balikpapan oilfields had been made by B-24s of the 380th BG on 13 August 1943 in a 17-hour sortie from Darwin, Australia. Two further raids were made and in September 1944 the airfield at Noemfoor in north-west New Guinea became available, reducing the flying time to 14 hours and allowing the B-24s to carry a 2,500 lb bomb load. (via Elmer Vogel)

visibility was zero. I knew we were somewhere in the Celebes area. Pretty soon we broke out of the storm after a good deal of bulleting up and down like a giant roller-coaster. Passing the Celebes group of islands I noticed the view below was anything but beautiful.

We started across Makassar Straight and approached the IP. The target was burning up ahead. Between 50–75 Japanese fighters hit us. They seemed as thick as flies and the flak was quite heavy. Their own flak knocked down some of their own. We were flying at about 9,000 ft, within range of most of their guns. Hits on our plane were from flak as well as fighters.

I felt the vibration of our guns being fired and felt some of the hits on our plane. We were hit often. I saw two or three B-24s go down. One was below me and on fire. This must have been hard on my nervous system. I got quite sick and had to use the oxygen several times due to vomiting in the turret. It seemed that as fast as I would fire at one fighter someone would call out 'fighters at 3 o'clock' etc. and I would turn the turret and try to line up the computing sight that the ball turret was famous for. With so many fighters against us I found this most difficult to do. I relied on knowing that every fifth round was a tracer and I could do a better job under those conditions.

One fighter came up under me. I started giving him short bursts and noticed he was not firing at me. Then I started with longer bursts from my twin fifties. He got so close I could actually make out his facial expression. He had on goggles and was gritting his teeth. It was then I noticed he was carrying a phosphorus bomb. Smoke began to pour from his engine when he turned away. He released the phosphorus bomb and it exploded off to our side. The last I saw of him he was spiralling toward the sea. I was credited with one probable.

I was running out of ammo and all of this happened after bombs away. The 10 250 lb bombs all fell in the target area. I did not know how bad we were hit until later. Everything seemed to be happening fast as someone called out over the interphone that John Warne, the nose gunner, was hit. I had no ammo left and stowed the guns straight down and proceeded to get out of the ball turret. I did not retract the ball as this was done later by the copilot.

The strangest feeling came over me when I heard John was hit. It was as if I knew it was going to happen. I believe God spoke to me and said 'Go help John.' I'll never believe otherwise. Also, since I was the nose gunner only three missions before, I felt very peculiar. This would have been me if we hadn't switched turrets. As I left the turret I felt a tremendous amount of wind and thought the bomb-bay doors were open but found it was coming from a large hole in front of the right waist window. I reached for my parachute to attach to my harness and saw it had three holes in it. I threw it out the opening as it was no longer of any use to me. I looked back and saw S/Sgt Rennaker on his knees. He was hit in the hand and someone was helping him.

I started up to the nose and as I passed under the command deck I noticed this red stuff dripping from above. I thought it was blood and wondered who was hit. Later, I found out it was hydraulic fluid as our brakes were shot out. When I got to the nose Lt John Pfirman, the bombardier, was having a difficult time getting John Warne out of the nose turret because he was hit in the back with a piece of shrapnel. When we got John out of the turret I thought he was dead. He was hit in the right chest and his right arm was

Paul Kimble's crew in the 380th BG. Front row, left to right: Harvey Cauntais, copilot; Paul Kimble, pilot; Lt John Pfirman, bombardier. Back row, left to right: Elmer Vogel, ball gunner; Dave McClintic, gunner; Dave Debusman, engineer/gunner; S/Sgt Thomas Rennaker, gunner; Peter Yanos, gunner; Bucky Walters, radio operator/gunner. (Elmer Vogel)

Paul Kimble's crew on 'Snooper' patrol over the Philippines in February 1944. (Elmer Vogel)

dangling. Fortunately, it wasn't serious. I took my pocket knife and sprinkled some morphine powder on the opening. As we were moving him from the turret, Lt Pfirman said, 'Elmer, there is one last Jap fighter still with us. Why don't you surprise him and get in the turret when he makes the next pass?' As I tried to turn the turret I saw the fighter turning towards us. The turret was inoperable.

We were 5–6 hours from home and we tied a tourniquet on John's arm. He was unconscious most of the time, but would come to and cry out for water and then pass out again. While this was going on Lt Kimble called and said he did not know whether we could stay in the air much longer and might have to ditch. We were flying at about 1,500 ft.

Pfirman and I proceeded to give John some blood. This wasn't easy as neither of us knew how to do this but we realized it had to be done or he would die. Pfirman and I read the instructions on mixing the plasma with water. We knew we couldn't have any air in the lines when we inserted the needle in his vein, but we had a difficult time getting it all done. We looked at each other as we tried unsuccessfully to insert the needle in the vein. Pfirman said, 'Elmer, let's pray. We need help'.

After we prayed aloud and cried out for God's help a miracle happened. We gave him six pints of blood

and kept him alive. Our B-24 sustained many holes, including the nose turret, which had received a direct hit, a large hole in the waist, many small holes throughout the fuselage, the hydraulic system shot out, two engines shot out, two large holes in the top of the fuselage in front of the pilot and copilot, all but one or two instruments shot out, and two large holes in the right wing outside the [number] four engine. The waist gunner was wounded in the right hand, Pfirman was hit in the back, Kimble, a piece of shrapnel in the right in-step and Harvey Cauntais, the copilot, had several wounds in each arm.

We were quite concerned whether we had enough gas left to reach Sansapar. I understand only one B-24 made it back to our base at Noemfoor. As we approached Sansapar we knew our hydraulic system was gone so the main landing-gear had to be cranked down. We could not get the nose wheel down. Knowing that we would have to land without brakes and without the nose wheel, we had to take added emergency measures. We threw the waist guns over-board and tied the parachutes to the gun mounts to act as brakes. As many crew members as possible were placed in the rear of the plane to keep the nose up until the parachutes opened and slowed us down enough so that when the nose touched the runway we would not tip over. Lt Kimble did a beautiful job of bringing us in. What a wonderful feeling it was to kiss the ground again.

Several other B-24s came in behind us with various problems. One from the 424th Squadron, whose crew included Sabu 'The Elephant Boy', who was a movie actor before enlisting as a gunner.

There was certainly a lot of things that happened that I can't explain but I do know [that] not many airplanes could still fly as this B-24 did with all the damage encountered. She sure took a beating but did get us back. With the total co-operation of all on board and with God's help, we lived to see another day. I guess it just wasn't our time to go.

The Philippines fell on 16 February 1945 and from August 1944 until 19 February 1945 the 7th AF was engaged in strikes on Iwo Jima and surrounding islands. By July 1945, all the Pacific air forces had begun moving northward for the final assault on Japan. The 5th AF was based at Okinawa and the 13th AF on Clark Field in the Philippines began attacking targets in Formosa and Indochina. The 5th AF flew explosive and fire raids on Japan but the honour of being the first group in the AAF to bomb Japan went to the 'Cobras' of the 494th BG, when its B-24s raided Omura Airfield on Kyushu. The armed forces of Japan were now being attacked from all sides and the chief weapon was the B-29 Superfortress.

Four B-29 groups of the 58th Wing had moved to India in spring 1944 but before they could fly operational missions these groups had to fly the 'Hump' (Himalayas), moving in supplies and munitions to forward bases in China. The first B-29 mission took place on 5 June 1944 when landing fields in China were used as staging posts to refuel and rearm 98 B-29s for the 2,000-mile round trip to bomb rail targets in Bangkok. Some 14 aborted and five crashed on landing. Only 18 bombs landed in the target area. On 15/16 June the first raid on the Japanese mainland was made when 47 B-29s made a night attack on the Imperial Iron and Steel Works at Yawata on the island of Kyushu. Seven B-29s were lost.

The 58th Wing continued to operate from their Chinese forward landing fields right up until March 1945. Among their missions was the longest of the war for a B-29; a 3,950-mile flight

from Ceylon to Palembang in Sumatra in August 1944. During the summer months of 1944, five B-29 bases were constructed in the newly captured Marianas where it was decided to concentrate all B-29s of XX AF. It was from here, on 24 November 1944, that the first raid on Tokyo took place when Brig Gen O'Donnell's 73rd Wing (the second B-29 wing to be formed) bombed the Musashima aircraft factory. All Japan would come to fear the dreaded *Bni-Ju's* as they came to call the B-29s.

Throughout late 1944 and early 1945 the B-29s continued high-level daylight raids on Japanese targets, but without success. Losses, too, were becoming prohibitive. Then in March 1945, Maj Gen Curtis E. LeMay, who had arrived in the China–Burma–India (CBI) Theatre the previous August to command XX BC in India, decided to completely change tactics to those he had used successfully in the 8th AF in

Headline in The Philippine Liberty News *of 25 May 1945 proclaiming the damage wreaked by 550 B-29s on Tokyo.*

England. LeMay, who in January 1945 took over XXI BC (and command of XX AF in July 1945), put the best and most experienced radar operators in XXI BC in lead planes and used them as pathfinders designated to mark the targets. LeMay reasoned that as the B-29s could not hit their targets accurately, they must area bomb using incendiaries to burn up large areas of Japanese towns and cities.

The first B-29 low-level incendiary attack on Tokyo took place on the night of 9/10 March 1945. Crews were astonished to be told that they were going to fly to the target, each plane by itself, and go in at 9,000 ft and at night! Over 300 B-29s followed the pathfinders across Cape Noijima and north over Tokyo Bay and across Tokyo at altitudes ranging from 4,900 to 9,200 ft. Each B-29 carried 8 tons of M69 incendiaries to drop to the pattern set by the fires started by the pathfinders. The M69s were set to burst at

2,000 ft, each in turn dividing into 38 separate sub-munitions covering a swath of Tokyo 500 ft by 2,500 ft with burning petrol. To B-29 crews it looked like 'the whole world was on fire'. The firestorm consumed so much oxygen that those who did not die by the flames simply suffocated. Almost 16 square miles of Tokyo was razed to the ground as gusting winds whipped up the flames, and over 80,000 Japanese died. Fourteen B-29s were lost and 42 received flak damage.

Despite the losses and the strain on the airmen and ground crews, LeMay scheduled a further five fire-bomb missions in 10 days. It was the beginning of the end for Japan, her industry and her people. Throughout early 1945, B-29s based on Saipan, Tinian and Guam made intensive raids on the Japanese mainland, her environs and oil refineries. For attacks on the refineries, B-29 Superfortresses in the 315th BW based on Guam were stripped of all armament, except the tail

Throughout early 1945, B-29s based on Saipan, Tinian and Guam made intensive raids on the Japanese mainland, her environs and oil refineries. Here, Censored *of the 39th BG taxies out at North Field, Guam. This group flew its first mission to Maug, in the northern Marianas, early in April 1945. (USAF)*

Propaganda leaflet dropped by the B-29s.

turret, and AN/APQ-7 *Eagle* radar bomb-sights were installed. The radar aerial was housed in a 14 ft radome 'wing' under the fuselage. Another unit, the 313th, carried out highly successful aerial mining of Japanese home waters and shipping lanes.

As enemy fighter opposition diminished it was possible to improve the speed of the B-29 by removing gun turrets and sighting blisters. These stripped versions were designated the B-29B, B-29A having been assigned to Renton-built aircraft which featured a different type of centre wing construction. LeMay wrote:

In the daylight runs, even during the last three months of the war, Japanese fighters would bother us occasionally—diving into the formation, dropping phosphorus bombs, or trying to ram the B-29s—but we'd bother them back. On the 7 May mission for example, our gunners shot down a hell of a lot of fighters—34 to be exact. We positioned our own fighter escorts out in front and made them stay there. This forced the Japanese fighters to attack from the rear, where the compensating gun-sights of the B-29s would handle them. It didn't make the Japanese very happy.

Despite the effective blockade and relentless bombing by an ever increasing number of B-29s—by April 1945 LeMay had four wings and up to 700 Superfortresses under his command—Japan refused to surrender. Commanders in the Pacific Theatre were told of the potential of a 9,700 lb atomic bomb early in 1945 and preparations began for the possibility of B-29s carrying these incredibly destructive bombs to Japanese cities. On 16 July 1945, scientists test-exploded the first atomic device at Alamogordo in the New Mexican desert. President Harry Truman authorized the use of the atomic bomb and a mission directive was sent to General Carl A. Spaatz, commander of the newly formed US Strategic Air Forces in the Pacific. A top secret squadron was ready with 15 specially modified B-29s in the 313th Wing, XXI BC based on Tinian, ready to deliver the first atomic bomb, code-named 'Little Boy', after 3 August 1945 as

P-51H 44-64164. A few 'lightweight' P-51Hs, the final production version of the Mustang, served in the Pacific War before the Japanese surrender. (North American)

soon as weather would permit visual bombing. So secret was the 393rd Bomb Squadron (the only squadron in the specially formed 509th Composite Group) that a verse, intended as a taunt, appeared in *Yank* magazine, on 7 September 1945.

> Up in the air, the secret rose
> Where they are going, nobody knows
> Tomorrow they'll return again,
> But we'll never know where they've been.
> Don't ask about results and such
> Unless you want to get in Dutch
> But take it from one who's sure of the score
> The 509th is winning the war.

A list of targets was issued to XXI BC: Hiroshima, Kokura, Niigata and Nagasaki. Hiroshima was selected and the mission was set for 6 August. Lt Col Paul Tibbets, commander of the 509th Composite Group, would command the attacking B-29. At Los Alamos back in September 1944, Capt William S. 'Deak' Parsons USN, had revealed that he would be going on the atomic mission with Tibbets. Tibbets had said: 'Good . . . if anything goes wrong, Captain, I can blame you.' Parsons had replied: 'If anything goes wrong, Colonel . . . neither of us will be around to be blamed.'

In 1942, Paul Tibbets, then a group commander, had led the first B-17 raid on occupied Europe. His navigator had been 'Dutch' Van Kirk and his bombardier, Tom Ferebee. They would fly in the same positions on the atomic bomb drop. Robert Schwartz, writing for *Yank* magazine, wrote:

The navigator was Capt Red (Dutch) Van Kirk, a young Pennsylvanian with a crew haircut that gave him a collegiate look. Van Kirk was a good friend of Major Tom W. Ferebee, the bombardier. They had flown together in North Africa and England, usually as navigator and bombardier for Col Tibbets. They were in on most of the colonel's firsts, and he had brought them into his atomic unit as soon as he was put in command.

Tibbets wrote:

My concern about civilian deaths . . . extended to the enemy homeland including Japan where . . . the atomic bomb took such a heavy toll of civilians. By this time it had become an all-out war in which the civil population had become virtually a part of the front: in London, Rotterdam, Coventry, Essen, Berlin, Tokyo, and all other cities where there was heavy loss of life.

Tibbets directed that his mother's name, *Enola Gay*, be painted beneath the pilot's cabin on the port side of the fuselage. Altogether, seven B-29s were used on the mission, including a reserve aircraft, three weather reconnaissance B-29s and two special observation aircraft, Maj Charles Sweeney's *The Great Artiste*, and Capt George Marquardt's *Necessary Evil*, both of which carried observers and recording equipment. Navy weapons expert Capt William 'Deke' Parsons, the Naval scientific observer, armed 'Little Boy'. It would be released from a height of 31,600 ft.

At 8:15:17, the bomb-bay doors sprang open and 'Little Boy' fell earthward. 'Bomb away!' cried Ferebee. Forty-three seconds later Hiroshima ceased to exist. Tibbets wrote

My teeth told me, more emphatically than my eyes,

of the Hiroshima explosion.

At the moment of the blast, there was a tingling sensation in my mouth and the very definite taste of lead upon my tongue. This, I was told later by scientists, was the result of electrolysis—an interaction between the fillings in my teeth and the radioactive forces that were loosed by the bomb

'Deke' Parsons records: 'It was 09.15 when we dropped our bomb and we turned the plane broadside to get the best view. Then we made as much distance from the ball of fire as we could.'

The destruction was on an unprecedented scale. Some 48,000 buildings were destroyed and 78,000 Japanese died immediately in the explosion (in the first great B-29 fire raid against Tokyo, 80,000 had died). By 8 August President Truman had still not received any official reaction from the Japanese government so a second atomic device was dropped on Japan. Kokura was selected as the primary target with Nagasaki as the alternative. On 9 August, B-29 *Bock's Car*, named after its commander, Capt Frederick C. Bock, but piloted on the mission by Maj Charles W. Sweeney, headed for Kokura. In the bomb-bay was 'Fat Man', a plutonium device ('Little Boy' had been a uranium device) and the

B-29 Enola Gay *of the 393rd Bomb Squadron (the only squadron in the specially formed 509th Composite Group) flown by Lt Col Paul Tibbets, commander of the 509th, for the dropping of the first atomic bomb to be used in warfare, on 6 August 1945.*

sole remaining atomic device in existence. Because of its more complex nature, 'Fat Man' had to be armed before take-off. Sweeney wrote:

The navigator made landfall perfectly. We passed over the primary target but for some reason it was obscured by smoke. There was no flak. We took another run, almost from the IP. Again smoke hid the target. 'Look harder,' I said to the bombardier, but it was no use. Then I asked Commander Frederick Ashworth (Naval advisor to the project) to come up for a little conference. We took a third run with no success. I had another conference with the Commander. We had now been 50 minutes over the target and might have to drop our bomb in the ocean. Our gas was getting low. We decided to head to Nagasaki, the secondary target. There we made 90 per cent of our run by radar. Only for the last few seconds was the target clear.

'Fat Man' was released over Nagasaki. An estimated 35,000 people died immediately in the explosion. The Japanese government surrendered five days later, on 14 August, when a record 804 B-29s bombed targets in Japan. The official surrender ceremony took place aboard the USS *Missouri* in Tokyo Bay on 2 September. By then, the B-29s had substituted bombs for food supplies and clothing parcels as the majority of these aircraft flew mercy missions to thousands of beleaguered Allied prisoners of war scattered throughout the crumbling Japanese Empire.

Postwar, the Superfortress saw service in bomb wings and training units in America. Captain Ped G. Magness, a WW2 B-24 pilot in the 15th AF, was an instructor pilot in B-29s with the 4th Ferrying Group, Memphis, Tennessee.

I had a student pilot in the left seat, and was practising landings at Biggs Army Air Base, El Paso, Texas in December 1945. When on approach, and approximately 300 ft in altitude from touchdown, a small liaison airplane taxied out on the runway for a take-off. I told the student pilot to go around the pattern for another try at landing. The student, being new in the aircraft, became excited and opened the throttles too fast, causing a top cylinder to burst, thus spraying 100-octane fuel over the engine, and the engine began burning furiously, melting the top engine mounts. I took control, made a left turn toward the burning engine, to line up with a runway at the municipal airport, 4 miles away. During the interim, the assistant crew chief, who rode in the rear of the B-29, and who had bailed out of a burning B-17 in combat, wanted to jump. I told him we were too low but there was no answer.

Heat melted the top engine mounts, and it fell, so that one-third of the engine nacelle extended below the main landing-gear. I dived the disabled plane onto the runway at excessive speed. When the propeller and nacelle of the dangling engine struck the runway, the force of the impact severed it from the mountings. I yanked back on the control column wheel, jumped over the severed engine and made a 'hot' landing. I had to burn out the brakes to stop the aircraft. After stopping all the crew ran. I ran to the rear aircraft door (17 ft from the ground) to find out why the assistant crew chief had not answered me on intercom. He had jumped before the 29 had stopped rolling, broke a knee cap and was at least 400 yards away, still running! The fire-fighters extinguished the fire and I flew the repaired airplane away one month later.

Magness was awarded the Army Commendation Medal.

In June 1947, Marham in England hosted a detachment of nine Boeing B-29s of the 97th BG and three of them conducted rocket bombing trials against German U-boat pens at Farge. The Air Force would initiate a training programme whereby B-29 very heavy bombardment units of the Strategic Air Command would rotate to Europe to acquaint the units with operating conditions in Europe because, as British Prime Minister Winston Churchill had put it at an address at Westminster College, Fulton, Missouri on 5 March 1946, an Iron Curtain had 'descended across the Continent'. The Cold War between the Soviets and the West resulted from this Iron Curtain. A continued American presence in Europe was clearly needed. Gen George C. Marshall, President Truman's Secretary of State, initiated the Marshall Plan, which gave financial and economic aid to European countries devastated by war, while military co-operation and humanitarian aid, which first floated down over Holland in April 1945, would herald a new era in postwar Europe.

Chapter Six

Fighting the Cold War: USAF in Europe 1945–94

In late April 1945, the RAF and USAAF had begun Operation *Manna* to airdrop food and medical supplies to the starving Dutch popula-tion. RAF DZs (drop zones) were marked by aircraft of the Pathfinder Force. On 1 May, 396 8th AF B-17s, each carrying 4,500 lb of canned

Forerunners of the aircraft supplied to European air forces after the defeat of Germany were types like the P-38 Lightning and F-51 Mustang, which are shown here in Italian Co-Belligerent Air Force markings. (Italian AF)

C-rations in 50 lb cases, flew over the Dutch coast at 500 ft, dropped down to 300 ft and released 700 tons in free fall to the starving population at two airfields, a racetrack at The Hague, and an open space near Rotterdam. The Germans had not yet surrendered and crews kept a wary eye on the enemy troops parading in their black uniforms with swastikas flying.

Within three months of the 8 May surrender of Germany, US air power in Europe had been markedly reduced. On VE-Day, USSTAF had 152 airbases and 226 other installations but these were due to be cut back as US forces moved into the US occupation zones of Germany and Austria. Of the more than 450,000 US airmen in the ETO, a third had been moved to the conti-

Germany at the end of the war presented a massive problem to the victorious Allies whose Air Force units took over former Luftwaffe airfields in the British and American zones of occupation.

nental USA, and the 17,000 aircraft, including some 11,000 first-line aircraft, were being cut back also. Forces were being moved to the Pacific Theatre to fight in the war against Japan. On 16 July, 8th AF HQ was moved to Okinawa. By August, USAFE had 315,747 personnel, about 10,000 aircraft, including 6,575 first-line aircraft, and 109 airfields in its inventory. The War Department directive of 7 August 1945 changed the designation of USSTAF to USAFE 'effective immediately'.

Lt Gen John K. Cannon's responsibilities as commanding general of USAFE embraced many activities, including redeployment of forces to the USA, and after the Japanese surrender on 14 August, demobilization. The USAFE was to become the air arm of the occupation force in Germany and Austria with the responsibility of disarming the Luftwaffe and standing ready to deal with possible outbreaks of Nazi resistance. On 28 September 1945, USAFE HQ officially opened at US Army Air Station Wiesbaden, Germany, having moved there from France earlier that month. The 12th AF was inactivated 31 August, the 15th AF on 15 September, and the 9th AF on 2 December.

On 2 March 1946, Maj Gen Idwal H. Edwards became Commanding General of USAFE. That year, the Luftwaffe was disarmed and the demobilization of US forces almost completed but chilly relations with the Soviets and the Eastern Bloc showed the first signs of freezing over. On 9 August, a European Air Transport Service C-47 on the Vienna–Udine run strayed into Yugoslav airspace and was fired on and forced down by Yugoslav fighters. Ten days later, another C-47 was shot down in the same area. From then until October, when the international crisis had been resolved, USAFE B-17s flew the endangered route. In mid-November, a flight of six SAC B-29s flew to Rhein-Main airfield (named after the confluence of the Rhine and Main rivers) at Frankfurt, and then began a series of visits to airbases in the free countries of Western Europe. The flight commander was to survey these for possible future use. The presence of these aircraft, with the capability of carrying atomic bombs, demonstrated US support for the countries visited. The SAC

B-17Gs of the 96th BG at Giebelstadt, Germany after VE Day. (M. D. Wilson)

aircraft returned home at the beginning of December.

In 1947, military personnel, and airfields and installations were cut by another third. Tactical units were cut to the minimum. Starting on 5 June, SAC initiated a series of training deployments of Superfortresses to Giebelstadt and Fürstenfeldbrück airbases. In September, USAFE flew its first humanitarian mission when aircraft lifted vaccines and special aircraft to spray insects to stem the spread of cholera in Egypt. On 18 September, the US Air Force became a separate service and USAFE was recognized as a major command of the Air Force, although remaining operationally a component of EUCOM, which was under the control of the Army. On 20 October, Lt Gen Curtis E. LeMay became Commanding General of USAFE. He remained in the post until 16 October 1948, when he was given command of Strategic Air Command. Lt Gen John Cannon took over USAFE again on that date.

The USAFE continued in the American tradition of policing trouble spots in Europe when,

From July 1947 to May 1948, USAFE ferried AT-6 aircraft and three C-47s aircraft to Greece together with a one-year supply of spare parts for both types of aircraft, as part of US assistance in suppressing a Communist guerrilla revolt in that country. (Greek AF)

from July 1947 to May 1948, it ferried AT-6 aircraft and three C-47s aircraft to Greece together with a one-year supply of spare parts for both types of aircraft, as part of US assistance in suppressing a Communist guerrilla revolt in that country.

Meanwhile, on 17 March, the Soviets walked out of the Allied Control Council meeting after the Allies rejected their demands for restrictions on air traffic between the Western Zones and Berlin. In April, the US Office of Military Government refused to submit to demands by transportation officers in the Soviet Zone of occupied Germany that military trains between Berlin and the Western Occupation Zones be inspected by Soviet personnel. In Berlin, the population of over 2.5 million was still recovering from the ravages of war and depended solely on surface transport links with the outside world.

When the Soviets closed all the border routes on 25 June 1948, Berlin was totally isolated. Medicines, foodstuffs and other goods could only be supplied to the beleaguered capital by air. A mini-airlift to Berlin resulted from the Soviets' severance of all passenger train services. The next step occurred on 16 June when the Russians withdrew from the four-power municipal government. Tension increased, particularly after an Allied currency reform on 20 June. Next day, Gen Lucius D. Clay, the Allied military governor, ordered an all-out airlift. The Soviets responded with a total blockade of railways, rivers, roads and canals. It also proclaimed East Berlin as a part of the Soviet Zone of Occupation.

The Berlin Airlift began on 26 June when the USAF started flights from Frankfurt and two other bases by C-54 Skymaster and C-47 Skytrain. A total of 32 flights by Skytrains carried 80 tons of supplies from Wiesbaden AFB to Tempelhof Airport. Two days later, Operation *Vittles* was organized under Gen Curtis E. LeMay and the RAF began Operation *Plain Fare*. Thirty-five C-54 aircraft were immediately transferred from bases in Alaska, the Caribbean, and the US to be used in transporting supplies to Berlin. Within three weeks the airlift was well under way with 54 C-54 Skymasters and 105 C-47 Skytrains carrying the load of the US effort

supported by 40 RAF Yorks and 50 RAF Dakotas. Together they delivered 2,250 tons of supplies to Berlin every day. By November 1948, the US Navy was unloading huge quantities of aviation fuel at Bremerhaven. By 1949, crews from the air forces of Australia, New Zealand and South Africa had joined the airlift and by now 8,000 tons a day was not uncommon. In mid-April 1949, 'Maximum Effort Day', resulted in 12,940 tons of cargo delivered to Berlin by 1,398 flights. The American-British airlift, which also included two US Navy squadrons, was commanded by Maj Gen William H. Tunner, a WW2 veteran of the CBI airlift. The force consisted of men and aircraft from USAFE, the RAF and flying units of the US Navy. French forces and the US Army Transport Corps provided cargo vehicles and airfield engineers.

Meanwhile, the increasing tension with the Soviet Union led on 16 July 1948 to the establishment of the 3rd Air Division (Provisional), at Marham, England. The Norfolk RAF station was a B-29 rotational base for SAC aircraft and the move marked the first time in history that US combat forces were stationed in a friendly foreign country during peacetime. On 23 August, the word 'Provisional' was deleted from the designation, and on 8 September the 3rd AD moved to the former USSTAF HQ building at Bushy Park. At the outset of the Berlin Airlift, SAC augmented its B-29 detachment at Fürstenfeldbrück. On 15 July, SAC HQ ordered two B-29 groups to less vulnerable bases in England and terminated the training deployments to Germany. USAFE's 3rd AD was to support the Superfortresses in England. In August, the 36th Fighter Bomber Wing arrived in Europe by ship with 75 F-80 jets. Stationed at Neubiberg in Germany, the 36th became the second combat group in USAFE.

The Soviet Union capitulated on the Berlin Blockade on 12 May 1949, but airlift stockpiling continued for five months more. In $10^1/_2$ months in 195,530 round trips, the Allies had delivered 1,583,686 tons of supplies, as well as 160,000 tons of material to build or improve airfields. On 30 September, the last Operation *Vittles* flight was successfully flown to West Berlin. Some

2,326,204 tons of food, coal and supplies had been transported in 15 months on 277,264 flights.

Following the signing of the North Atlantic Pact which established the North Atlantic Treaty Organization (NATO) on 4 April, the US Congress passed the Mutual Defence Assistance Program (MDAP) legislation. Under this act, USAFE began training pilots of other NATO countries in November. Also in April, USAFE forces took part, for the first time, in a EUCOM

On 26 June 1948, the Berlin Airlift began when the USAF started flights with C-47s and C-54 Skymasters from Frankfurt and two other bases. Thirty-five C-54s were transferred from bases in Alaska, the Caribbean, and the US to be used in transporting supplies to Berlin. Within three weeks, the airlift was well under way with 54 C-54 Skymasters and 105 C-47 Skytrains carrying the load of the US effort. (USAF)

Above *On 18 September 1950, the first USAFE F-84Es arrived in Europe and the old F-80s were returned to the USA, and the P-47s were turned over to the Italian Air Force.*

Left *Republic F-84F-51RE Thunderstreaks of the Royal Netherlands Air Force supplied by the US under its Mutual Defence Assistance Program. (RNAF)*

field exercise, Operation *Showers*. This was part of the effort to bring US forces in Germany to a high state of combat readiness.

On 18 September 1950, the first F-84Es arrived in theatre and the old F-80s were returned to the USA, and the P-47s were turned over to the Italian Air Force. The Communist attack on South Korea in 1950 again increased international tensions and compelled the US to strengthen its air and ground forces in Europe. The growing impact of the Cold War resulted in an expansion of USAFE and a shift in mission emphasis. On 19 December, the NATO Council appointed General Dwight D. Eisenhower as the first Supreme Allied Commander Europe (SACEUR), and on Christmas Day, the US Government announced that its military forces in Europe were at the disposal of the NATO command.

On 5 June 1952, the 49th Air Division, a former TAC unit, moved from Langley AFB Virginia to RAF Sculthorpe, and the 47th BW (Light) was equipped with North American B-45 Tornado and F-84 aircraft modified to carry nuclear weapons. Pictured is an RB-45C Tornado which served with the 19th Tactical Reconnaissance Squadron in Germany. RAF pilots based at Sculthorpe regularly flew spy missions over the Soviet Union in this type of aircraft. (USAF)

On 21 January 1951, the 12th AF was re-activated at Wiesbaden and the 3rd AF was established in England. Both commands were assigned to USAFE. Next day, Lt Gen Lauris Norstad became USAFE Commander-in-Chief in place of Lt Gen Cannon, who took over Tactical Air Command. In February, negotiations with France led to the establishment of USAFE bases at Chaumont, Laon and Toul in eastern France, airfield sites in the French Zone of Occupation west of the Rhine, and bases in French Morocco. By the end of 1951, USAFE had a compliment of 75,856 personnel, 18 primary bases, and 668 aircraft. The aircraft inventory included 222 F-84s, but many were older types, including 62 B-26 bombers and 11 B-17s, while just over 200 were mostly twin-engined C-47, C-119 and C-54 types in two troop carrier wings. By the end of 1952, the personnel strength had risen to 98,302 and 1,025 aircraft. Turkey became a member of NATO on

18 February 1952, and American personnel were sent there. During the summer, the 49th Air Division, equipped with B-45s and F-84s modified to carry atomic weapons, arrived in England. As a part of the NATO build-up, new bases were acquired at Landstuhl and Ramstein in Germany and four other sites, Bitburg, Spangdahlem, Hahn and Sembach, were negotiated for in the French Zone of Occupation. In December, the F-86 Sabre began arriving in Europe with the 86th Fighter Bomber Wing the first to convert from the F-84.

In 1953, Lt Gen William H. Tunner became Commander-in-Chief of USAFE, which now numbered 96,679 personnel and 1,509 aircraft, including 525 F-86 Sabres and 202 F-84Gs. In April 1953, 17th AF was formed at Rabat, Morocco and the 322nd Air Division (Combat Cargo) was activated as the USAFE's airlift support arm. Humanitarian operations continued throughout the year and included rendering flood disaster aid to England and the Netherlands. USAFE also provided earthquake aid to Turkey and the Ionian Islands and, in August, began Operation *Kinderlift*, which annually from 1953 to 1958 flew underprivileged West Berlin children to West Germany for summer holidays in German and American homes. In January 1954, an avalanche struck the mountainous region near Blons, Austria and the USAFE evacuated 68 people from the disaster area and flew in relief supplies and communications equipment.

On 20 May, the first Matador surface-to-air guided missiles arrived in theatre at Hahn, Germany. Later, missile squadrons were established at Bitburg and Sembach and formed the 701st Tactical Missile Wing, the first in the USAF. On 16 November, the 512th Fighter-Day-Squadron moved from England to Soesterberg AFB in Holland, making it the first military unit to be based in the Netherlands in peacetime. In

1954, flood disaster aid was extended to Syria and Iraq and earthquake recovery assistance was given to Larissa, Greece and Orleansville, Algeria. The following year, USAFE gave flood recovery assistance in the Rhineland area of Germany and earthquake recovery aid to Valles, Greece. When a destructive hailstorm struck Lyon, France on 27 August, USAFE delivered 100,000 sq ft of canvas tarpaulin to be used as temporary cover for factory roofs.

There were more human disasters in 1956, some of them man-made, and the USAFE repeatedly sent aid and assistance. The worst snowstorm to hit the Mediterranean region in the twentieth century occurred in February. Three C-119s para-dropped over 100,000 lb of food and clothing to suffering Greeks snowbound in rugged mountain regions after an appeal for help from the US ambassador to Greece. Next came Operation *Snowbound* when USAFE transports carried some 700,000 lb of food, clothing and

In 1958, 59 B-66B Destroyers were assigned to USAFE. On 28 November 1956, the first RB-66C to arrive in Europe to replace RB-45 and RB-57 aircraft, was assigned to the 42nd TRS, 10th TRW at Spangdahlem AB, Germany. (Douglas)

blankets from Germany to thousands of cold and hungry Italians, Sicilians and Sardinians who had been cut off from normal food and fuel supplies. In mid-March, C-119s flew 178,000 lb of rice, cheese, butter and dried milk, and 125 tents to destitute families in Turkey, stricken by earthquakes, floods and fires. Later in March, USAFE aircraft rushed 37,000 lb of blankets, tents and medical supplies to victims of earthquakes in Lebanon and in the spring similar assistance was given for flood recovery assistance in Iran. In September, USAFE C-124s ferried 226 tons of supplies and equipment and 1,196 UN troops to a staging area at Naples, Italy from where they were rushed to the Gaza Strip of the Egypt–Israel border as a UN truce force. USAFE aircraft also operated in conjunction with US Navy vessels in evacuating American citizens from the Middle East. Nearly 500 people were airlifted to Athens and Rome.

USAFE was also called upon to help airlift emergency supplies to Austria for use in relief of victims of the Hungarian uprising. A C-119 flew an iron lung and 5 tons of medical supplies from England to Vienna. Later, bedding and mess gear for 5,000 people were hauled from Germany and France to Munich for rail shipment to Vienna. USAFE furnished extensive logistic support for Operation *Safe Haven I*. Some 9,700 Hungarian refugees were airlifted to new homes in the USA from 11 December 1956 to 2 January 1957 and another 4,616 were flown from Europe during the first seven months of 1957 under *Safe Haven II*.

In 1956, the first F-100Cs had arrived at Bitburg and, in November, the first RB-66s had begun arriving in theatre to replace the RB-45s and RB-57s. On 24 September, the first 10 jet pilots of the new German Air Force trained by USAFE received their wings at Fürstenfeldbrück AFB. By December, USAFE had a strength of

On 1 May 1960, the Soviets shot down a U-2 flown by Francis Gary Powers near Sverdlovsk, Russia while on a reconnaissance mission from Incirlik, Turkey via Peshawar, Pakistan, across the Soviet Union to Norway. Operated by the CIA, the U-2 was also flown from Watton, Norfolk in the late 1950s by four RAF pilots who trained on the 'Black Lady of Espionage' at Laughlin AFB, Texas. (Lockheed)

When on 13 August 1961 the Soviets began erecting the Berlin Wall USAF units were immediately deployed to Europe. From November, F-104s of the 157th FIS of the South Carolina ANG, the 151st FIS of the Tennessee ANG, and the 197th FIS, Arizona ANG were ferried to Spain (for onward flight to Germany), using MATS C-124 Globemasters. (Douglas)

bombers and 453 were transports. Its major subordinate commands were the 3rd AF in England, the 12th AF in Germany, 17th AF in Libya and various smaller units in France and Turkey.

New types of strike aircraft and missile arrived in theatre to counter a growing Soviet threat. In January 1958, the McDonnell F-101 Voodoo arrived, and in 1959 F-84F and RF-84Fs were phased out in favour of the F-101A and C. That same year, fighter pilots at Bitburg began converting to the F-102 Delta Dagger interceptor, which began replacing the F-86D. TM-76 Mace missiles began replacing the TM-61 Matadors in 1959. In July that year, following President de Gaulle's refusal to grant US atomic storage rights in France, the 48th, 49th and 50th Tactical Fighter Wings were withdrawn from France under Project *Red Richard*, and were relocated at Lakenheath. On 30 June 1961, the first F-105 Thunderchiefs arrived in theatre. Two years later, on 1 April 1963, USAFE received its first F-105 rotational TAC squadron with the arrival of the 344th Tactical Fighter Squadron at Moron AFB, Spain when SAC KC-135 tankers were used. On 13 August 1961, the Soviets

over 113,000 personnel and just over 2,000 aircraft of which 972 were fighters, 204 were

In 1965, the first F-4 Phantoms were introduced to Europe when the RF-4C began arriving at the 10th Tactical Reconnaissance Wing at RAF Alconbury on 12 May, and the first F-4C arrived at the 81st Tactical Fighter Wing at RAF Bentwaters on 4 October. On 22 March 1966, the first F-4D arrived at the 36th Tactical Fighter Wing, Bitburg. (USAF)

began erecting the Berlin Wall as a challenge to the Four-Power Status of the city. Eight TAC squadrons were immediately deployed to Europe and were replaced in October by 11 squadrons equipped mainly with F-84s and F-86s, of the Air National Guard. Five additional bases were activated by the 17th AF in France while F-104 units were ferried to Spain, for onward flight to Germany, using MATS C-124 Globemasters. In August 1958, C-124s had been used to airlift Pacific Air Force F-104A Starfighters and their support equipment to Ching Chuan Kang AFB on Formosa (now Taiwan) after China, supported by Russia, had partitioned two Formosan islands and threatened to occupy them. On 10 November, C-124s at McEntire AFB in the USA were loaded with partly dismantled F-104 Starfighters of the 157th FIS of the South Carolina ANG for delivery to Moron AFB in Spain. Later, F-104s of the 151st FIS of the Tennessee ANG and the 197th FIS, Arizona ANG were delivered to Europe by C-124s.

In 1965, the first F-4 Phantoms were introduced to Europe. The RF-4C began arriving at the 10th Tactical Reconnaissance Wing at RAF Alconbury on 12 May and the first F-4C arrived at the 81st Tactical Fighter Wing at RAF Bentwaters on 4 October. That same year the

During the Cuban Missile Crisis in 1962, F-104Cs of the 479th TFW were stationed at Moron AB in Spain. (Lockheed)

first EC-135 airborne command post arrived at RAF Mildenhall on 1 November. On 22 March 1966, the first F-4D arrived at the 36th Tactical Fighter Wing, Bitburg.

In times of natural disaster and during operational deployments, the USAFE transport fleet continued to provide service. During 1957 the C-130 Hercules transport and the C-131 Samaritan aeromedical evacuation aircraft were

On 1 November 1965, the first EC-135 airborne command post arrived at RAF Mildenhall. (USAF)

introduced into the USAFE inventory. In mid-July 1958 a USAFE airlift moved 2,000 troops and 7,900 passengers from Germany to the Middle East in response to the Lebanon crisis. Over 4.5 million lb of equipment was transported, including a complete 100-bed hospital and its 179-man medical staff, all within 12 hours. In 1960, USAFE transports were used in relief operations during the Agadir earthquake and Pakistan cyclones, and provided an airlift of UNEF troops and cargo to the strife-torn former Belgian Congo. For four years, 1961–65, USAFE flew airlift missions to the war-ravaged African state. In 1961, USAFE C-130s airlifted relief supplies to fire-ravaged Yemen and assisted flood disaster operations in Germany and Libya in 1962 and carried out relief operations in Iran the same year after an earthquake devastated vast areas in the north-west of the country.

From 22 October to 21 November 1963, the largest and fastest deployment of troops in US Military history took place when MATS deployed 14,893 troops and 116 tons of equipment of the 2nd Armoured Division from Texas to USAFE bases in Germany and France in Operation *Big Lift*. The operation took just over 63 hours to complete. In addition, a TAC Composite Air Strike Force of 69 aircraft with support aircraft and over 680 personnel were also deployed. Another massive airlift took place from 2 November 1962 to 29 August 1963, when USAFE transported men and materièl to India after Communist Chinese incursions along its northern border. In the same year, flood disaster aid was provided by fixed-wing transports and helicopters to Morocco, and C-130s moved earthquake disaster aid to Libya, Yugoslavia and Iran. During the Moroccan operation, a T-39 Sabreliner was used on a mercy mission for the first time when it delivered typhoid vaccine from Germany to Sidi Slimane in $3^1/_2$ hours. In April 1964, USAFE's tactical airlift functions were re-assigned to Military Air Transport Service (MATS).

Operations got off to a bad start in 1966 with

The collision between a SAC B-52 and a KC-135 tanker during a refuelling operation over the southern coast of Spain on 17 January 1966 got operations off to a bad start. USAFE provided support during the ensuing clean-up operations and the search for a lost atomic weapon.

Top *Visits to East Anglia during the 1980s for bombing competitions were quite common. This B-52H, 60046, pictured at RAF Marham on 16 June 1981 for the* Giant Strike *competition is from the 5th BW at Minot AFB. (Author)*

Above *B-52H 60026 of the 319th BW from Grand Forks AFB at RAF Marham for* Giant Strike *on 16 June 1981. (Author)*

Right *B-52Ds of the 96th BW at RAF Marham on 23 September 1981. Its WW2 predecessor, the 96th BG, operated B-17s from Snetterton Heath. (Author)*

the collision, on 17 January, between a SAC B-52 and a KC-135 tanker during a refuelling operation over the southern coast of Spain. USAFE provided support during the ensuing clean-up operations and the search for a lost atomic weapon. On 7 March 1966, Gen Charles de Gaulle announced his intention to withdraw French forces from NATO and directed that NATO HQ and forces stationed in France should

The 48th TFW at RAF Lakenheath received the remainder of its F-4D aircraft in September 1974 and was the last in USAFE to convert to the Phantom. (USAFE)

be removed by 1 April 1967. Nine major bases and 78 installations in France were closed. Throughout the summer of 1966, troop carrier wings evacuated US forces to Mildenhall, Lakenheath, Upper Heyford and High Wycombe in England, and to the USA and West Germany. The operation continued into 1967, when USAFE completed the relocation of about 33,000 personnel and dependants. In 1970, the first F-111E arrived on 12 September at 20th Tactical Fighter Wing, RAF Upper Heyford. By August 1971, it had become the first overseas wing to be completely equipped with the F-111 and, by the early spring of 1972, the last of the F-100 Super Sabres had left the command. USAFE had become a tactical air force that operated only Phantoms and F-111s, and represented the most powerful air arm commitment in the history of NATO.

In March 1973, USAFE HQ transferred from Lindsey Air Station, Germany to Ramstein Air Base. NATO's Allied Air Forces Central Europe was established at Ramstein in June 1974. That same year, the first two OV-10A aircraft arrived on 21 June at Wiesbaden and were assigned to the 601st Tactical Control Wing. The 48th TFW at RAF Lakenheath received the remainder of its F-4D aircraft in September. The wing was the last to convert to F-4s. In 1976, 20 F-5E Tiger II fighters arrived at Alconbury in May–June to

form the equipment for the 527th Tactical Fighter Training Aggressor Squadron, which was to help train the command's crews in air-to-air combat. On 27 April 1977, the first F-15 Eagle air superiority fighters of the 525th TFS, 36th TFW arrived at Bitburg and on 25 January 1979 the first A-10s of the 92nd TFS arrived at Bentwaters and Woodbridge.

In the early 1970s, USAFE aircraft strength averaged around 600–800 aircraft each year. Humanitarian relief operations to victims of earthquake, flood and war-ravaged regions in the Mediterranean, Africa and the Middle East were carried out by the troop carrier wings. Operation *Fig Hill*, 28 September–31 October 1970, involved the USAFE airlift of two US military hospitals and medical personnel to Jordan to treat victims of the civil war. On 20 June 1975, supported by OV-10s of the 601st Tactical Control Wing at Sembach and by aircraft of the Air Rescue and Recovery Service, US naval forces evacuated US citizens from strife-torn Beirut. On 27 July, another evacuation took place, the naval force on this occasion supported by a C-130 of the Joint Airborne Communications Centre/Command Post. During November and December 1976, MAC C-141s delivered relief supplies, mainly tents and heaters, to Incirlik after more than 3,600 people died in an earthquake near Caldiran in eastern Turkey.

On 27 April 1977, the first F-15A Eagle air superiority fighters of the 525th TFS, 36th TFW arrived at Bitburg. (USAFE)

From Incirlik MAC C-130s flew 40 missions to move supplies to Van Airport, often under difficult weather conditions.

To compensate for a reduction in support by SAC KC-135s, *Creek-Party* exercises in logistics and unit movements, and air-refuelling support was sometimes provided by ANG KC-97L units. Operations which had begun on 1

RF-4C Phantom and F-5E Tiger II of the 527th Tactical Fighter Training Aggressor Squadron at Alconbury. In May–June 1976, 20 F-5E Tiger II fighters arrived at Alconbury where the 527th was assigned to the 10th TRW, to form the equipment for the Aggressor Squadron, which was to help train the command's crews in air-to-air combat. In mid-1983 the unit became the 527th Aggressor Squadron and moved to Bentwaters where it was inactivated on 30 September 1990. (USAFE)

A-10A Thunderbolt II 81-0988 of the 78th TFS, 81st TFW comes into land at Bentwaters late in 1991. Note the ALQ-131 ECM pod (under right wing) and LANTIRN navigation pod (under left wing). Thunderbolt 81-988 was one of the last A-10s at Bentwaters before the wing left on 23 March 1993. Over 35 A-10As were transferred to the 10th TRW, later the 10th TFW, at Alconbury in 1988, and 18 in the 511th TFS deployed to Saudi Arabia for the Gulf War of 1991. (Author)

May 1967 ended on 28 April 1977. During 18 May–15 June 1978, MAC conducted an airlift of French, Belgian and West African troops into Zaire's Shaba province to combat an invasion from Angola. During the operation, C-5s, C-141s and C-130s flew more than 200 missions.

On 12 December 1979, NATO voted to deploy cruise and Pershing II missiles in Europe. Two weeks later, Soviet troops invaded Afghanistan. Just two years later, in February 1982, the United States presented the Soviet Union with a draft treaty, based on President Ronald W. Reagan's 'zero option' proposal, to cancel Pershing II and ground launched cruise missile deployments, provided the Soviets dismantled their SS-20, SS-4, and SS-5 missiles. Next day, the Soviet Union counter-proposed a two-thirds cut in all US and Soviet medium-range nuclear weapons in Europe by 1990. In 1988, the Intermediate-Range Nuclear Forces Treaty was ratified and mandated, the first ever elimination of an entire class of weapons from

US and Soviet inventories. USAFE completed the removal of ground-launched cruise missiles and other weaponry in March 1991 when the last 16 missiles were removed from Comiso Air Station in Italy. The Soviet threat in western Europe had finally diminished. In January 1989, a major political upheaval began in Eastern Europe that ended 45 years of Soviet domination. The Hungarian Parliament passed legislation permitting a multi-party political system and during the year, the communist regimes in other Eastern European countries fell to democratic pressures. In April, the first Soviet tanks began to be withdrawn from Eastern Europe and on 9 November 1989 the German Democratic Republic opened the Berlin Wall. By December the communist government in the GDR had resigned. On 3 October 1990, Germany was re-unified after 45 years.

With the Cold War now fully thawed, the US announced plans in 1990 to close 35 domestic bases and reduce forces at more than 20 other

The last four F-4G Wild Weasels of the 81st FS left Spangdahlem AB in Germany in February 1994 for Nellis AFB, Nevada where they joined the 561st FS.

locations and close 12 bases overseas. Since the 1950s, many of these bases had been used to help maintain the peace and to carry out repeated humanitarian airlifts in Africa and the Balkans (of which more later) and to mount counter-offensives in South-East Asia where Communist take-over was a powerful threat to world peace. In the vanguard once again, were US forces.

Chapter Seven

War in the Land of the Morning Calm: Korea 1950–53

Break Left,
Break Right,
Streamers on the wing.
Flick Roll,
Slow Roll,
We do anything.
Sabre Song

On 25 June 1950, five years after the end of WW2, the North Korean Army crossed the 38th Parallel and invaded South Korea. The invasion caught the Army of the Republic of Korea (ROK) and its American advisors completely off balance and from the outset the North Koreans enjoyed total air superiority. Of just 26 B-26Bs in the 3rd Bomb Wing at Ashiya Air Base on Kyushu, Japan, which were immediately available, only 10 could be made ready for standing patrols in the Yellow Sea during the evacuation of US personnel by C-54s and C-47s from Kimpo and Suwon in South Korea. F-80Cs of the 8th Fighter Bomber Wing, 5th AF, based in Japan flew high-altitude escort for the transports. Later that day four F-80Cs of the 8th FBW inter-

Lockheed F-80C Shooting Star 49-1820 in flight. On 7 November 1950, Lt Russell J. Brown, pilot of a 51st Fighter Interceptor Wing F-80, managed to destroy a MiG-15 in a diving attack in the first jet versus jet confrontation in history. (Lockheed)

cepted eight Il-10s and shot down four of them. On the night of 27/28 June, four B-26s of the 8th Bomb Squadron (the other six could not be spared from patrol duty) tried to find Red armour north of Seoul and returned to Japan without dropping their bombs. A second attempt fared equally badly.

The first successful bombing mission of the war occurred on At on 28 June. At 07:30 hrs, 12 B-26s of the 13th Bomb Squadron 3rd Bomb Wing took off from Ashiya to bomb the rail complex at Munsan near the 38th Parallel, and Communist troops and vehicles. The targets were well hit with bombs, rockets and machine-gun fire but almost all of the Invaders were damaged by intense ground fire. One crash-landed at Suwon and was destroyed by a Yak-9 later in the day, another crashed on landing at Ashiya, killing the crew, and a third had to be written off after its return. Later on 28 June, nine B-26s attacked targets north of Seoul, and all returned safely.

Next day, Invaders attacked bridges along the Han River, and 18 B-26s made intensive raids on enemy troop convoys near Seoul. One convoy was caught cold along a road leading to a bridge which was under repair and the Invaders destroyed the vehicles in a 5-minute broadside of rockets and machine-gun fire. B-26s in Korea were modified to carry 18 machine-guns, an internal bomb load of 4,000 lb and either four bombs or 14.5-inch underwing rockets. Most of the 197 vehicles and 44 tanks destroyed in the Pyongtaek–Seoul area, 7–9 July, were the result of Invader strikes by the 8th and 13th Bomb Squadrons of the 3rd BW.

By late 1950, the North Koreans had the Allies penned in around Pusan and in August the Communists attempted to cut the Pusan Perimeter in half. B-26s of the 3rd BW dropped flares and made night attacks on enemy armour and artillery until the Perimeter was secured. Invaders and F-82 Twin Mustangs shouldered the burden of night intruder work without short-range navigation radar or blind-bombing equipment during the counter-attacks around Pusan.

F-94B FA-882 in flight. The Starfire was the first all-weather jet fighter to enter USAF service and the 319th Squadron, 325th FIW was the first F-94 unit to be transferred to Korea, in March 1952, where it replaced the F-82. On 30 January 1953, an F-94B scored the first Starfire victory when a prop-driven LA-9 was brought down. Two more enemy aircraft were shot down in the spring; one a Po-2 (a light biplane of 1926 vintage) 'Bed Check Charlie' (nuisance raider) which the Starfire destroyed after throttling back and lowering landing gear and flaps to reduce speed, but the jet fighter stalled immediately afterwards and crashed, killing the crew. Another Po-2 collided with a Starfire on 12 June and both aircraft were lost. (Lockheed)

At the time of the North Korean invasion of the South, on Sunday 25 June 1950, the North American F-82 Twin Mustang equipped the 5th AF's 68th Fighter All-Weather Squadron at Itazuke and the 339th F(AW) Squadron at Yokota in Japan, and the 20th AF's 4th F(AW) Squadron at Okinawa. F-82s covered the evacuation of American civilians from Seoul and Inchon on 26 June and on 27 June an F-82 piloted by Lt William G. Hudson of the 68th Squadron had the distinction of destroying the first enemy aircraft over Korea when he shot down a Yak-7. (North American)

The siege of Pusan was lifted in September. Mainstay of the US 5th AF was the Lockheed F-80C Shooting Star jet interceptor of which three wings were based on Japan supported by two wings of F-82 Twin Mustangs. In addition, the 20th AF had one F-80C wing and an F-82 wing based on Okinawa, main base for the command's B-29 operations over Korea. These new types of USAF aircraft were ill-suited to operate in a close air support and interdiction campaign in Korea. They needed paved runways 6,000 ft long and these only existed in Japan which meant that air operations over Korea were restricted to only a few minutes.

Since the start of the war in Korea, US commanders had no reason to fear the Communist air threat because only piston-engined aircraft had confronted the USAF F-51s and F-80s and the Navy fighter-bombers. Gen Emmett O'Donnell's B-29s had made repeated raids on industrial targets in the North with impunity. United Nations Forces broke out of

the Pusan perimeter on 19 September and within a week had virtually annihilated the North Korean Army. The 5th AF had accounted for 8,000 enemy troops in just five days in the face of disintegrating North Korean air activity. Fighter-bomber wings based in Japan were sent to re-occupy hastily repaired airfields in South Korea and to be ready for the imminent invasion of the North. All went well until the United Nations advance reached the banks of the Yalu River which formed the border between North Korea and the Republic of China which had threatened to intervene if its territory was threatened. The overwhelming balance of air power changed dramatically with the intervention by Communist China and the appearance of the Soviet-built jets in North Korean airspace.

On the morning of 1 November 1950, the Allies received a rude shock. A B-26 of the 730th Bomb Squadron, 452nd BW was attacked by three Yak-9s in Chinese Air Force markings. One of the Invader's gunners shot down a Yak

At the start of the war in Korea many of the 1,804 Mustangs with the ANG and in storage were put back into service and within a year three USAF wings were serving in Korea. By the end of the Korean War the F-51 had flown 62,607 sorties, primarily in the ground support role, for the loss of 194 aircraft. For his actions on 4 or 5 August 1951, Maj Louis J. Sebille of the 67th FBW was awarded a posthumous Congressional Medal of Honor (one of only four to be awarded, all posthumously, to Air Force personnel in Korea) for deliberately sacrificing his life to destroy enemy forces that were threatening UN troops. The Mustang pictured is an RF-51D in Japan at the time of the Korean War. (USAF)

but the appearance of Chinese Air Force units was a serious setback to operations in North Korea. Even worse, six MiG-15 jet fighters, bearing the red star of the Republic of China on their stubby fuselages and swept back wings, took off from the safety of their airbase at Antung in Manchuria, climbed rapidly to 30,000 ft and crossed the Yalu River into North Korea. The formation of American F-51 Mustangs and F-80 Shooting Stars flying on the North Korean side of the river were surprised at the devastating closing speed of the Communist jets whose pilots only failed to wipe out the American aircraft through their own inexperience. The MiG-15 was the result of a Soviet project in 1946 which benefited from German research into swept wings and the British development of the Rolls Royce Nene turbojet (25 were sold to the Soviets under the Anglo-Soviet Trade Agreement of 1946). The MiG-15 could fly at near sonic speed and was armed with one 37 mm and two 20 mm cannons.

On 5 November, when B-29s carried out the first of many incendiary raids, Gen Douglas MacArthur, the US Supreme Commander in Korea, issued a directive for an all-out, unrestricted air campaign against the North. B-29s were to fire-bomb four North Korean cities and burn them from end to end with incendiaries, just as the bombers had done in the war against Japan. On the same day, Communist Chinese forces poured across the bridges on the Yalu but President Harry Truman decreed that the bridges were not to be bombed. Maj Gen Earle E. Partridge, commander of the 5th AF, pressed for fighter-bomber attacks on Communist airfields in Manchuria but Gen George E. Stratemeyer, CIC, FEAF (Far East Air Force), refused permission. He did, however, allow the most experienced fighter pilots in the 5th AF and Task Force 77 to bomb enemy targets up to the banks of the Yalu. An area, 100 miles deep between Sinuiju on the Yalu and Sinanju on the Chongchon River, soon became known as MiG Alley.

On 8 November, when F-51s and F-80s strafed enemy anti-aircraft emplacements on the south bank of the Yalu, six MiG-15s left the safety of their own airspace in Manchuria and crossed the Yalu to attack the American fighters. The straight-winged F-80C should have been no match for the advanced Communist jet but the battle-hardened American pilots used their hard-won experience gained in the war against Germany and Japan to greater effect. Lt Russell J. Brown of the 51st Fighter Interceptor Wing, 20th AF based on Okinawa, became the first ever jet pilot to shoot down another jet in combat when he dived onto the tail of one of the MiGs as it passed in front at 20,000 ft and shot it down from a range of 1,000 ft. That same day, a Grumman Panther shot down a MiG-15 to become the first US Navy jet to down another jet aircraft.

On 26 November, 18 Chinese divisions entered the battle and soon the United Nations Forces were in headlong retreat southwards.

American high command recognized that only air power could halt the reverses until the ground troops could be reorganized to meet the Communist threat. The 27th Fighter Escort Wing, equipped with Republic F-84E Thunderjets, was already on its way to Korea. So, too, was the 4th Fighter Interceptor Wing, commanded by Col John C. Meyer, a veteran fighter pilot in WW2 with 24 victories, and equipped with North American F-86A Sabres. These had been shipped to Korea aboard an aircraft carrier almost as soon as the MiG-15 threat had materialized.

The F-86, like the MiG-15, had benefited from German research into wing design. The first Sabre design was a straight-wing version and had flown for the first time in November 1946 but the results of German wartime research into swept wings led to a 35° sweep angle being adopted by its North American designers. The XP-86 made its maiden flight on 1 October 1947 and the following spring it exceeded Mach 1 for the first time, in a shallow dive. In September 1949, an F-86A set a world speed record of

The first Republic F-84E Thunderjets to see combat in Korea equipped the 27th FEW which began flying missions over Korea on 6 December 1950, scoring its first MiG victory on 21 January 1951. The slow, straight-winged jet was inferior to the swept-wing MiG in air-to-air combat, shooting down only nine enemy aircraft for the loss of 18 F-84s. Some 122 more were lost on fighter-bomber sorties over Korea. The Thunderjet pictured is an F-84G of the 49th FBW based in Japan at the time of the Korean War. (USAF)

Unarmed RF-86F Sabre of the 4th FIW at dispersal in Korea with black-painted fake gun ports to scare off MiG, and large camera bulge on the port side. (USAF)

671 mph. In Korea, the Sabre was found to be the equal of the MiG-15 but the lighter enemy jet proved to have the edge over the F-86A in climb and altitude performance and was more manoeuvrable.

The 4th Fighter Interceptor Wing took up residence at Kimpo (K-14) a few miles south of the 38th Parallel and to the north of Seoul, the South Korean capital. They were soon in action. Four F-86A Sabres of the 336th Fighter Interceptor Squadron engaged in combat with the MiG-15 for the first time on 17 December 1950, 11 days after the 27th Fighter Escort Wing had begun operations with the F-84E, when four MiGs were sighted near the Yalu. Lt Col Bruce H. Hinton, CO of the 336th Squadron, shot down the first MiG and the other three, too fast for the pursuing F-86s, made for the border. Hinton's was the first of 792 MiGs to be destroyed in the Korean War.

Sabres and MiGs clashed again on the morning of 19 December when one of the enemy jets was damaged by Lt Col Glenn T. Eagleston. He also claimed a probable two days later when eight of the Sabres tried to intercept two MiGs flying at 34,000 ft. On the morning of 22 December, the first Sabre was shot down in combat with a MiG but the F-86 pilots gained revenge later that day when the 4th Wing destroyed six MiGs in one combat.

On New Year's Day 1951, the Chinese launched a new invasion of South Korea which succeeded in removing the United Nations Forces from Seoul. Next day, the 4th Fighter Interceptor Wing was forced to evacuate to Johnson AFB in Japan. In desperation, a detachment of Sabres arrived at Taegu on 14 January to begin ground attack sorties over the enemy lines. However, they were of limited success—only two 5-inch rockets could be carried in addition to the Sabre's machine-guns because of the need to carry drop tanks—and the extreme operating range meant that pilots only had a short time to locate and hit targets. By 31 January, though, the F-86s had completed 150 valuable close-support sorties.

Ten days earlier, on 21 January, the 27th Fighter Escort Wing scored its first MiG kill when Lt Col William E. Bertram, CO of the 523rd Squadron, destroyed one of the Communist jets. An F-80 and an F-84E Thunderjet were also lost. Two days later, the

Lockheed F-80C Shooting Star Butch, *FT-590, at a base in Japan at the time of the Korean War. (USAF)*

Wing downed four more MiGs, including two which fell to the guns of Lt Jacob Kratt. Three probables and four damaged were added to the score.

The United Nations Forces launched a counter-offensive which succeeded in recapturing Seoul but airbases at Suwon (which fell on 25 January), Kimpo (10 February) and the South Korean capital were too badly damaged for occupancy by the USAF who would have to wait for the engineering battalions to make them habitable again. On 22 February, the 4th Fighter Interceptor Wing's 334th Squadron took over Taegu (K-5) in the south of the country but it was too far for the Sabres to hunt MiG-15s over MiG Alley. The furthest the Sabres could fly was to Pyongyang. Finally, on 10 March, the single concrete runway at Suwon (K-13) was able to take jets again and the 334th Squadron took over occupancy of the battered airfield. The vacated dispersals at Taegu, meanwhile, were taken over by Sabres of the 336th Squadron, which flew in from Japan.

In the meantime, B-29s, escorted by the slower F-80s and F-84Es, were sent on bombing raids to the area south of the Yalu with almost disastrous results. On the first mission, on 1 March, the 18 bombers of the 98th BG missed the rendezvous with the Shooting Stars and were

bounced by nine MiGs. The enemy damaged 10 B-29s and three only just managed to crash land at Taegu. On 12 March, a dozen MiGs completely surprised a flight of four F-80s of the 8th Fighter-Bomber Group but the Shooting Stars escaped when the Communist pilots failed to press home their attacks. The American pilots damaged four of the enemy jets and two MiGs collided and crashed to earth. Another mid-air collision occurred on 17 March when a MiG and an F-80 crashed into one another during a dogfight between the 8th Fighter-Bomber Group and three MiGs. Two full-scale raids by B-29s and their Sabre and F-84 escorts were made on 23 March and 30 March. On the latter raid, the MiGs brushed aside the F-80 escort but the B-29 gunners claimed two enemy jets shot down.

Meanwhile, night operations were mounted using Invaders—on occasion aided by C-47 'Lightning Bugs' which dropped flares to illuminate their targets on close-support missions. The C-47s even dropped tacks at night to puncture enemy vehicles' tyres to permit B-26s to finish them off at first light. In March 1951 when enemy anti-aircaft fire became too hot for the C-47s in the Sinuiju sector, 3rd BW B-26s were modified to carry their own flares on their underwing rocket rails. The naval flares were fused to ignite at about 3,500 ft and burn long enough to allow two or three strafing runs on the enemy. Many pilots, however, chose to make a single pass with 100 lb fire bombs and 260 lb fragmentation bombs and hit enemy vehicles while they still had their lights on.

On 7 April, the B-29s bombed rail and road bridges at Sinuiju and Uiju escorted by 48 F-84 Thunderjets of the 27th Wing. Some 30 MiGs attacked the bombers during bombs away, destroying one B-29. Five days later on 12 April, 50 MiG-15s intercepted a formation of 48 B-29s of the 19th, 98th and 307th Bomb Groups which were being escorted to their target, the bridges at Antung-Sinuiju (Antung is on the Chinese side of the border while Sinuiju is in North Korea) by 33 Sabres of the 4th Wing flying top cover, and 39 F-84s of the 27th Wing. A 19th Bomb Group B-29 was shot down in flames and five other bombers were badly damaged. A diving attack on the bombers by a second group of 20 MiGs forced the Thunderjets to scatter as the enemy jets blazed away with their cannons. Hits brought down a B-29 in the 307th BG and the third B-29 lost was so badly shot up that it limped back to Suwon where it was destroyed in a crash-landing. The American fighters' claims of seven enemy jets destroyed and six damaged was small consolation and as a result of the débâcle that had unfurled, B-29 raids were halted until more effective escort tactics could be adopted.

Equally worrying was that even the Sabre pilots were finding it increasingly difficult to maintain air superiority over the Communist air force. Enemy tactics in April showed a marked reluctance to continue with large formations of 50-plus MiGs. They were replaced by more flexible formations of 16 fighters in four flights of four. To combat these new tactics, the USAF dispatched small patrols of 12 Sabres backed up by supporting flights which could be called upon when the first group had flushed the MiGs. This manoeuvre totally outwitted the Communists on 22 April when four enemy jets were shot down and four more damaged.

One of the kills went to Captain James Jabara of the 4th Fighter Interceptor Wing, who shot down his fourth MiG of the war. Jabara, who had downed 3.5 German aircraft in WW2, now needed only one more to become the first jet ace of the Korean War. Jabara had to wait until 20 May. The patrol of 14 F-86As was intercepted by 50 MiGs over Sinuiju. Jabara, who was in the second wave of 14 Sabres, tacked on to three MiGs at 35,000 ft and singled out the last one. He blasted the MiG with cannon fire and the pilot bailed out at 10,000 ft just before the fighter disintegrated. Jabara climbed back to 20,000 ft and bounced six more MiGs. He fired at one and the enemy fighter began to smoke and catch fire before falling into an uncontrollable spin. Jabara completed his tour but returned to Korea and increased his score to 15 to finish the war as the second highest scoring ace.

At the end of May, the UN Forces began Operation *Strangle* which was designed to wipe out the Communists' lines of communication in the North. Initially, attacks by the 5th AF, together with carrier-borne aircraft of the US Navy and the 1st Marine Corps, went well but once the Communists had recovered from their early surprise they skilfully concealed dumps and repaired blown bridges and roads as quickly as they were destroyed. B-26s of the 3rd BW operating from Kusan sowed road junctions and choke points between the 39th Parallel and the front line with clusters of butterfly bombs which detonated when disturbed. During April–May 1951, Invaders accounted for 211 locomotives and over 850 vehicles. In June, the 3rd BW destroyed over 400 vehicles and damaged 1,048 more. Invaders in the 452nd BW (later re-designated the 17th Bomb Wing) moved up to Pusan and converted to night intruder operations and destroyed 151 vehicles and damaged 224 more between 11 and 20 June. In July, the 3rd Wing began to operate B-26s in pairs, one Invader lighting the target for the other to attack. These tactics accounted for 240 vehicles destroyed and over 690 damaged. The 452nd, operating its Invaders singly, destroyed over 450 vehicles and damaged 880 others. The most spectacular action occurred on 14 July when Capt William L. Ford of the 452nd BW came across two enemy convoys just before dawn and destroyed 38 trucks and damaged about 30 more. On 14 September 1951, John Walmsley earned the Congressional Medal of Honor when his B-26 night intruder crashed while on a mission near Yangdok, killing the entire crew.

F-80s were fitted with long range, 265-gallon 'Misawa' elongated tanks beneath the wing tips for missions from Japan. Later, new centre-line tip tanks, containing 230 gallons, were fitted as standard. On 6 July 1951, three RF-80As of the 67th TRW were each refuelled three times by a Boeing KB-29M to make the world's first air-refuelled combat mission. After a further trial, the experiment was discontinued.

Meanwhile, it had become obvious by the summer of 1951 that the Communists were increasing the size of their jet fighter force in China. It was estimated that the Chinese Air Force now had 1,050 Soviet-built combat aircraft, including 445 MiG-15s (only 89 Sabres were available) and new airfields were under construction in the Antung area to accommodate 300 of the jet fighters. On 17 June, Sabres shot down one MiG and damaged six others without loss.

An attack by 40 MiGs on 32 Sabres the next day added weight to the theory but the Sabres still destroyed five of the enemy jets for the loss

of one F-86. On 19 June, one Sabre was shot down with no loss to the MiGs. The enemy pilots seemed to grow in stature. Sometimes they flew in singles and pairs with drop tanks fitted to their MiG-15s as far south as the 38th Parallel. The enemy attacks bore all the hall-marks of being carried out either by Red Chinese instructors or Soviet pilots—'Honchos' (from the Japanese word meaning 'boss') as the Americans called them. Tactics against the bombers were right out of the Luftwaffe hand-book and veteran American fighter pilots noticed the similarity between these attacks and those mounted by the Germans against B-17s and B-24s in WW2. The Soviets had learned very quickly.

A worried Gen Otto P. Weyland, who assumed command of the Far East Air Force on 10 June, saw the immediate need for four more Sabre wings (two to be sent to Korea and two to Japan) and they needed to be equipped with the latest F-86E model instead of the F-86A. The F-86E largely eliminated the shortcomings of the earlier model. It was fitted with a 'flying tail', power-operated controls and a slatted wing.

Douglas WB-26C Invader in Japan at the time of the Korean War. In Korea, Invaders were used mostly at night. On 14 September 1951, John Walmsley earned the Congressional Medal of Honor when his B-26 night intruder crashed while on a mission near Yangdok, killing the entire crew. In all, B-26/RB-26 Invaders flew over 72,000 sorties in Korea for the loss of 56 B-26s to enemy action and 170 to other causes. (USAF)

Although the 136th Fighter-Bomber Wing equipped with F-84 Thunderjets arrived in Korea and scored its first success on 24 June and in June–August 1951 the 49th FBW converted to the F-84E, Weyland's requests for more Sabres fell on deaf ears. The 44 F-86As of the 4th Fighter Wing were left to soldier on alone as the only F-86 wing in Korea for a few months more.

The news was made worse by the start of a new Communist air offensive at the beginning of September. By this time there were no less than 525 MiG-15s in the enemy inventory. The Sabre was the only fighter able to compete on roughly level terms with the MiG-15. Sabres continued to knock down MiGs at a good rate but the Communist air force posed a very real threat to American fighter-bomber operations in the North. When a further request for more Sabres was rejected, Gen Frank F. Everest, commander of the 5th AF, withdrew his fighter-bombers from MiG Alley in the face of the increased Communist opposition. However, the enemy could not be allowed to build airfields which would enable its jets to range further into South Korea so patrols over MiG Alley were stepped up in October before the B-29s were unleashed on targets in North Korea. The tactics worked, for in the first week of operations the 4th Fighter Wing destroyed 19 MiGs (including nine on 16 October) and two more were claimed destroyed by F-80 pilots of the 8th Fighter-Bomber Wing.

The first night raids on 13 and 14 October and the daylight raids beginning on 18 October proved disappointing. A B-29 was shot down by a MiG on 22 October and worse was to follow on 23 October when eight B-29s escorted by 55 F-84 Thunderjets and 34 Sabres headed for Namsi airfield in North Korea. Over 100 MiGs assailed the Sabres and while the American fighters were thus engaged, another 50 MiGs took on the F-84s and B-29s. The F-84s fought valiantly but one Thunderjet and two bombers were shot down and a third B-29 flew on badly damaged before crashing into the sea. Three MiGs were shot down by B-29 gunners and three more were shot down by the F-86s and F-84s. Four B-29s were badly damaged and the survivors landed at bases in South Korea and Japan with dead and wounded aboard.

Col Francis 'Gabby' Gabreski, CO of the 51st FIW in Korea, pictured in the cockpit of his 56th FG Thunderbolt in WW2. Gabreski shot down 31 German aircraft in WW2 and added 6.5 MiG kills before the Korean War ended. (USAF)

During October, 32 MiGs had been destroyed but the Americans lost 10 jet fighters and five B-29s. Encouraged by this success, the Communists dispatched their fighters further south of the Yalu and based fleets of bombers at Sinuiju. Fortunately, USAF commanders recognized the new Chinese threat. The 4th Fighter Interceptor Wing, including the 335th Squadron in Japan, was moved up to Kimpo and on 22 October, 75 of the latest F-86E Sabres were transferred from Air Defence Command to Korea. They were used to convert the 51st FIW which formed at Suwon on 6 November, and an equal number of F-80E crews returned Stateside in exchange. The 51st was commanded by the legendary WW2 fighter ace, Col Francis 'Gabby' Gabreski, who had flown P-47 Thunderbolts in the 56th FG based in England, destroying 28 German aircraft. Gabreski had added two MiGs to his score while flying missions as deputy CO of the 4th Wing in Korea and he went on to add 4.5 while commanding the 51st. (The half MiG was shared with Maj Bill Whisner, another WW2 ace, who finished the Korean War with 5.5 kills.)

The 51st Wing's new Sabres went into action on 1 December. (Beginning in September, a few 'E's had filtered through to the 4th Wing, but the 'A' was not completely replaced in 4th Wing service until July 1952.) The Communists also boasted a new fighter, the MiG-15Bis, which had an uprated VK-I turbojet in place of the original RD-45. In good hands, the new jet easily outclassed the F-86A.

In December, Operation *Strangle* was extended to include fighter-bomber attacks on the Communist railway system. Losses in aircraft mounted on both sides. On 13 December, 4th Wing Sabres took on 145 MiGs and shot down 13 of the enemy jets in a bitter engagement. Maj George A. Davis Jr, CO of 334th Squadron, 4th FIW, shot down four—a Korean record. A total of 28 MiGs were shot down in December for the loss of seven Sabres.

In January 1952, the enemy launched a New Year air offensive, sending as many as 200 MiGs across the Yalu at any one time. The canny MiG pilots avoided combat below 30,000 ft and the 4th Wing had a lean time, downing only 11 MiGs during January–February. The higher-performance F-86Es of the 51st Fighter Wing, which could climb to 45,000 ft before engaging the enemy, took on the MiGs on equal terms and shot down 36 aircraft in the same period. Lack of spares and poor maintenance grounded many Sabres but during January, only five F-86s were lost in the air.

In February, the Communists raised their operational altitude to above the F-86E's 48,000 ft service ceiling to avoid battle with the new Sabre. It did them no good: 17 MiGs were destroyed for the loss of only two F-86s. One of them occurred on 10 February. Maj George A. Davis Jr, who was the leading jet ace with 12 kills, was leading 18 Sabres on an escort mission to the railway yards at Kumu-ri when he spotted a formation of MiGs at 32,000 ft closing on the fighter-bombers he was protecting. He turned to meet the threat, joined only by his wingman, intending to break up the attacking force before it could get among the bombers. Davis destroyed two of the MiGs and was closing on a third when his Sabre was hit and it crashed into a mountainside. Davis was awarded a posthumous Congressional Medal of Honor for his heroic action.

In March 1952, USAF tactics changed to concentrate on selected parts of the North Korean railway system and keep the tracks out of action permanently by the use of repeated bombing. Operation *Saturate*, as it was called,

On 10 February 1952, Major George A. Davis Jr of the 4th FIW, who was the leading jet ace with twelve kills, attacked a large force of MiGs during an escort mission to Kumu-ri before the enemy could get among the bombers. Davis destroyed two of the MiGs before he was hit and crashed into a mountainside. He was awarded a posthumous Congressional Medal of Honor for his heroic action. At the end of the war, Davis's 14 victories (all achieved in less than three months) made him the fourth ranking fighter ace in Korea. (USAF)

was a great success, greatly reducing the flow of supplies to the fronts and preventing the Communists from launching any new offensives. For 44 days, beginning on 26 January 1952, just over 200 B-26s and B-29s began a rail interdiction campaign, saturating road and rail targets near the village of Wadong. On 25 March, eight B-26s dropped 21,000 lb of bombs on a stretch of railroad track between Chongju and Sinanju. Meanwhile, night intruder B-26s of the 3rd and 452nd Wings, made attacks on rolling-stock at night, first marking their location with incendiaries and then using 80 million candlepower searchlights to illuminate the targets for strafing runs to be made. Unfortunately, the B-26s were also illuminated and led to unacceptable losses using this mode of attack, so the searchlights were removed. B-26 operations generally were on the wane early in 1952 when increased enemy AA capability, coupled with inexperienced replacement crews and poor B-26 stock from the USA which contained equipment and features unsuitable for a Korean winter, resulted in less effective bombing and high losses.

The enemy also lost heavily in the air. In March, F-86 pilots claimed 39 MiGs for the loss of only three Sabres and two F-84s. April was even better, with 44 MiGs claimed destroyed for the loss of four F-86s and one F-80 although the total would have been higher if the American pilots had been allowed to cross the Yalu into Manchuria and make strafing runs on bases there. On 13 April, they could quite clearly see 400 MiGs based on one airfield, immune from UN attack.

However, American pilots were permitted to make strafing and bombing attacks on Communist airfields south of the Yalu and these proved very successful during April–May. On 22 April, 51st Wing ace Capt Iven C. Kincheloe and Maj Elmer W. Harris destroyed two Yak-9s at Sinuiju airfield in strafing runs. They returned on 4 May to strafe 24 Yak-9s and five were destroyed in the attack. (Kincheloe, who accounted for three Yak-9s in the attack, survived the war and in 1956 took the experimental Bell X-2 to Mach 2.93.) On 13 May, 4th Wing Sabres, each carrying two 1,000 lb bombs below their wings, made their first dive-bombing attack on Sinuiju. In another attack, on the railway yards at Kumu-ri, Col Walker H. 'Bud' Mahurin, the 4th Wing CO, was shot down by flak and was taken prisoner. Mahurin, who had shot down 21 German aircraft in WW2 flying in the 56th FG as well as a Japanese bomber while serving in the Pacific, was credited with 3.5 MiGs at the time of his capture. Altogether, the enemy lost 27 MiGs during May while the Americans lost five Sabres, three F-84s and one F-51 in combat during a record 5,190 sorties. This total was unsurpassed by the time hostilities ended in 1953.

Early in June, the 51st FIW had been strengthened with the arrival, from the 18th Wing, of the 39th FIS, which was equipped with the latest F-86F Sabre model. The new fighter showed considerable improvement over the 'E' model. Sabre pilots had reported that intermittent opening of wing slats on the F-86E caused them gun-

Col Walker M. 'Bud' Mahurin, CO of the 4th FIW, poses on the wing of his F-86 Sabre. Mahurin was a WW2 ace with 22 victories and had destroyed 3.5 MiGs before he was shot down and captured on 13 May 1952 during an attack on the railway yards at Kumu-ri. (via Ian Mclachlan)

sighting problems during combat. The wing slats were omitted on the F-86F version and a new wing leading edge, extended by 9 inches, was added to improve manoeuvrability at high altitudes.

Between 23 June and 27 June, USAF and US Navy bombers, B-29s and fighter-bombers, carried out a systematic destruction of the North's hydroelectric plants. The co-ordinated operation cost the US forces just two aircraft. It had been hoped that a knock-out blow against such a valuable part of the enemy war machine would expedite peace moves and bring to an end the protracted cease-fire negotiations which were then taking place with the North Koreans, but still the war dragged on.

In July 1952, the FEAF began a reorganization programme and the F-86 wings were brought up to strength. The Communists also made a concerted effort in July. On 4 July, 50 MiGs crossed the Yalu and UN pilots claimed 13 destroyed for the loss of two Sabres. That month, 19 MiGs were shot down while four Sabres failed to return. In August, 35 MiGs were shot down, including six which were destroyed in a battle between 35 Sabres and 52 MiGs on the 6th.

In August–September, the F-84 Thunderjet wings began to be strengthened with the introduction of the F-84G model to replace the stop-gap F-84D which had given problems since its arrival in Korea. Also, in September, the 335th Squadron of the 4th Wing received the F-86F to replace the older 'E'. It was just as well because September saw the Communist pilots attack in some strength. One of the heaviest battles took place on 4 September when 13 MiGs were shot down for the loss of four Sabres. Five days later, 175 MiGs penetrated the Sabre escort and intercepted F-84s attacking Sakchu, shooting down one of the Thunderjets.

Mounting losses restricted enemy air activity in November and only the more experienced MiG pilots dived down from the safety of numbers at 40,000 ft to take on the American formations. On occasions, smaller formations of up to 24 MiGs took on flights of four Sabres and tried to box them in. The Americans responded by increasing the flights to six or eight, with the

higher-performance F-86Fs operating at 40,000 ft covering the more vulnerable 'E's' at lower altitudes. The new tactics worked, for only two Sabres were lost in combat while 28 MiGs were destroyed in the air. One of the F-80s lost in November was flown by 34-year-old Maj Charles Loring, squadron operations officer in the 8th FBW. Loring had flown 55 strafing missions and dive-bombing missions in WW2 and had been shot down on Christmas Eve 1944 during the Battle of the Bulge and taken prisoner. On 22 November, Loring led a flight of four F-80s to the area around Sniper Ridge (he led 51 artillery-strafing missions between June and November) on an artillery dive-bombing mission. Loring was hit by ground fire but made no attempt to retreat. He pulled his crippled aircraft around and deliberately dived on an artillery position which exploded in flames. He was awarded a posthumous Congressional Medal of Honor.

Although Soviet pilots were identified flying strangely coloured MiGs with the plain red star of the Soviet Air Force in some of the January battles when 37 MiGs were destroyed, the winter of 1953 saw little enemy activity until February when the B-29s blasted industrial targets once more. Meanwhile, USAF fighter-bombers attacked bridges and supply routes in the North. On 18 February, four Sabres attacked 48 MiGs, shooting down two and forcing two more to spin and crash. In all, 25 MiGs and four Sabres were lost in combat during February.

In March, 34 MiGs and three Sabres were lost. On 8 April, the 8th Fighter-Bomber Wing at Suwon, which had converted from the F-80C to the F-86F, flew their first Sabre sortie to MiG Alley. (The 18th Fighter-Bomber Wing at Osan had also converted to the F-86F, from F-51 Mustangs, beginning on 28 January, leaving the RF-80As of the 67th TRW as the only Shooting Stars in combat.) Air combats during April were few and far between but, even so, the Sabres claimed 27 MiGs destroyed for the loss of four F-86s. A fifth Sabre was shot down by flak. On 27 April, Capt Manuel J. Fernandez of the 334th Squadron, 4th Fighter Interceptor Wing, destroyed his eleventh enemy fighter to lead the table of Korean aces. Close behind came Capt

Joseph McConnell Jr of the 16th Fighter Squadron, 51st FIW, with 10.

May 1953 was a highly successful month for marauding UN fighter pilots, who no longer faced Soviet and Chinese pilots in combat. The Red Chinese and Soviet Union now had no need to further their experience in Korea. The remaining Communist pilots were not of the same calibre as the departing Honchos; some resorting to their ejection seats when an F-86 appeared on their tail, while others crashed once they got into difficulties. Gen Weyland gave the fighter pilots free reign and the American aces used the advantage to increase their scores. On 18 May, Capt Joseph McConnell scored his sixteenth and final victory when he destroyed a total of three MiGs. Both he and Fernandez, who finished the war with 14.5 kills, were pulled out of the war on 19 May and sent Stateside. McConnell's score remained unbeaten at the end of the war in Korea, making him the leading ace of the Korean War. Tragically, he was killed testing an F-86H on 24 August 1954. UN fighter pilots finished the month of May with a total of 56 MiG kills chalked up on the score sheet.

Meanwhile, sensing victory, the USAF fighter-bombers were directed to destroy North Korean irrigation dams to cause widespread destruction, and to cut lines of communication. F-84 Thunderjets carried out the first raid, on the Toksan Dam, on 13 May with great success. In desperation, the Communists launched a final offensive on 28 May against UN troops. The offensive petered out in the face of overwhelming air operations mounted by the 5th AF and the US Navy. The B-29s played their part, carrying out highly effective radar-directed bombing raids on enemy supply lines.

In June, 77 enemy fighters were shot down without loss to UN forces. In July, Sabres alone shot down 32 enemy fighters. Maj James Jabara, who had been the first ace of the war, and who had returned to the USA with six kills, had returned to combat in January 1953. By 26 May, he had downed three MiGs and on 10 June the 4th Wing ace shot down his tenth and eleventh MiGs. He added three more that month before claiming his fifteenth and final MiG victim on 15 July. Jabara's 15 victories put him into

This photo was taken on 18 February 1953, moments after Captain Manuel Fernandez (right) became the war's twenty-sixth ace. He finished the war as third ranking ace with 14.5 victories behind Captain James Jabara (left)—the first jet ace of the Korean War—of the 4th FIW who notched 15 victories, and Capt Joseph McConnell who led with 16 victories. (USAF)

second place overall behind McConnell.

By 20 July, the Communist offensive had spluttered to a halt. Two days later, the last combat between MiG and Sabre occurred, when Lt Sam P. Young of the 51st Fighter Wing shot down his first MiG, over MiG Alley during an offensive patrol. On 27 July, an Armistice was signed. With less than half an hour to go before the cease-fire agreement took effect—signed that morning at Panmunjom—a B-26 of the 8th BS, 3rd BW made the final close-support mission of the war when it dropped its bombs near the front line. It was trailed by an RB-26C of the 67th Tactical Reconnaissance Wing a few minutes later. That same day, Capt Ralph S. Parr of the 4th FIW destroyed an Ilyushin Il-12 transport. It was the last aircraft to fall in the Korean War.

Chapter Eight
In the Dragon's Jaw: Air War in Vietnam, 1964–66

Vietnam, formerly French Indo-China, which borders China, Laos and Cambodia, had been split into two countries in July 1954 after the defeat of the French forces, using the 17th Parallel to form the Republic of South Vietnam and the Communist North. The victors, the Communist Viet Minh forces led by Gen Giap, planned to take over control of the South using a new Communist guerrilla force called the Viet Cong (VC) or National Liberation Front (NLF). The VC campaign increased in intensity in 1957

and finally, in 1960, Premier Diem appealed to the United States for help and special 'advisors' were sent in. On 18 October 1961, four McDonnell RF-101A Voodoos arrived at Tan Son Nhut to become the first USAF unit to operate from Vietnam. On 26 December, the first USAF bombing mission of the Vietnam War was flown by two T-28s of the 'Farm Gate' Detachment—4400th Combat Crew Training Squadron flying from Tan Son Nhut—in support of two Vietnamese AD-6s and attacked Viet

When US 'Farm Gate' forces were deployed to South-East Asia in 1961, four B-26Bs were among those aircraft re-commissioned for use as COunter-INsurgency (COIN) operations from Bien Hoa. On 11 February 1964, after an Invader lost a wing in combat, all B-26s were grounded. Forty B-26Ks with completely rebuilt wings and fuselage, wing-tip tanks and new electronics equipment were produced and in June 1964, 18 B-26Ks were dispatched to Nakhom Phanom RTAFB. Treaty regulations forbad bombers to be stationed in Thailand, so in 1967 they reverted to the A-26A ('Attack') designation. They operated on interdiction missions over the Ho Chi Minh Trail at night from 1966 until the last sorties on 9 November 1969. (McDonnell Douglas)

Cong facilities north of Saigon. Finally, in 1964 President Lyndon B. Johnson began the moves which led to total American involvement.

The Korean War had shaken the military might of America and had led to far-reaching changes in the equipment it would need to fight any similar war anywhere in the world. Propeller-driven combat aircraft could no longer survive in the front line of any new conflict that flared up in the 1960s, and in the aftermath of the Korean War, American designers sat down with their design teams to conceive powerful new replacements for the USAF, US Navy and US Marine Corps.

In February 1965, the Viet Cong stepped up its guerrilla war and the first American casualties in Vietnam occurred when the VC attacked US installations in the South. In retaliation, the order was given for a strike code-named *Flaming Dart I* by 83 US Navy aircraft from carriers in the Gulf of Tonkin against VC installations at Dong Hoi and Vit Thu Lu.

The guerrilla war escalated and finally, in 1965, when the South Vietnamese administration was on the point of collapse, a squadron of F-105 Thunderchiefs arrived at Korat, Thailand to begin bombing operations. On 8 March, US Marines landed at Da Nang. A total of 111 aircraft were involved in the first strike on 2

March against the Xom Bong ammunition dump some 35 miles north of the DMZ (Demilitarized Zone). Some 44 Thuds, 40 F-100D Super Sabres, 20 B-57Bs and seven RF-101C Voodoos, were involved in the operation, called *Rolling Thunder*, as the air offensive against North Vietnam was called. Only moderate results were achieved and five aircraft, including two F-105s, were shot down by 'triple A' (anti-aircraft artillery).

The F-105 Thunderchief, or 'Thud' as it was known, had been designed as a successor to the F-84F and flew for the first time on 22 October 1955. It was the largest single-seat, single-engined combat aircraft in history. The Thunderchief was to bear the brunt of raids on the North because other types, such as the B-57, were too slow and the F-104 and F-5 did not have the range or payload to be effective. In the first five years of operations in Vietnam, F-105s flew 75 per cent of all USAF attack missions and losses were in proportion.

In March, the decision to interdict the North Vietnamese rail system south of the 20th parallel led immediately to the 3 April strike against the giant Ham Rong (Dragon's Jaw) road and rail bridge over the Song Ma River 3 miles north of Thanh Hoa, the capital of Annam Province, in North Vietnam's bloody Iron Triangle

F-105 Thunderchief in flight. Thuds were used throughout the Vietnam conflict, starting with the first Rolling Thunder *Operation against Xom Bong on 2 March 1965. (USAF)*

(Haiphong, Hanoi and Thanh Hoa). The 540 ft long, 56 ft wide Chinese-engineered bridge, which stood 50 ft above the river, was a replacement for the original French-built bridge destroyed by the Viet Minh in 1945, blown up by simply loading two locomotives with explosives and running them together in the middle of the bridge.

Lt Col Robinson Risner, a jet ace with eight victories in the Korean War, was designated overall mission co-ordinator for the attack. He assembled a force consisting of 79 aircraft made up of 46 F-105s, 21 F-100D Super Sabres, two RF-101 Voodoos and 10 KC-135A tankers. The F-100s came from bases in South Vietnam, while the rest of the aircraft were from squadrons TDY (temporary duty) at various Thailand bases. Sixteen of the 46 Thuds were loaded with pairs of AGM-12 Bullpup guided missiles, and each of the remaining 30 carried eight 750 lb general-purpose bombs.

The aircraft that carried the missiles, and half of the bombers were scheduled to strike the bridge; the remaining 15 would provide flak suppression. The plan called for individual flights of four F-105s from Korat and Takhli which would be air-refuelled over the Mekong River before tracking across Laos to an Initial Point (IP) 3 minutes south of the bridge. The plan called for all aircraft to continue east after weapon release until over the Gulf of Tonkin where they would rejoin and a Navy destroyer would be available to recover anyone who had to eject due to battle damage or other causes. After rejoining, all aircraft would return to their bases, hopefully to the tune of 'The Ham Rong Bridge is falling down'.

Shortly after noon on 3 April, *Rolling Thunder* aircraft on Mission 9-Alpha, climbed into the South-East Asian skies on their journey to the Thanh Hoa Bridge. The sun glinting through the haze, made the target a little difficult to acquire, but Risner led the way 'down the chute' and 250 lb missiles were soon exploding on the target. Since only one Bullpup missile could be fired at a time, each pilot had to make two firing passes. On his second pass, Lt Col Risner's aircraft took a hit just as the Bullpup hit the bridge. Fighting a serious fuel leak and a smoke-filled cockpit in addition to AAA fire from the enemy, he nursed his crippled aircraft to Da Nang and to safety. (On 16 September 1965, Risner was shot down a few miles north of the bridge. As he landed, he tore his knee painfully, a condition which contributed to his ultimate capture by the North Vietnamese. Risner was held at the Hanoi Hilton and other PoW camps around the capital until his release in 1973 but while a PoW, he was held in solitary confinement for $4^1/2$ years. Besides the normal malaise and illnesses common to PoWs, Risner also suffered from kidney stones, which severely debilitated him in the spring and summer of 1967.)

The first two flights had already left the target when Capt Bill Meyerholt, number three man in

Lt Col Robinson Risner, a jet ace with eight victories in the Korean War, led the first Rolling Thunder *attack on the notorious Dragon's Jaw bridge on 3 April 1965. On 16 September, Risner was shot down a few miles north of the bridge, captured, and held in solitary confinement for $4^1/2$ years. (USAF)*

F-100D similar to the one in which 1/Lt George C. Smith was shot down on 3 April 1965 when 21 F-100D Super Sabres were included in a force of 79 aircraft which tried unsuccessfully to destroy the giant Ham Rong (Dragon's Jaw) road and rail bridge over the Song Ma River 3 miles north of Thanh Hoa. (North American)

the third flight, rolled his Thud into a dive and squeezed off a Bullpup. The missile streaked toward the bridge and as smoke cleared from the previous attacks, Capt Meyerholt was shocked to see no visible damage to the bridge. The Bullpups were merely charring the heavy steel and concrete structure. The remaining missile attacks confirmed that firing Bullpups at the Dragon was about as effective as firing shotgun pellets at a tank.

The bombers, undaunted, came in for their attack only to see their payload drift to the far bank because of a very strong south-west wind. First Lieutenant George C. Smith's F-100D was shot down near the target point as he suppressed flak. The AAA fire was much stronger than anticipated. No radio contact could be made with Smith, nor could other aircraft locate him.

The last flight of the day, led by Capt Carlyle S. 'Smitty' Harris, adjusted their aiming points and scored several good hits on the roadway and superstructure. Smitty tried to assess bomb damage but could not because of the smoke coming from the Dragon's Jaw. The smoke would prove to be an ominous warning of things

to come. A Navy A-4C Skyhawk was shot down and a US Navy F-8 Crusader was damaged when four F-8Es tried to bomb the bridge and were attacked by MiG-17s. In addition, Capt Herschel S. Morgan's RF-101 was hit and went down some 75 miles south-west of the target area, seriously injuring the pilot. Morgan was captured and held in and around Hanoi until his release in February 1973.

When the smoke cleared, observer aircraft found that the two steel through-truss spans which rested in the centre on a massive reinforced-concrete pier 16 ft in diameter, were still standing. Numerous hits from the 32 Bullpups and 10 dozen 750 lb bombs aimed at it had charred the structure, yet it showed no sign of going down. A re-strike was ordered for the next day.

On 4 April, 48 F-105Ds and the 'Cadillac' BDA (bomb damage assessment) flight returned once more to try and destroy the giant bridge but although over 300 bombs scored hits, the bridge still refused to fall down. The attack force was jumped by MiG-15s and MiG-17s of the NVAF (North Vietnamese Air Force) about 76 miles south of Hanoi. One Thud was shot down by AAA fire and two others, an F-105D piloted by Capt Carlyle 'Smitty' Harris, and an F-105D flown by Capt James A. Magnusson, were shot down by MiG-17s. (Some 60 F-105s were shot down in 1965, mostly by AAA and missiles.)

Harris was flying as call sign 'Steel 3'. He took the lead and orientated himself for his run on a 300° heading. Harris reported that his bombs had impacted on the target on the eastern end of the bridge. However, he was on fire as soon as he left the target. Radio contact was garbled. 'Steel Lead', 'Steel 2' and 'Steel 4' watched helplessly as Smitty's Thunderchief, emitting flame 20 ft behind, headed due west of the target. All flight members had him in sight until the fire died out but observed no parachute, nor did they see the aircraft hit the ground. Smitty was captured by the North Vietnamese and held prisoner for eight years.

'Zine 2', an F-105D flown by Capt Magnusson, had its flight bounced by MiG-17s. As 'Zine Lead' was breaking to shake a MiG off his tail, 'Zine 2' was hit and radioed that he was heading for the Gulf of Tonkin if he could maintain control of his aircraft. The other Thunderchiefs were busy evading the MiGs and Magnusson radioed several times before Steel Lead responded and instructed him to tune his radio to the rescue frequency. Magnusson finally ditched over the Gulf of Tonkin near the island of Hon Me and he was not seen or heard from again.

Capt Walter F. Draeger's A-1H Skyraider (probably an escort for rescue teams) was shot down over the Gulf just north-east of the Dragon that day. Draeger's aircraft was seen to crash in flames but no parachute was observed and he was listed MIA. (From April to September 1965, 19 more pilots were shot down in the general vicinity of the Dragon, including many who were captured and released.)

Meanwhile, in April 1965, McDonnell F-4C Phantoms of the 45th Tactical Fighter Squadron arrived at Ubon, in south-east Thailand to be used initially to provide combat air patrols to protect F-105 strikes. The F-4 had resulted from a US Navy requirement for a new shipboard fighter which had led to an order for two prototypes on 18 October 1954. It is probably the most famous of all the aircraft to emerge from the post-Korea era. It was the world's first truly multi-role supersonic combat aircraft.

After a lull in operations to give peace negotiations a chance (which soon failed), the USAF F-4Cs were in action against the MiGs. On 10

F-4C Phantoms refuel from a KC-135A. F-4Cs of the 45th TFW which were deployed to Ubon AB in April 1965 were the first USAF Phantoms deployed to South-East Asia. (McDonnell Douglas)

July, two Phantom crews in the 45th TFS shot down two enemy MiG-17s with Sidewinder missiles to chalk up the first USAF victories of the war. One month later, on 24 July, an F-4C was brought down by a Soviet-built SA-2 SAM (Surface-to-air) missile. The SA-2 Guideline was a 35 ft two-stage rocket with a 349 lb high explosive warhead and a ceiling of almost 60,000 ft. Pilots who encountered them described them as 'telegraph poles.' In 1965, SAMs brought down five USAF and six USN aircraft.

In December 1965, Operation *Tiger Hound* was started by the US Air Force to strike at targets in the southern panhandle of Laos next to the South Vietnamese border to interdict troop and supply movements. On Christmas Day, President Johnson suspended the *Rolling Thunder* bombing campaign to induce the Communists to negotiate. The VC responded with a counter-offensive campaign and the *Rolling Thunder* Campaign was re-started again on 31 January 1966. The war in Laos was no less fierce than in Vietnam and triple A fire was often no less of a hazard, particularly when slow, propeller-driven aircraft such as the Cessna O-1E Bird Dog, Grumman OV-1A Mohawk observation aircraft, and the A-1 Skyraider were involved.

On 10 March 1966, an A-1E Skyraider piloted by Maj Dafford W. 'Jump' Myers, was shot down during an air strike in support of the Green Berets (US Special Forces) near A Shau camp on the Vietnamese border where some 20 Green Berets and 375 South Vietnamese fought a bloody two-day battle against 2,000 NVA (North Vietnamese Army) troops. Outnumbered, the Green Berets had to evacuate the camp on 10 March. Myers' A-1E caught fire as a result of strikes by .50-calibre machine-gun fire but he managed to crash-land on the runway at A Shau. Overhead, Maj Bernard F. Fisher radioed for a rescue helicopter but he decided time was running out and landed his Skyraider with the intention of rescuing Myers from the advancing enemy. Despite intense small-arms fire, Fisher landed and plucked Myers to safety. Both men landed safely at Pleiku. Fisher's Skyraider had 19 bullet holes in it. On 19 January 1967,

President Johnson presented Maj Fisher with the first Congressional Medal of Honor to be awarded to an Air Force officer during the Vietnam War for his daring rescue. Eighteen months later, another A-1 pilot, Lt Col William Jones, was similarly awarded for repeated attacks against VC positions during a rescue of a Phantom pilot near Dong Hoi in North Vietnam.

Flying slow, unarmed, single-engined FAC (Forward Air Control) aircraft such as the Bird Dog over VC infested Laos was equally dangerous. Maj William W. McAllister had distinguished himself on 9/10 March 1965 when, despite intense ground fire and with complete disregard for his own safety, he sought out targets for A-1Es near Qui Nhon AFB, at times taking on the VC with just an M16 automatic rifle. Mac's actions enabled two American casualties to be evacuated. Later that night, he returned to assist US positions in darkness and under extremely bad weather conditions in mountainous terrain. His actions earned him the AFC. A few weeks later, Mac was killed when his O-1F stalled on take-off from Phu Cat, just north of Qui Nhon.

At about 13:00 hrs on 15 March 1966, a USAF O-1E Bird Dog, piloted by David Holmes, was shot down on the east side of the Se Nam Kok River valley 11 miles north-west of Tchepone, Laos. There was a large number of NVA in the area maintaining a vehicle park along the Ho Chi Minh Trail, as well as six gun emplacements. Another O-1E, call sign 'Hound Dog 50', was dispatched immediately. He observed Holmes, apparently unconscious, sitting in the cockpit of his Bird Dog. At about 14:35 hrs, 'Hound Dog 50' also observed an OV-1A Mohawk flown by Maj Glenn McElroy and Capt Mike Nash of the 20th Aviation Detachment, US Army on a *Tiger Hound* photo run along Route 91 on the west side of the Se Nam Kok River valley. The OV-1A was hit by AAA fire and crashed. One parachute was seen and it is believed that it contained Nash, because the pilot ejected from the right side of the damaged aircraft.

Because of the loss of the two aircraft and the discovery of troops and gun emplacements, F-4 Phantoms (call sign 'Oxwood 95') and A-1E

Skyraiders were called in and the ensuing battle raged for about 5 hours. Next day, a search and rescue team flew to the crash site of David Holmes' O-1E and found his plane empty. URC-10 emergency radio signals were heard four times in the next six days but it was thought that the signals were initiated by the enemy as voice contact was never made. Holmes, Nash and McElroy all had URC-10 radios. The fates of all three are unknown. None of the 600 Americans missing in Laos have ever been released.

On 25 April 1966, the MiG-21 was seen for the first time and the following day, two MiG-21s attacked three USAF Phantoms escorting two RB-66s. One of the F-4 pilots fired two Sidewinder missiles at one of the MiGs and the enemy pilot was seen to eject from the doomed fighter. As in Korea, it proved that in the hands of an accomplished pilot, a heavier machine could still beat a more manoeuvrable enemy fighter.

In May 1966, the USAF again turned its attentions to the notorious Dragon Jaw bridge at Thanh Hoa. Since the shooting down of Col Robbie Risner in September 1965, 15 more pilots had been downed in the bridge area without any lasting damage being registered. Now the Air Force decided to try out an innovative concept—mass focusing the energy of certain high explosive weapons—against the stubborn structure. Operation *Carolina Moon* used two specially modified C-130A Hercules transport aircraft to drop the weapon, a rather large pancake-shaped bomb 8 ft in diameter, 2.5 ft thick and weighing 5,000 lb. The C-130s would fly below 500 ft to evade radar along a 43-mile route (which meant the C-130s would be vulnerable to enemy attack for about 17 minutes) and drop the bombs which would float down the Song Ma River that passed under the Dragon's Jaw, and detonate when sensors in the bombs detected the metal of the bridge structure.

Because the slow-moving C-130s would need protection, F-4 Phantoms would fly a diversionary attack to the south, using flares and bombs on the highway just before the C-130s were to drop their ordnance. The F-4s were to enter their target area at 300 ft, attack at 50 ft and pull up to 300 ft for subsequent attacks. Additionally, an EB-66 was tasked to jam the radar in the area during the attack.

The first C-130 was to be flown by Maj Richard T. Renners and the second by Maj Thomas F. Case, both of whom had been through extensive training for this mission at Eglin AFB, Florida and had been deployed to Vietnam only two weeks before. Ten mass-focus weapons were provided, allowing for a second mission should the first fail to accomplish the desired results. Last minute changes to coincide with up-to-date intelligence included one that would be very significant. Maj Renners felt that the aircraft was tough enough to survive moderate AAA hits and gain enough altitude should bailing out be necessary. Maj Case agreed that the aircraft could take the hits, but the low-level flight would preclude a controlled bail-out. With these conflicting philosophies, and the fact that either parachutes or flak vests could be worn—but not both—Maj Renners decided that his crew would wear parachutes and stack their flak vests on the floor of the aircraft. Maj Case decided that his crew would wear only flak vests and store the parachutes.

On the night of 30 May, Maj Renners and his crew, including navigators Capt Norman G. Clanton and 1/Lt William 'Rocky' Edmondson, departed Da Nang at 25 minutes past midnight and headed north under radio silence. Although the Herky-Bird met no resistance at the beginning of its approach, heavy—although fortunately inaccurate—ground fire was encountered after it was too late to turn back. The five weapons were dropped successfully in the river and Maj Renners made for the safety of the Gulf of Tonkin. The operation had gone flawlessly, and the Hercules was safe. Although the diversionary attack had drawn fire, both F-4s returned to Thailand unscathed. Unfortunately, the excitement of the crew was short lived because recconnaissance photos taken at dawn showed that there was no noticeable damage to the bridge, nor was any trace of the bombs found. A second mission was planned for the night of 31 May.

The plan for Maj Case's crew was basically the same with the exception of a minor time change and slight modification to the flight

C-130A 54-1625 in flight. A C-130A piloted by Maj Tom Case was lost on the second abortive Carolina Moon *mission to destroy the Dragon Jaw bridge at Thanh Hoa on 31 May 1966. (Lockheed)*

Col Dayton W. Ragland who was shot down on 31 May 1966 and is still listed as missing. (US Veterans And News Report)

route. A crew change was made when Maj Case asked 1/Lt Edmondson, the navigator from the previous night's mission, to go along on this one because of his experience gained on the first 'pancake bomb' mission. The C-130 departed Da Nang at 01:10 hrs. Two F-4 Phantoms again flew as a diversion for the Herky-Bird strike. One of the back-seaters was Col Dayton W. Ragland, a crack US fighter pilot during the Korean War and the veteran of many missions in MiG Alley. On 18 November 1951, he accompanied Capt Kenneth D. Chandler in a strafing run which destroyed four enemy jets on the ground at Uiju. That same month, Ragland was shot down and he spent two years as a prisoner of the Red Chinese before being released in 1953 during Operation *Big Switch*. Having flown 97 combat missions in Vietnam, Ragland was about ready to be rotated back to the US but the colonel agreed to fly in the back seat of one of the F-4s piloted by 1/Lt Ned R. Herrold to give the younger man more combat flight time while he operated the sophisticated technical navigational and bombing equipment.

The two Phantoms left Thailand and headed for the area south of the Dragon flying at times only 50 ft above the ground. At about 2 minutes prior to the scheduled C-130 drop time, the F-4s were in the middle of creating the diversion when crew members saw AA fire and a large ground flash in the vicinity of the bridge. Maj Case and his crew were never seen or heard from again. During the F-4 attack, Herrold and Ragland's jet was hit. On its final pass, the Phantom did not pull up but went out to sea. The damaged jet made it nearly 5 miles off shore

before it exploded. The two crew may have ejected before the explosion because a search and rescue aircraft discovered a dinghy in the water the following day. No trace of the C-130 or its crew could be found. In late 1986, the remains of Case and two of his crew were returned to the US. Herrold and Ragland are among the 2,303 Americans still listed as unaccounted for in South-East Asia.

Almost 700 sorties were flown against the bridge at a cost of 104 crewmen shot down over an area of 75 square miles around the Dragon. In March 1967, the US Navy attacked the charmed bridge with new Walleye missiles but failed to knock out the structure despite three direct hits. The spans were finally brought down on 13 May

Six USAF F-4C Phantoms led by a EB-66B ECM aircraft drop bombs on military targets in North Vietnam. (McDonnell Douglas)

F-4E-35-MC of the 469th TFS/388th TFW based at Korat in Thailand. (McDonnell Douglas)

1972, by laser-guided 'smart' bombs dropped by F-4Ds of the 8th TFW. Unfortunately, by then the Communists had built several other back-up routes around the bridge and the flow of supplies across the Ma River were not seriously affected.

On 14 July, F-4C Phantoms of the 480th TFS of the 35th TFW shot down two MiG-21s. Altogether, the NVNAF lost 13 MiG-17s and four MiG-21s in combat in 1966. The year 1966 was a bad year for the US Air Forces. Altogether, 379 aircraft were lost, including 34 victims of SA-2 SAM missiles. Some 126 F-105 Thunderchiefs and 42 F-4s were lost in combat. Something had to be done to drive the MiGs from the skies over North Vietnam.

Chapter Nine

The Bloody Iron Triangle: Air War in Vietnam, 1967–75

The USAF stepped up its operations in the New Year. On 2 January 1967, a formation of F-4Cs of the 8th TFW using electronic jamming pods made a spoof F-105 strike to lure the MiG-21s into combat. They were so successful that seven MiGs fell to the Phantoms' fire-power. Two more MiG-21s were shot down in similar fashion four days later. On 10 March, a F-105 pilot, Capt Max C. Brestel of the 354th TFS of the 355th TFW, became the first USAF pilot in South-East Asia to destroy two enemy aircraft in one sortie.

Phantoms and MiGs met each other over Vietnam on many occasions throughout the first half of 1967 and American crews also continued to run the gauntlet of SAM missiles and ground fire.

Raids on Communist airbases provoked a

Against a backdrop of mountainous terrain in North Vietnam, an F-4C Phantom dives toward a target. On 2 January 1967, a formation of F-4Cs of the 8th TFW, using electronic jamming pods, made a spoof F-105 strike to lure the MiG-21s into combat and shot down seven MiGs. Two more MiG-21s were shot down by F-4Cs on 6 January. From January to June 1967, USAF jets shot down 46 MiGs, including seven MiG-17s by two Phantoms and five F-105s on 13 May. (McDonnell Douglas)

furious response from the defending enemy jets. Remarkably, from January to June 1967, USAF jets shot down 46 MiGs, including seven MiG-17s by two Phantoms and five F-105s on one day, 13 May. In a 16-month period ending 27 October 1967, F-105Ds of the 355th and 388th TFWs, using 20 mm cannon and Sidewinder heat-seeking missiles, destroyed 27 MiG-17s in the air. From April to July 1967, the US Navy accounted for another dozen enemy aircraft. On 17 December 1967, Capt Doyle Baker, a Marine pilot on exchange duty flying an F-4D of the 13th TFS of the 432nd TRW with 1/Lt John D. Ryan Jr in the back seat, became the first Marine pilot to down a MiG. By the end of the year, 20 F-4s and F-105s had been shot down by the MiGs and a further 20 aircraft by SAMs.

One of the worst days occurred on 21 August 1967 when two F-105Ds flown by Maj Merwin L. Morrill and 1/Lt Lynn K. Powell, and three Grumman A-6A Intruders from a four-plane strike force from VA-196 aboard the USS *Constellation* were shot down during a raid on the Duc Noi rail yards 4 miles north of Hanoi. A month later, on 1 September, 42-year-old Maj George 'Bud' Day, an F-100 Super Sabre pilot and veteran of both WW2 and Korea, was shot down on his sixty-seventh mission near Vinh Linh. Day had joined the USMC in 1942 and served 30 months in the South Pacific as a non-commissioned officer. In 1951, Day was called to active duty service. He served two tours in the Far East as a fighter-bomber pilot during the Korean War. Day recalls: 'We had launched to take out a surface-to-air missile site. When we got close we started taking a lot of flak. We knew it was good [a good target]. Once we spotted the missile site we headed for the target. That's when we took a direct hit.' At an altitude of 4,000 ft, the controls failed and Day ejected while the aircraft was inverted. He recalls: 'You're not supposed to eject that way. I hit the ground in bad shape.' (Day had previously bailed out from a burning F-84F over England and his parachute had not deployed. He had plummeted 300 ft before landing in a heavily wooded area which cushioned his fall.)

Ejecting over Vietnam, Day struck the canopy of the F-100. This time he broke his arm in three places and temporarily lost the sight of his left eye, in addition to numerous cuts and bruises he received. He was subsequently captured. 'I made up my mind that I was going to escape. So when the opportunity presented itself, I did.' Day was held in an underground bunker, guarded by teenage soldiers. He convinced them that he could not move, then made his getaway. Day fled to the south. He was shot twice and he survived a mortar attack. 'I was bleeding pretty good from a lot of places. It took a lot of steam out of me.'

Eventually, Day was recaptured. He was tortured unmercifully. 'It was barbaric but I kept the faith. I'm an optimist so I never doubted my country would come to get us.' Day spent 5½ years as a PoW, 38 of those 67 months being spent in solitary confinement. (On his release in 1973, Day, along with Captain Lance P. Sijan, another air force pilot who died in captivity, and Cmdr James Bond Stockdale, a US Navy pilot shot down in 1965, were each recommended by their fellow prisoners for the Congressional Medal of Honor for their conduct as PoWs. On 4 March 1976, Day, Stockdale and Sijan's family were presented with the medals by President Gerald Ford.)

One of the ways of preventing aircraft losses to SAM missiles was the use of F-105F Wild Weasels in a SAM neutralization role. The F-105F featured radar homing and warning gear. Upon pinpointing the radar at a missile site, the Wild Weasel attacked with Shrike missiles that homed in on radar emissions. The F-105F was a 'stretch-limo' F-105, with a longer fuselage to permit an electronic warfare officer to be carried. As modified for the 'G', the F-105 launched a standard anti-radiation missile (ARM) rather than the shorter-range AGM-45A Shrike normally carried by the F-105F.

On 19 April 1967, Maj Leo K. Thorsness, Head Weasel of the 357th TAC Fighter Squadron at Takhli AFB, Thailand and his back-seater, Capt Harry Johnson, were flying an F-105 on a Wild Weasel mission with three other aircraft when a few miles south-east of the Xuan Mai army base, 60 kilometres south-west of Hanoi, the Wild Weasel's radar picked up a SAM site ahead of them. Thorsness launched a

Major (later Lt Colonel) Leo Thorsness. For his actions on 19 April 1967 Maj Leo K. Thorsness, Head Weasel of the 357th TAC Fighter Squadron at Takhli AFB in Thailand, received the Congressional Medal of Honor. (USAF)

Shrike missile and the blip disappeared, indicating that the SAM site no longer existed.

Thorsness headed north for another SAM site with his wingman, Capt Tom Madison, which the major destroyed with a cluster bomb. Both F-105s stayed low, on the lookout for more SAM sites. Ground fire enveloped their aircraft and Madison and his back-seater, Capt Tom Sterling, were forced to eject. Thorsness gave cover and dispatched a MiG-17 which could have attacked the two fliers in their chutes. After taking on fuel from a tanker over Laos, despite having only 500 rounds of ammunition remaining, Thorsness returned to Xuan Mai to give support to two A-1E Sandys and a rescue helicopter heading for the downed pilot and his back-seater. Johnson picked up four MiGs on

their tail and Thorsness spotted three MiGs in front. He managed to outrun them through a series of mountain valleys and at least one MiG crashed during the pursuit. Low on fuel and out of ammunition, Thorsness headed for the remaining MiGs before reinforcements arrived. In a final act of bravery, Thorsness, his F-105 by now almost on empty, guided the tanker to a lost A-1E pilot before he landed, almost out of fuel, at Udorn.

Despite Thorsness's valiant efforts Sterling and Madison were captured and spent six years in captivity. On 30 April while on another Wild Weasel mission, Thorsness (on his ninety-third mission) and Johnson were shot down by a MiG. The two men ejected at 600 knots and both suffered severe back injuries before they too were captured and incarcerated. They spent almost six years as PoWs and Thorsness was tortured and denied medical attention because of his 'uncooperative' attitude. On 15 October 1973, President Nixon presented the Congressional Medal of Honor to Lt Col Leo K. Thorsness. Harold Johnson was later awarded the Air Force Cross.

Early in 1968, President Johnson forbade all strikes beyond the 19th Parallel and on 1 November he ordered a halt to all bombing of North Vietnam. As a consequence losses in the F-105 and F-4 wings dropped while the NVNAF lost only five MiG-17s and three MiG-21s in combat that year. The policy of halting the bombing of the North was confirmed in January 1969 by the incoming President, Richard E. Nixon. Two months later, on 24 February, 23-year-old Airman 1st Class John L. Levitow, the only enlisted man and the youngest to receive America's highest award during the Vietnam War, received the Congressional Medal of Honor for saving his AC-47 gunship after it was hit by an enemy 82 mm shell near Long Binh during a *Spooky* night mission. AC-47s were nicknamed 'Puff the Magic Dragon' because they were equipped with three multi-barrelled 7.62 mm Miniguns, and magnesium illumination flares in 23 ft long cylinders to provide ground lighting for ground troops below or to hit a target. The 82 mm shell blew a 3 ft hole in the gunship just as Sgt Ellis Owen was pulling the lanyard from a

The famous Douglas C-47 Dakota was used in a variety of roles throughout the Vietnam War. Pictured here is an AC-47D gunship of the 4th SOS, 14th SOW. (Douglas)

magnesium flare (which triggered the time-delay firing mechanism) prior to dropping it out the open cargo door. Ellis and the flare fell to the floor. Levitow, the gunship loadmaster that night, had been hit 40 times by shrapnel in his right leg and hip. Nonetheless, he helped the wounded and managed to throw the flare out of the AC-47 before it exploded with a brilliant white flash. Maj Ken Carpenter, the pilot, landed safely back at Bien Hoa airfield near Saigon where, after seeing the trail of blood, pieced together the loadmaster's actions, and recommended Levitow for the Congressional Medal of Honor.

The AC-47 was an adaptation of the famous C-47 Dakota, one of the most versatile aircraft in the history of aviation. During the period 1965–1972, few aircraft in Vietnam were as versatile as the F-105. The Thud performed on many diverse missions in South-East Asia, including SAM attack, bombing, and armed escort and diversion. On 28 January 1970, an F-105G Wild Weasel crewed by pilot Capt Richard J. Mallon and Capt Robert J. Panek, his EWO, were sent as escort to a reconnaissance aircraft on a mission in North Vietnam. The F-105 was shot down during the mission and they both successfully ejected safely into an enemy

controlled area about 20 miles north-east of the Mu Gia Pass on the mountainous North

A1C John Levitow, loadmaster on an AC-47 gunship Spooky 71, was the only USAF enlisted man to receive the Congressional Medal of Honor, for his actions on 24 February 1969. (McDonnell Douglas/USAF)

Vietnam–Laos border. Mallon landed on a road near the pass and was captured almost immediately. Panek landed in nearby trees and his parachute was seen 30 minutes later being pulled from the trees. Both men were seen in a clearing within the hour, surrounded, stripped to their shorts, and holding their hands in the air.

A helicopter, piloted by Maj Holly G. Bell with four crew and a passenger aboard, was immediately dispatched to pick up the two downed airmen. When the aircraft was about 50 miles north-west of the location of the F-105 crash, it was hit by a MiG and exploded. The Vietnamese denied any knowledge of any of the eight men missing that day but in December 1988 the Vietnamese returned a number of remains they stated were those of American servicemen. The remains of Mallon, Panek and Holly Bell were subsequently positively identified by the US Casualty Identification Laboratory in Hawaii.

The ban on bombing of the North remained in force throughout 1970 but covert operations continued, sometimes inside Laos. The *Steve Canyon* programme was a highly classified FAC (Forward Air Control) operation covering the military regions of Laos. US military actions inside this country were severely restricted during the Vietnam War because Laos had been declared neutral by the Geneva Accords. The non-communist forces in Laos, however, had a critical need for military support in order to defend territory used by Lao and North Vietnamese Communist forces. The US, in conjunction with non-Communist forces in Laos, devised a system whereby US military personnel could be 'in the black' or 'sheep dipped' (clandestine vernacular for mustered out of the military to perform military duties as a civilian) to operate in Laos under supervision of the US Ambassador to Laos.

'Raven' was the radio call-sign which identified the flyers of the *Steve Canyon* programme. Men recruited for the programme were rated Air Force officers with at least six months experience in Vietnam. They tended to be the very best of pilots but by definition this meant that they were also mavericks and considered a bit wild by the mainstream military establishment.

The Ravens came under the formal command of CINPAC and the 7/13th AF 56th Special Operations Wing at Nakhon Phanom, but their pay records were maintained at Udorn with Detachment 1. Officially, they were on loan to the US Air Attaché at Vientiane. Unofficially, they were sent to outposts like Long Tieng where their field commanders were the CIA, the Meo Generals and the US Ambassador. Once on duty, they flew FAC missions which controlled all US air strikes over Laos.

All tactical strike aircraft had to be under the control of a FAC who was familiar with the locale, the populous, and the tactical situation. The FAC would find the target, order up US fighter-bombers from an airborne command and control centre, mark the target accurately with white phosphorus (Willy Pete) rockets, and control the operation throughout the time the planes remained on station. After the fighters had departed, the FAC stayed over the target to make a bomb-damage assessment (BDA).

The FAC also had to ensure that there were no attacks on civilians, a complex problem in a war where there were no front lines and any hamlet could suddenly become part of the combat zone. An FAC needed a fighter pilot's mentality but was obliged to fly slow and low in such unarmed and vulnerable aircraft as the 105 mph Cessna O-1 Bird Dog and the Cessna O-2. Consequently, aircraft used by the Ravens were continually peppered with ground fire.

Ravens were hopelessly overworked by the war. The need for secrecy kept their numbers low (never more than 22 at one time) and the critical need of the Meo sometimes demanded each pilot fly 10-hour and 12-hour days. Some Ravens completed a tour of approximately six months with a total of over 500 combat missions. On 24 February 1967, Capt Hilliard Wilbanks, an O-1 pilot and veteran of 487 combat missions, deliberately drew intense VC fire to divert attention from an outnumbered Ranger battalion and made strafing runs at 100 ft armed only with an M16 rifle before being shot down. Wilbanks was picked up by a rescue helicopter but died of his wounds en route to hospital. For his actions, Wilbanks was posthumously awarded the Congressional Medal of Honor to

FAC Cessna O-2A armed with two Minigun pods for suppressive fire and two white phosphorus rocket pods for target marking. An FAC needed a fighter pilot's mentality but was obliged to fly slow and low in such unarmed and vulnerable aircraft as the 105 mph Cessna O-1 Bird Dog and the Cessna O-2. Consequently, aircraft used by the Ravens were continually peppered with ground fire. (Cessna)

go with his DFC and 17 Air Medals.

The Ravens at Long Tieng in Military region II, had the most difficult area in Laos for several years. The base, just on the southern edge of the Plain of Jars, was also the headquarters for the CIA-funded Meo Army commanded by Gen

In Vietnam, aircraft such as the Ryan Navion (left) the L-5 liaison aircraft were used for FAC work. (Author)

Vang Pao. On 30 December 1970, Capt Park George Bunker was lost when his O-1 was brought down after AAA fire knocked out his engine and he was forced to put down on a flat patch in the horseshoe bend of a river but not before he had sent out a mayday message. Four Ravens picked up the transmission and headed for Bunker's crash site which was now under attack from three sides. They heard Bunker say over the radio: 'I've been hit, I'm hit . . . God I've been shot five times. I'm not going to make it. I'm as good as dead.' One of the Ravens, Chuck Engle, braved the enemy fire for a closer look but he had to break off after seeing something under a tree. A Skyraider pilot later confirmed that there was a blood-soaked body under the tree. Next day, it had been removed. Bunker only had 30 days of his tour remaining when he was lost.

Lam Son 719 was a large offensive operation against North Vietnamese communications lines in the southern Laotian panhandle adjacent to the two northern provinces of South Vietnam. The operation was a raid in which ARVN (Army of the Republic of Vietnam) troops would drive west from Khe Sanh on Route 9, cut the Ho Chi Minh Trail, seize Tchepone some 25 miles away, and then return to Vietnam. The ARVN would provide and command the ground forces while the US Air Force and Army would furnish airlift and firepower support. The 101st Airborne Division (Airmobile) commanded all US Army Aviation units in direct support of the operation. Most of the first part of the operation, begun on 30 January 1971, was called Operation *Dewey Canyon II* and was conducted by US ground forces in Vietnam.

On 8 February, ARVN began pushing along Route 9 into Laos. The NVA reacted fiercely, committing some 36,000 troops to the area. The ARVN held its positions supported by US air strikes and re-supply runs by Army helicopters. President Nguyen Van Thieu ordered a helicopter assault on Tchepone and the abandoned village was seized on 6 March. Two weeks of hard combat were necessary for the ARVN task force to fight its way back to Vietnam.

Randy Ard of the 1st Squadron, 1st Cavalry, 23rd Infantry Division, US Army had been in Vietnam only a few weeks when an emergency call came in for him to fly the squadron commander to a platoon command post to work his way down to his Third Platoon, which was in ambush in the north-west segment of South Vietnam. He flew his OH-58A Kiowa Scout helicopter from the 5th Mech and picked up Lt Col Sheldon Burnett, the squadron commander, Capt Phil Bodenhorn, Alpha Company commander and SP4 Mike Castillo, Third Platoon RTO.

Ard mistakenly flew past the command post and entered Laos. Seeing yellow marking smoke he took the chopper down lower. It was too late to pull up when they heard the sound of an RPD machine-gun and AK-47s. They had been tricked into a North Vietnamese ambush. The helicopter went down fast and smashed into the brush, coming down on its side (or upside down, depending on the version of the account). Ard and Burnett were trapped in the wreckage, but alive. Ard got on the radio and began mayday calls. Bodenhorn and Castillo, who had been in the rear seat, got out of the helicopter. Bodenhorn managed to free Ard but he had two broken legs and possibly a broken hip. Burnett was completely pinned within the wreckage, injured but alive. Bodenhorn and Castillo positioned themselves on opposite sides of the aircraft for security and expended all the coloured smoke grenades they had, marking the position for rescue.

Bodenhorn and Castillo soon heard NVA approaching and killed them. The two listened for nearly an hour as others advanced towards their position from two directions, and 155 mm artillery rounds impacted very near them. They could not understand why they were not being rescued, unless it was because the enemy was so close to them. A helicopter flew over, but they took heavy fire and left. They decided to leave Ard and Burnett and escape themselves. They told Ard who nodded wordlessly. Burnett was drifting in and out of consciousness. Both men were alive.

Bodenhorn and Castillo were rescued by ARVN troops an hour later. Ard and Burnett were classified MIA. Eleven days later, the 11th ARVN Airborne Battalion fought their way into the area where the helicopter had crashed. They searched the wreckage and the surrounding area for several days but found no sign of the two missing men. Losses in *Lam Son 719* were heavy. Aviation units lost 168 helicopters and another 618 were damaged. Some 55 aircrewmen were killed in action, 178 were wounded and 34 MIA. Four US newsmen were killed when their helicopter was shot down by enemy ground fire. There were 19,360 known enemy casualties from the operation which lasted until 6 April 1971.

Although bombing of the North was still out of the question, raids continued to be made near the DMZ. One such raid, which occurred on the afternoon of 2 April 1972, reveals the incredible lengths to which the US military went in trying to recover downed airmen from behind enemy lines. Once again, it was one of the ubiquitous helicopter crews—who so often performed such heroic work to pluck men from the jungles of Vietnam—who were used to try and rescue the crew of an EB-66C aircraft (Bat 21) based in Korat in Thailand, which was lost while flying with a second EB-66C (Bat 22) while flying pathfinder escort for a cell of B-52s bombing near the DMZ. The two EB-66s were from the

42nd Tactical Electronic Warfare Squadron, 388th TFW.

Bat 21 took a direct SAM hit and the plane went down. The aircraft was observed by Bat 22 flight members to break apart and crash. A single beeper signal was heard, that of navigator Col Iceal E. Hambleton. At this time, it was assumed that the rest of the crew died in the crash. The crew included the pilot Maj Wayne Bolte, and 1/Lt Robin Gatwood, Lt Col Anthony Giannangeli, Lt Col Charles Levis and Maj Henry Serex. It should be noted that the lowest ranking man aboard was Gatwood, a 1st lieutenant. This was no ordinary crew and its members, particularly Hambleton, would be prize captures for the enemy. It became critical, therefore, that the US locate Hambleton and any other surviving crew members before the Vietnamese did—and the Vietnamese were trying very hard to find them first.

An Army search and rescue team was nearby and dispatched two UH-1H 'Slicks' and two AH-1G HueyCobras. When they approached Hambleton's position just before dark, at about 50 ft, with one of the Cobra gunships flying at 300 ft for cover, two of the helicopters were shot

An EB-66E converted from an RB-66B for electronic counter-measures missions, similar to Bat-21 of the 42nd TEWS, 388th TFW which was brought down by a SAM on 2 April 1972. (Harry Gann/McDonnell Douglas)

down. The downed Cobra ('Blue Ghost 28') reached safety and the crew was picked up without having seen the other downed helicopter, a UH-1H from F Troop, 8th Cavalry, 196th Brigade. The UH-1H had just flown over some huts into a clearing when they encountered ground fire, and the helicopter exploded.

Jose Astorga, the gunner on the UH-1H, was injured in the chest and knee by the gunfire. Astorga became unconscious and when he came round, the helicopter was on the ground. He found the pilot, 1/Lt Byron Kulland, lying outside the helicopter. WO John Frank, the copilot, was still strapped in his seat and conscious. The crew chief, SP5 Ronald Paschall, was pinned by his leg in the helicopter, but alive. WO Franks urged Astorga to leave them, which he did and was captured. He soon observed the aircraft to be hit by automatic weapons fire and to explode with the rest of the crew inside. He never saw the rest of the crew again. Astorga was released by the Vietnamese in 1973.

The following day, 3 April 1972, 'Nail 38', an OV-10A Bronco, equipped with electronic rescue gear enabling its crew to get a rapid fix on its rescue target, entered Hambleton's area and was shot down. The crew, William J. Henderson and Mark Clark, both parachuted out safely. Henderson was captured and released in 1973. Clark evaded for 12 days and was subsequently rescued. On the same day, a UH-1H 'Slick' went down in the area carrying a crew of four enlisted Army personnel. They had no direct connection to the rescue of Bat 21 but were very probably shot down by the same SAM installations that downed Bat 21. The helicopter (from H/HQ, 37th Signal Battalion, 1st Signal Brigade) had left Marble Mountain airfield, Da Nang on a standard re-supply mission to signal units in and around Quang Tri City. The crew, consisting of pilot WO Douglas O'Neil, copilot CW2 Larry Zich, crew chief SP5 Allen Christensen, and gunner SP4 Edward Williams, remain missing in action.

Three months later, on 29 June 1972, another OV-10A FAC pilot, Capt Steven L. Bennett from Da Nang, was directing US close-air-support fighters near Quang Tri. The strip between Hue

USAF North American OV-10A Bronco light attack aircraft, which was used by the USMC and the USAF on FAC operations. For his actions on just such a mission on 29 June 1972, USAF OV-10A pilot Capt Steven L. Bennett was awarded a posthumous Congressional Medal of Honor when he was killed on his fourth strafing run while attacking the VC with machine-gun fire. (USAF)

and Quang Tri had been nicknamed by the French during the colonial war of the late 1940s – early 1950s as the 'Street Without Joy'. The Americans knew it as 'SAM-7 Alley' because of the number of Soviet missiles there. Bennett's back-seater, USMC Capt Mike Brown, was laying the firepower from ships of the US Navy in the Gulf of Tonkin. At dusk, Bennett got an emergency call from a South Vietnamese platoon that was about to be overrun by a several hundred North Vietnamese. With no fighters in the area, Bennett decided to take a lone hand, making four runs and attacking the VC with 7.62 mm machine-gun fire. On the fifth run, however, a SAM-7 hit the Bronco and caused the aircraft to catch fire, shedding debris as it flew on.

The fire threatened to engulf the OV-10A and Bennett prepared to 'punch out'. However, Brown's parachute had been ripped apart by the explosion. Bennett refused to go alone but the situation eased when the fire abated, and he decided to try and make Da Nang, only 25 precious minutes distant. However, north of Hue, the fire started up again and Bennett had no option but to ditch off the Gulf of Tonkin. The Bronco bucked hard, cartwheeled and landed on its back, nose in the water. Brown scrambled free but Bennett drowned. On 8 August Mrs Linda Bennett accepted the Congressional Medal of Honor presented posthumously to her husband.

Meanwhile, on 6 April, an attempt had been made to pick up Clark and Hambleton which resulted in a Sikorsky HH-53C being shot down. The Super Jolly Green Giant combat rescue helicopter was badly hit. It landed on its side and continued to burn, consuming the entire craft, and presumably all six men on board. Next day, another USAF OV-10A Bronco went down in the area with Larry Potts, an Air Force pilot, and Bruce Walker, a USMC officer, aboard. Walker's last radio transmission to search and rescue was for SAR not to make an attempt to rescue, the enemy was closing in. Walker evaded capture for 11 days while it is reported that Potts was captured and died in Quang Binh prison.

Hambleton and Clark were rescued after 12 incredible days. Hambleton continually changed

positions and reported on enemy activity as he went, even to the extent of calling in close air strikes near his position. He was tracked by a code he devised relating to the length and lie directions of various golf holes he knew well. Another 20 or so Americans were not so fortunate. A week after all search and rescue had been called off for BAT 21, another mission was mounted to recover 'another downed crew-member' from BAT 21 but strangely, no additional information has so far been released as to who this crew member was.

Bombing of the North finally resumed with a vengeance on 10 May 1972, with *Linebacker I* raids aimed at the enemy's road and rail system to prevent supplies reaching the Communists operating in South Vietnam. This was two days after squadrons of Navy A-6 Intruders had sowed minefields in Haiphong, Hon Gai and Cam Pha in the north, and in five ports in the south. At this time, the North Vietnamese had one of the best air defence systems in the world with excellent radar integration of SA-2 SAMs, MiGs and AAA. The North Vietnam defence system could counter US forces from ground level up to 19 miles in the air. MiG fighters were on ready alert and after takeoff, were vectored by ground-control radar. Soviet advisors devised attack strategies, manned a number of the SAM sites, and also trained North Vietnamese crews.

In a seven month period starting on 10 May and ending 15 October 1972, the USAF lost 44 aircraft, including 27 to MiGs and 17 to SAMs and AAA, while the enemy lost 34 MiG-21s and eight MiG-19s in the same period. On the first *Linebacker I* strike day, the entire US strike force encountered heavy concentrations of AAA fire and 16 MiGs were seen. Three of the MiGs were downed, but the USAF lost an F-4E flown by Capt Jeffrey L. Harris and his WSO, Capt Dennis E. Wilkinson.

The period 10 May to 15 October is memorable in that it produced all four American aces (three USAF and one US Navy) of the Vietnam War. The three USAF aces all belonged to the 432nd TRW, flying F-4 Phantoms (by this time, F-105 units were used only in the Wild Weasel anti-SAM role). Two of the aces were WSO (Weapons Systems Officer) crewmen. Capt

Charles B. DeBellevue, a WSO in the 555th Tactical Fighter Squadron, destroyed four MiG-21s and two MiG-19s between 10 May and 9 September 1972, and Capt Jeffrey S. Feinstein, a WSO in the 13th Tactical Fighter Squadron, destroyed five MiG-21s between 16 April and 13 October 1972. Capt Richard S. Ritchie of the 555th Tactical Fighter Squadron was the USAF's only fighter pilot ace of the war in South-East Asia. On 10 May 1972, he crewed an F-4 Phantom with WSO Capt Charles B. DeBellevue, and shot down a MiG-21, two more on 8 July and one on 28 August. His fifth kill, a MiG-21, occurred on 31 May when he was accompanied by WSO Capt Lawrence H. Pettit. *Linebacker II* operations began on 18 December

1972 and lasted until the 29th. The USAF, Navy and Marines carried out an intensive aerial bombardment against industrial and communications targets, ports, supply depots and airfields in the Hanoi and Haiphong areas. USAF F-4Ds and F-4Es flew MiGCAPs (MiG combat air patrols) as well as day and night escort missions for strike aircraft and B-52s. During *Linebacker II* sorties, the F-4Ds of the 555th TFS destroyed five enemy aircraft in the air and B-52 gunners shot down another two.

The *Linebacker I* and *Linebacker II* offensives were the most effective strikes against enemy defences in the war. According to pilots who flew the missions, the North Vietnamese had 'nothing left to shoot at us as we flew over. It

B-52Hs were added to the Stratofortress fleet in time for Linebacker II *operations 18–29 December 1972, when B-52D, Fs and Gs escorted by F-4D/Es delivered almost three-quarters of the bombs dropped during the sustained 11 day and night offensive against industrial and communications targets, ports, supply depots and airfields in the Hanoi and Haiphong areas. On 18 June 1965, the first USAF heavy bombing mission of the Vietnam War was flown by 27 B-52s (Arc Light) of the 7th and 320th Bomb Wings, flying from Andersen AFB, Guam, in an attack on the VC base at Ben Cat. (Boeing)*

was like flying over New York City'. The unrestricted use of air warfare had a great effect on the Communists and by October 1972 the on-off negotiations in Paris finally looked like resulting in a ceasefire agreement. President Nixon therefore ordered the cessation of the bombing of the North to the 29th parallel. However, this resulted in the North going about the task of rebuilding their shattered war economy and the Communists refused to negotiate a peace settlement. On 13 December 1972 Le Duc Tho and his negotiation team arrogantly walked out of the Paris peace talks with Henry Kissinger and Nixon was forced to call for a resumption of the bombing. On the night of 18 December a mighty force of B-52s and F-111s and planes of the US Navy bombed Hanoi and Haiphong and *Linebacker II* bombing strikes went on day and night for eleven days. They finally stopped on 29 December but only after the Communists had been persuaded that their Government should seek an end to the war.

The USAF and US Navy could at least draw some solace in the fact that their final, intensive campaign had finally persuaded the Hanoi Government to seek an end to the war. On 3 January 1973, all US bombing ceased above the 20th parallel but bombing and strafing missions below the line continued. On 8 January 1973, Capt Paul D. Howman and 1/Lt Lawrence K. Kullman of the 4th TFS of the 432nd TRW, flying an F-4D, destroyed a MiG-21. It was the 137th and final USAF victory of the war.

Finally, on 23 January, Kissinger and Le Duc Tho reached an agreement and a ceasefire was announced. During 12 years of war the Vietnam conflict had cost the Americans 58,022 dead and brought its Government worldwide condemnation for its role in South-East Asia. On 12 February the first of 651 American PoWs released by the North were flown home from Hanoi.

Although all US ground forces were withdrawn from South Vietnam, air raids into neighbouring Cambodia and Laos continued until August 1973. Both countries then fell to the Communists and the North turned its attentions to the final take-over of South Vietnam. Inevitably, the South, now without US military support, collapsed under the full might of the Communists' spring offensive. On 12 April 1975 the American Embassy in Saigon was evacuated and 287 staff were flown to US carriers offshore. On 29 April 900 Americans were airlifted by the US Navy to five carriers. Next day Saigon was in Communist hands and the South was now under control of North Vietnam.

The aerial battles fought in South-East Asia bore little similarity to the dog-fighting of Korea. Aircraft had become so sophisticated and operated at such high speeds that it took a team of men to knock down a MiG. More often than not, pilots had the services of a back-seater system operator, while kills would have been impossible without the help of radar aids that separated MiGs from friendly aircraft in South-East Asia. Vietnam was also the last war in which airmen fought a sustained series of engagements, month after month, year after year.

Vietnam began the process of using high-tech weapons capable of great destruction to bring major conflicts to a much speedier end. This was never more true than in the late 1980s and early 1990s when a world, already well acquainted with the images of war on their television screens, viewed live transmissions from the troubled spots of Central America, North Africa and the Middle East showing space-age battlefield weapons of incredible accuracy and destructive might. Once again, America led the way.

Chapter Ten

Raging Storms

War is the remedy that our enemy has chosen.
Therefore let them have as much as they want.
Gen Norman Schwarzkopf quoting Gen Sherman in
an interview after *Desert Storm*

US military personnel and American civilians have not only come under fire while fighting oppressive regimes in time of war. Since the 1970s, personnel stationed in foreign countries have faced terrorist attack, often on or near their bases. In December 1976, a bomb was planted in the officers' club at Rhein-Main AFB, fortunately injuring no one. Rhein-Main was, from 1956, the primary arrival and departure point in Europe for US military personnel. On 8 August 1985, terrorists detonated a car bomb near the wing headquarters building, killing two people, injuring 20 and significantly damaging several buildings.

Following the abortive Iranian Rescue Mission in April 1980 and the subsequent acts of terrorism and hostage taking, 23rd AF was activated at Scott AFB, Illinois on 1 March 1983, consisting of forces trained in air rescue and special operations. In October 1983, 23rd AF took part in operations in Grenada. Four years later, US Special Operations Command was set up, with the special forces of each branch of the armed services coming under a central operational control. The 23rd AF became its USAF component and in August 1987, moved to Hurlburt Field situated in the vast Eglin AFB complex in north-west Florida. Special Operations personnel have trained there since 1942 when they prepared for the Doolittle raid on Tokyo.

From 20 December 1989 to 1 January 1990, the US launched Operation *Just Cause*, the US invasion of Panama. Military Airlift Command (MAC) flew 408 missions using C-130, C-141 and C-5 aircraft to land or airdrop 19,500 troops and 11,700 tons of cargo. Troops from the 82nd Airborne were parachuted onto drop zones at the Madden Dam and the Tocumen/Torrijos International Airport. Twenty-one AC-130 gunships, MC-130E Combat Talons and MH-53E/J Pave Low helicopters of AF Special Operations Command (AFSOC), flew over 400 missions during *Just Cause*. AC-130 gunships were among the first in action early on the morning of 20 December, destroying the Panamanian Defence Force's Comandancia HQ with devastating fusillades of cannon and machine gun-fire. The MC-130E Combat Talons and MH-53E Pave Low helicopters were used to infiltrate US Army Rangers and Navy SEALS into Panamanian positions. It was 23rd AF's final operation before its deactivation. On 22 May 1990, AF Special Operations Command was established at Hurlburt Field with a directive to organize, train, equip and educate Air Force special operations forces.

Meanwhile, in August 1981, Colonel Gadaffi, President of Libya, had established his so-called 'line of death' in the Gulf of Sidra from a point just south of Tripoli across to Benghazi, and warned that any American aircraft or surface vessel crossing it would be destroyed. Undeterred, USS *Nimitz* had moved south on 3 August to join up with the *Forrestal* for training exercises which would culminate in a live missile firing in the Gulf of Sidra area. On 18 August, two Libyan Sukhoi Su-22 Fitter-Js attempted to shoot down two F-14As of VF-41 from the *Nimitz* but were promptly dispatched by the Tomcats.

On 27 December 1985, terrorists attacked the El Al check-in counters at airports in Rome and Vienna, killing 14 people including an 11-year-old American girl and injuring 50 others. The attack was thought to be Libyan backed. America's patience was exhausted. In February 1986, Operation *Prairie Fire* was launched to provoke Libya into a direct military confrontation. Three carrier battle groups crossed the 'line of death' and on 24 March, two SA-5 Gammon missiles were fired at the 6th Fleet but both missed their targets. Later that day, two Tomcats chased off a pair of MiG-25 Foxbat-A interceptors, and tension increased as more missiles were fired at the carrier groups. The US Navy retaliated and two Grumman A-6E Intruders sank a Libyan fast attack craft with AGM-84A Harpoon anti-ship missiles and Rockeye cluster bombs. Vought A-7E Corsairs badly damaged a shore installation with AGM-88A High Speed Anti-Radiation (HARM) missiles and further attacks on Libyan targets were carried out by more A-6Es and A-7Es. A total of four Libyan vessels were destroyed or damaged and one or two SAM sites knocked out.

Regrettably, terrorist action continued on 5 April when a bomb exploded in the LaBelle disco in West Berlin, which was frequented by hundreds of off-duty US personnel. A US Army sergeant and a Turkish woman were killed and 230 people were injured, including 79 US servicemen. The Libyan regime clearly backed the attack. More bomb plots were uncovered by intelligence sources, aimed at US military targets around the world with 10 planned for Berlin alone. Certainly, swift action was needed to deter the terrorists and their Libyan paymasters. President Ronald Reagan kept a five-year-old promise to the American people to meet terrorism with 'swift and effective retribution' and the decision was taken to bomb terrorist-related targets at Tripoli and Benghazi, using air force squadrons on mainland Europe and carrier-borne aircraft of the US Navy in the

Mediterranean. NATO countries would not allow US aircraft stationed in its countries to use European bases or overfly their airspace for attacks on Libya. Britain's Prime Minister, Margaret Thatcher, had no such qualms and no restrictions were placed on strike aircraft based in eastern England. This allowed the US planners the option of using F-111F tactical strike bombers based in East Anglia for a retaliatory strike against Tripoli, the Libyan capital, while US Navy A-6E Intruder carrierborne attack planes bombed Benghazi.

At the time, over 150 F-111E/Fs were based in Britain for NATO duty. The F-111E equipped the 20th TFW at Upper Heyford in Oxfordshire while the 48th TFW, 'The Liberty Wing' based at RAF Lakenheath in Suffolk, was equipped with four squadrons of F-111Fs. The F-111F was equipped with the Ford Aerospace AVQ-26 Pave Tack infrared target acquisition and laser-designating pod mounted under the fuselage centre-line. Armed with laser-guided bombs, the FB-111F could be particularly effective for bombing by night. The WSO operates an IR scope in the cockpit to lock the designator pod onto the target and a thin laser beam keeps the target 'spotted' for laser-guided Paveway bombs to follow the beam transmission directly onto the target no matter what manoeuvres the pilot puts the bomber through. Despite this incredibly accurate method of bombing, crews were briefed not to launch their bombs unless they also gained a positive radar identification. Civilian casualties had to be avoided where possible.

At around 18:15 hrs on 14 April 1986, Lakenheath dispatched 24 F-111Fs while nearby, RAF Mildenhall had earlier sent off six KC-135 Stratotankers followed by a KC-135A and two KC-10As and finally 10 KC-10A Extender refuellers. A further seven KC-10As and two KC-135As left RAF Fairford for Libya. Operation *El Dorado Canyon* as it was code-named, marked the first operational use of the Grumman/General Dynamics EF-111A Raven ECM aircraft. Five Ravens of the 42nd Electronic Combat Squadron of the 20th TFW took off from their home base at Upper Heyford and flew to Fairford to escort the F-111Fs. Off the north-west coast of Spain, the KC-10s took

A KC-135 Stratotanker and four F-111Fs of the 48th TFW re-enact the 14/15 April 1986 El Dorado Canyon *operation during the Mildenhall Air Fete of May 1986. (Author)*

on fuel from other KC-10s. Shortly afterwards, between 20:30 and 21:30 hrs, six F-111Fs acting as spares, returned to Lakenheath, and one of the EF-111As also returned to base, leaving the second spare Raven to continue to the target area as an airborne reserve. The F-111Fs each carried free-fall and laser-guided bombs which meant there was no room for external fuel tanks. Three

KC-10A Extender 83-0079 of the 2nd BW at Mildenhall which was one of 19 Extenders used on the 14/15 April 1986 El Dorado Canyon *operation to refuel the F-111Fs of the 48th TFW en route to Libya. (Author)*

Five Grumman/General Dynamics EF-111A Raven ECM aircraft of the 42nd Electronic Combat Squadron of the 20th TFW were first used operationally during the El Dorado Canyon *operation of 14/15 April 1986. Ravens were also used in* Desert Storm. *(Grumman)*

'silent' in-flight refuelling operations were therefore carried out off Portugal, south of Spain (after passing through the Straits of Gibraltar), and near Sicily.

Three F-111Fs of the 48th TFW over the Mediterranean in 1991. The 'Liberty Wing' carried out daring precision-bombing attacks at night against Libyan targets in 1986 and against Iraqi bunkers, vehicles and buildings in Desert Storm. *(USAFE)*

Meanwhile, the USS *America* and USS *Coral Sea* were at their positions off Libya ready to strike at military targets in Benghazi. Near Tripoli, the three EF-111A Ravens began their ECM jamming of Libyan radars at 23.54, while the Navy's A-7E Corsair IIs and F/A-18A Hornets blasted the SAM and radar installations around Benghazi with anti-radiation missiles. USAF and US Navy bombing runs started simultaneously at 00.01. The 18 F-111Fs of the 48th TFW roared in 200 ft below the Libyan radar sites on the coast and headed for the brightly lit streets of the capital. Nearing the city, the force split into three cells of six aircraft. Two cells headed for the Terrorist Training camp at Sidi Bilal naval base and the barracks at Bab al Aziziya where Gadaffi resided. The third cell flew on to the south before swinging round to bomb the military airport.

Pilots had been briefed to bomb only if they had positive radar and IR scope target acquisition. Four F-111Fs in the naval base and

Two days after the El Dorado Canyon *operation of 14/15 April 1986, post-strike reconnaissance was carried out by two Lockheed SR-71As from 'Detachment 4' at RAF Mildenhall and confirmed that all five targets had been well hit. (Lockheed)*

barracks attack, and one in the attack on Tripoli, did not bomb after experiencing problems with their equipment or failing to obtain the necessary electronic validation of their targets. The eight remaining bombers in the raid on the naval base and barracks made low-level single-pass attacks and each toss-bombed four 2,000 lb laser-guided bombs onto the targets before climbing away to a height of 250 ft at 518 mph for their rendezvous point over the Mediterranean. One F-111F, flown by Capt Fernando L. Ribas-Dominicci and WSO Capt Paul F. Lorence, which had been involved in the attack on the barracks, crashed and exploded as they re-crossed the coast. A long sea search was mounted but no trace of the crew was found.

The third group of six F-111Fs attacked the military airport with 500 lb Mk 82 low-drag retarded bombs, although one bomber was forced to carry its bombs home after a systems malfunction. US Navy A-6E Intruders destroyed at least four MiG-23s, a Fokker F-27 and two Mil Mi-8 helicopters at Benina airfield. Crews began landing back on their carriers while the F-111Fs headed for their tankers and the long flight back to Britain. One F-111F was forced to land at Rota in Spain suffering problems from engine overheating. Despite the limitations of crossing international boundaries and the loss of one fighter-bomber, *El Dorado Canyon* had been a great success. Two days after the attacks, post-strike reconnaissance by two Lockheed SR-71As from Mildenhall confirmed that all five targets had been well hit.

When the F-111F crews of the 48th TFW began touching down at Lakenheath at 06:30 on 15 April, few could have imagined how important their experience had been and that they would be heading back over the Mediterranean only four years later to participate in another series of pin-point bombing missions at night. As befits a crack specialist unit, the 48th TFW commanded by Col Tom Lennon, was the first wing in the USAFE to be deployed to the Middle East as part of *Desert Shield*. The wing deployed 18 F-111Fs of the 493rd TFS on 25 August 1990. By the time the war started, the 48th TFW had deployed 66 of its 70 F-111Fs to Taif airbase near Mecca in Saudi Arabia.

In August 1990, conflict in the Persian Gulf began after talks between the representatives from Iraq and Kuwait did not resolve grievances over oil pricing. On 2 August, President Saddam Hussein of Iraq massed seven divisions, totalling 120,000 troops and 2,000 tanks, along the Iraq–Kuwait border and invaded Kuwait in the early hours of the morning. On 8 August, Saddam Hussein announced that Kuwait was the 19th province of Iraq. President George Bush immediately put Iraq under a US economic embargo. The United Nations Security Council quickly followed suit. On 7 August, after Saddam Hussein refused to remove his troops from Kuwait, President Bush had ordered the start of *Desert Shield*, the US contingency commitment, ordering warplanes and ground forces to Saudi Arabia, stating that the country faced the 'imminent threat' of an Iraqi attack. More than 55,000 Air Force personnel would be ultimately dispatched to the Gulf, including more than 180 aircraft and 5,400 personnel assigned to USAFE units.

The US Central Command HQ, which would direct the coalition of allied forces against Iraq under the command of Army General H. Norman Schwarzkopf, immediately set pre-planned preparations in motion. CENTCOM's function was to co-ordinate US force deployment to the Gulf region to help defend Saudi Arabia and provide security to other Arab states. Lt Gen Charles A. Horner, USAF, the allied coalition's supreme air commander, began co-ordinating all air actions related to the build-up, and within days, established Central Command Air Forces (Forward) HQ in Saudi Arabia. From his HQ, the air actions that would bring an end to the war were put into operation.

Five fighter squadrons, a contingent of AWACS, and part of the 82nd Airborne Division moved into theatre within five days. In total, 25 fighter squadrons flew non-stop to the Gulf. Some 256 KC-135s and 46 KC-10 refuellers were deployed to the Gulf and 4,967 tanker sorties were flown during *Desert Shield*. Within 35 days, the USAF deployed a fighter force that numerically equalled Iraq's fighter capability.

More than 145 C-130 Hercules were deployed in support of *Desert Shield* and *Desert Storm*.

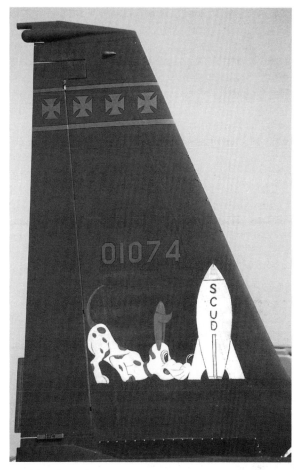

Lockheed TR-1A (renamed U-2R in December 1991) 80-1074 of SAC's 17th RW at Alconbury. On 23 August 1990, two TR-1As of the 17th RW were among the first Europe-based US aircraft to be sent to the Gulf when they deployed to Taif, Saudi Arabia. (Author)

These aircraft moved units to forward bases once they arrived in theatre. From 10 August 1990 to the cease-fire, C-130s flew 46,500 sorties and moved more than 209,000 personnel and 300,000 tons of supplies within the theatre. C-5 Galaxy and C-141 Starlifters moved 72 per cent of air cargo and a third of the personnel, while 95 commercial passenger and 63 cargo aircraft airlifted the rest.

In late August 1990, President Bush signed an order authorizing members of the armed forces reserves to be called up for active duty. Throughout the campaign, Air Force Reserve and Air National Guard members flew and maintained aircraft for strategic and tactical airlift, fighter and reconnaissance operations, as well as tanker support. Efforts by the UN Security Council to find a peaceful resolution with Iraq proved futile. On the morning of 15 January 1991, an eleventh-hour appeal by the Council for Iraq to withdraw from Kuwait drew only silence and at 12 noon the deadline for peace passed. Next day, at approximately 7 p.m. Eastern Standard Time, Operation *Desert Storm* began as Allied forces answered Iraq's silence with attacks by strike aircraft based in Saudi Arabia and Turkey. On 26 December, Joint Task Force *Proven Force* had been formed at Incirlik in Turkey and by 16 January, four F-111Es of the 79th TFS, 20th TFW were redeployed there with 14 F-15Cs of the 525th TFS, 36th TFW and six EF-111As of the 42nd Electronic Combat Squadron, 66th ECW, plus three EC-130s of the 43rd ECS, 66th ECW and five F-15Cs of the 32nd TFG as well as 11 F-16Cs and 13 F-4G Wild Weasels from the 23rd TFS, 52nd TFW, all from bases in England, Holland and Germany. *Proven Force* had to wait for Turkish parliamentary approval and as a result joined the war one day after it started.

The air campaign commenced when three USAF MH-53J Pave Low special operations helicopters leading nine Army AH-64 Apache attack helicopters, destroyed two early warning radar sites in Iraq with 30 mm cannon and AGM-114 Hellfire missiles. Meanwhile, TLAMs (Tomahawk Land Attack Missiles) launched from US ships in the Gulf and the Red Sea, struck targets in Baghdad. F-117A stealth fighter-bombers of the 37th TFW, which because of their construction are almost invisible to radar, flew deep into Iraq, hitting 34 targets, including hardened command and control bunkers, communications sites, and chemical, biological and nuclear production and storage facilities.

The 4th TFW F-15E Eagles, equipped for the night precision-bombing role (which were used against Scud missile sites) and B-52s also joined the attack. Before the night ended virtually every aircraft in the USAF inventory had participated in the massive air strike. Of 668 aircraft in the assault, 530 were USAF, 90 were USMC and Navy, 24 were RAF, 12 were French, and 12 were Saudi Arabian. F-16Cs of the 401st TFW based at Doha attacked Ali Salem airfield in Kuwait and Tallil airfield in Iraq, while F-16Cs of the 50th TFW attacked Al Taqaddum airfield near Baghdad. Some 55 F-111Fs of the 48th TFW attacked Iraqi airfields and chemical stor-

F-117A stealth fighter of the 37th TFW. During the Gulf War more than 40 F-117As flew 1,200 missions from Khamis Mushait AB in Saudi Arabia. (Lockheed Photo by Eric Schulzinger)

F-16C of the 52nd TFW from Spangdahlem AB, Germany. During Desert Storm, *11 F-16s from the 23rd TFS, 52nd TFW (and 13 F-4Gs) operated from Incirlik AB in Turkey. F-16Cs were the most numerous aircraft used in the war—249 F-16Cs flew more than 13,450 sorties, mainly fighter-bomber missions. (Author)*

age bunkers in a dozen attack cells each of four to six aircraft. Each cell was supported by 10 US Navy A-7E Corsair SAM suppression aircraft equipped with AGM-88A HARM missiles and three EA-6B Prowlers for ECM jamming while four F-14C Tomcats flew top cover. For these first strikes, the F-111Fs carried 2,500 lb Rockwell GBU-15 electro-optical glide bombs fitted with imaging infrared guidance specially developed for night bombing, 2,000 lb GBU-24A/B laser-guided bombs (LGBs), and CBU-89 mines for cratering runways. Royal Saudi Air Force Tornadoes also attacked the runways with JP233 cratering bombs.

Col Dennis R. Ertler of the 48th TFW earned the Silver Star, the third-highest American combat award, for his actions this first night of the war. After Iraqi defensive fire forced half the attack force to turn back he continued with the remaining aircraft on an attack against a HAS (hardened aircraft shelter) near Ali Al Salem airfield, Kuwait. He also out-manoeuvred a SAM on the way to the target. During delivery of a GBU-24A/B, and in the centre of intense defensive fire, Col Ertler again avoided a SAM while his WSO, Capt Keith Zuegel, marked the target with his laser and scored a direct hit, destroying the HAS. As their aircraft departed

the target area north of Kuwait City, Col Ertler released chaff and used other escape tactics to avoid a third SAM. Ertler recounts:

We were getting AAA, radar warnings and SAM activity so I set the jet on automatic terrain following

A 2,500 lb Rockwell GBU-15 glide bomb fitted with imaging infrared guidance for night attacks ready for delivery to its target on 25 February 1991. (USAFE)

radar when I saw the first launch of a SAM on the left side of the aircraft. The TFR seemed to be flying us directly into the path of climbing AAA. I was forced to fly the jet manually at low-level because of that . . .

During the weapons release, Ertler received a second warning of a SAM closing in on his aircraft.

I saw it coming at us at the same time we were trying to put our weapons through the door of the shelter, but that second SAM forced me to pull off at the last second. I released some chaff and the SAM blew up

A Grumman Aerospace & Electronics Group Joint STARS MTI scope image of the 'Mother of All Retreats'. During the Gulf War, E-8 Joint STARS (USAF USAFE/Army Joint Surveillance & Target Attack Radar System) undertook ground surveillance, targeting, and battle management missions. One E-8A (707-320 airframe modified by Boeing) was airborne every night of the Gulf War and its success prompted expansion into other roles including bomb-damage assessment, suppression of enemy air defences, and theatre missile defence, with emphasis on the detection of mobile missile launchers. (Grumman Aerospace & Electronics Group)

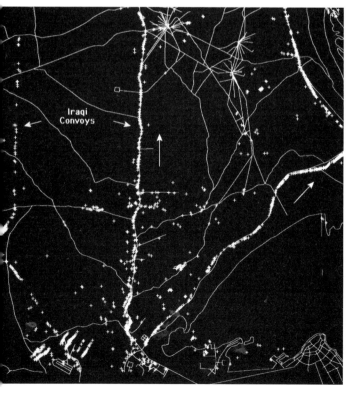

right behind us. Our bombs were still on target and they hit dead centre.

The Iraqis threw everything they had into the night sky. Ertler continues:

They still had all their defence capabilities and used them. We read about avoiding SAMs in our training manual but when you see a missile with your name on it coming your way, you don't really have time to think about it. You just do what you're trained to do.

The raids were a great success and despite their worst fears there were no losses and only two F-111Fs received minor battle damage. Thereafter, senior officers felt confident in replacing the 'small' strike units with larger formations of up to 24 F-111Fs against one airfield at a time.

Shortly after midnight on 17/18 January *Proven Force* carried out its first combat operations in support of *Desert Storm*, with attacks on four radar sites in northern Iraq by 20th TFW F-111s carrying 500 lb bombs. Air cover was furnished by F-15Cs of the 525th TFS, while F-4G Wild Weasels of the 52nd TFW carried HARM anti-radiation missiles, and EF-111 Ravens of the 42nd ECS provided ECM support. Complementing the Ravens were EC-130 Compass Call aircraft which monitored radar emissions from the radar sites about to be attacked. Of the eight radars in the Iraqi radar complex, seven were destroyed in the attack. The USAF lost its first aircraft when an F-15E Strike Eagle was lost, flown by Maj Donnie R. Holland and Maj Thomas F. Koritz.

Early in the Gulf War, the Eagles were assigned mainly Scud missile targets while the stealth fighter-bombers were tasked to hit selected targets in highly defended areas. During Operations *Desert Shield* and *Desert Storm*, 120 F-15Cs and Ds deployed to the Gulf and flew more than 5,900 sorties. Every Iraqi fixed-wing aircraft destroyed in air-to-air combat, including five Soviet-made MiG-29 Fulcrums, were shot down by F-15Cs. Some 48 F-15Es were deployed to the Gulf and flew more than 2,200 sorties. They were used to hunt Scud missiles and launchers at night, employed laser systems to hit hard targets, and attacked armoured vehi-

During early missions in the Gulf War a few F-111F crews encountered Iraqi MiG-29 Fulcrums and escape was made by fully sweeping the F-111's wing and accelerating to 1,110 kph then descending to 200 ft using terrain-following radar. At least one pilot in the 48th TFW used the 'flamer' technique (dumping fuel and igniting it) to avoid Iraqi Triple A fire after his chaff dispenser failed. The resulting 30 ft stream of fire convinced his attackers that he had been hit and the guns fell silent. (Author)

cles, tanks and artillery. Primary targets included command and control centres, armour, electrical facilities, and Scuds as well as carrying out road interdiction. The F-15Es used the LANTIRN navigation and targeting pods with spectacular results. The first air-to-air kills by F-15Cs took place on 17 January when three MiG-29s and three Mirage F.1EQs were downed using AIM-7s. Two nights later, six Iraqi MiGs and Mirages were brought down in air-to-air combat with the Eagles.

That day, Capt Michael V. McKelvey and his WSO, Capt Mark A. Chance, became the next members in the 48th TFW to receive the Silver Star for their actions during the attack on the heavily defended Al Habbaniyah airfield, 35 miles west of Baghdad. They were in a 14 aircraft package which included F-111Fs, EF-111As, F-4G Wild Weasels and F-15C Eagles. During the pre-strike air refuelling, the lead and deputy lead F-111Fs aborted with

Iraqi Scud Seeker, one of the six RF-4C Phantoms of the 106th TRS 117th Reconnaissance Wing, ANG from Birmingham, Alabama which were used during Desert Storm by active-duty 192nd TRS 152nd Recce Group ANG from Reno, Nevada. In daylight these unique RF-4Cs used their KS-127 LOROP (Long-Range Oblique Photography) cameras to spy on Iraqi forces from up to 50 miles away, looking for Scuds. (Author)

avionics malfunctions. Capt McKelvey assumed command of the attack group. The Chance–McKelvey team encountered radar warnings of an air-to-air missile launch to their right. McKelvey dispensed chaff and initiated a 5 g turn causing the missile to overshoot and explode in the clouds overhead. Chance guided his bombs onto the target and they severely cratered the runway, effectively stopping take-offs and landings at the MiG-29 airfield. On the way out, heavy defences and a confirmed air-to-

On 28 January 1991, Capt Brad Seipel of the 493rd TFS, 48th TFW flew 70-2390, Miss Liberty II, *from which two GBU-15 bombs were accurately guided onto the Al Almadi pumping station in occupied Kuwait on 28 January 1991 thus halting the flow of oil into the Gulf. The artwork is inspired by WW2 8th AF bombers. At least four B-17s and two B-24s in East Anglia had this name. (USAFE/Steve Jefferson)*

air threat forced them down to 200 ft using terrain following radar.

In an attack on the Kirkuk research facility, pilots reported a 'brilliant flash' about a minute after F-111s of the 20th TFW had attacked, 'with a fireball reaching to at least 15,000 ft'. Four aircraft were lost. The crew of an F-4G Wild Weasel were recovered but the crews of two F-16Cs and a F-15E were made PoW by the Iraqis. By the third day of *Desert Storm*, more than 7,000 coalition sorties had been flown, and 10 aircraft lost. Iraqi aircraft loses totalled 15. The Iraqis had lost eight aircraft in air-to-air combat on the first day of *Desert Storm* and 35 more would follow before the end of the war.

On 23 January, attacks were made by F-117A stealth fighters and F-16s on the Tuwaitha Nuclear Research Facility on the outskirts of Baghdad. The facility was the focal point of Iraq's nuclear research programme and was described by the US Defence Intelligence Agency as 'the most heavily defended facility in the Middle East'. Originally it had been bombed by the Israeli Air Force in 1981. In all, 19 SAM systems and more than 200 anti-aircraft guns could be brought to bear on attacking aircraft. No significant damage was caused to the plant and on 24 January an F-16 and its pilot were lost over the target area, shot down by Iraqi defences. The pilot was later recovered.

Also on 23 January, Lt Gen Charles 'Chuck' Horner, commander of all Central Command's air forces, ordered attacks on hardened aircraft shelters (HAS) by F-117s and F-111s. At the start of the war, Iraq had an estimated 594 HASs. Pilots of the 48th TFW reported 'sending hardened penetrating laser guided-bombs into shelter after shelter'. Bombing accuracy remained good enough to justify the change of tactics, although manoeuvrability suffered, especially for the F-111. One pilot likened flying the F-111 at 25,000 ft to trying to get 'a drunken elephant on ice skates to dance'. But aircrews adjusted and found that higher altitudes in the F-111 'gave an ever better look at targets on the Pave Tack system and allowed for even higher success rates'. Three days later, approximately 137 Iraqi aircraft flew to Iran, apparently seeking to escape the shelter attacks.

Above *Ford Aerospace AVQ-26 Pave Tack infrared target acquisition and laser-designating pod beneath the centre fuselage of a 48th TFW F-111F. (Author)*

Below *An F-111F of the 48th TFW takes off from Taif in Saudi Arabia on a bombing mission against Iraqi positions. (USAFE)*

Bottom *Maintainers load an F-111F of the 48th TFW at Taif during Operation* Desert Storm. *(USAFE)*

On 28 January, Capt Brad Seipel of the 493rd TFS, 48th TFW, flying *Miss Liberty II*, was responsible for one of the most famous bombing missions of the war when two GBU-15 electro-optical-guided bombs were toss-launched into the Al Almadi pumping stations in occupied Kuwait which were dumping millions of gallons of crude oil into the Persian Gulf, cutting the spill off at its source. The next night, 29/30 January, the 48th TFW opened its campaign against bridges using GBU-24 laser-guided bombs and GBU-15s. When the campaign finished the 48th TFW had scored 160 hits, destroyed 12 bridges and damaging 52 more. The 48th TFW proved equally adept at destroying Iraqi tanks and armoured vehicles at night; a role carried out in daylight hours by A-10s and F-16s. The Pave Tack pods of the F-111Fs easily picked up the heat signatures left in the soil during the day by the tracks of the enemy tanks and armour, now dug in for the night. Called 'tank plinking', the forward looking infrared equipment paved the way for 500 lb laser-guided bombs and more accurate assessment of numbers of Iraqi tanks destroyed. The 48th TFW

A US soldier scribbles an appropriate message on the casing of a laser-guided bomb beneath the wing of a 48th TFW F-111F at Taif, Saudi Arabia. (USAFE)

scored 920 hits on tanks and armour and a further 252 strikes on artillery pieces, using GBU-12s in single-bomb attacks, all at night. The greatest success occurred on the night of 13/14 February when 46 F-111Fs, each carrying four GBU-12s, scored hits on 132 tanks and armoured vehicles from 184 bombs dropped. One EF-111 Raven was lost.

Planners had divided Kuwait into 'kill boxes' in which aircraft like the F-111s, F-16Cs and A-10As concentrated their fire. F-16C pilots in the 401st TFW reported:

Flying in the area of the Republican Guard was a fighter pilot's dream come true. There were revetments full of tanks, APCs, ammunition, AAA, and artillery as far as the eye could see. To destroy the Republican Guard, the BAI (battlefield air interdiction) campaign would have to be tank by tank, one at a time, and the F-16 was just the aircraft to do that.

An A-10A pilot in the 10th TFW reported:

I was No. 4 in an eight ship package of Hogs going to visit the vaunted Republican Guard . . . Well, it turns out the Republican Guard wasn't so tough. There was the odd SAM, a sprinkling of AAA, but nothing this stalwart group of fighter pilots couldn't handle. So, we battered the armour we found, left a bunch of smoking holes and turned for home to make 'slot time' for take-off for our second mission.

By mid-February, Central Command was estimating that 35 per cent of Iraq's tanks, 31 per cent of its armoured vehicles, and 40 per cent of its artillery had been destroyed.

The US Air Force's 249 F-16Cs flew more than 13,450 sorties—more than any other aircraft in the war. The Air Force sent 144 A-10A Warthogs to the theatre. While flying only 30 per cent of the USAF's total sorties, these aircraft achieved more than half of the confirmed Iraqi equipment losses and fired 90 per cent of the precision-guided AGM-65 Maverick missiles launched during *Desert Storm*. They demonstrated versatility as daytime Scud hunters in Iraq and even recorded two helicopter kills with their 30mm cannon. Although A-10As flew more than 8,000 sorties in *Desert Storm*, only five were lost in combat. The first occurred on 2 February when Capt Richard D. Storr was made a PoW.

On 4 February, 18 48th TFW F-111Fs led by Lt Col James F. Slaton and supported by four F-15Cs, four F-4Gs and two EF-111Fs, attacked the Tuwaitha Nuclear Research Facility. As Slaton and his WSO, Capt John F. Daughtry, approached the target, their F-111F was engulfed by triple A fire. There were so many missile launches by the Iraqis that the F-4Gs had to fire all their HARMs within the first few moments of the attack. The fire was so intense that only three aircraft reached their targets. Lt Col Slaton led the remaining aircraft below the cloud cover into the heart of the AAA where they destroyed three of the critical nuclear component buildings. Despite having a weapons system problem which forced Capt Daughtry to an extremely difficult manual back-up delivery mode, the Slaton–Daughtry team hit and destroyed their target. Lt Col Slaton recalls: 'The clouds were too thick for our equipment, so we had to fly lower to get a good look at our targets. The only problem was, this put us within the heart of their defences.' To add to the excitement, their Pave Tack pod malfunctioned. Capt Daughtry recalls: 'Luckily, after going through three or four back-up modes, it came back up just in time for the weapons release.'

Lt Col Slaton recalled: 'Bear (Capt Daughtry's call-sign) guided the bombs directly on target and we got out of there. By that time the whole sky was lit up; at least that's how it looked to me.' Capt Daughtry confirmed that 'it was a pretty awesome light show'. Capt Slaton added: 'The Tuwaitha Nuclear Research Facility's primary purpose wasn't supplying electricity to Baghdad. It was for building

Twenty seconds to target! A WSO's view on the scope during a Gulf War infrared laser-guided bomb launch from an F-111F of the 48th TFW on a night attack of Iraqi targets. (USAFE)

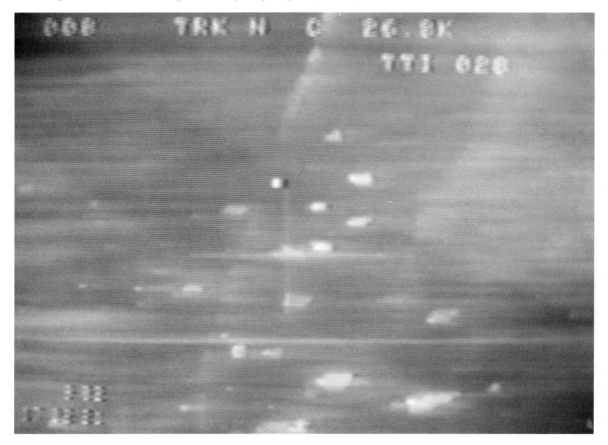

nuclear weapons. We put a stop to that.' The weapon used in the attack was the GBU-24A/B 2,000 lb laser-guided bomb. Slaton describes the weapon: 'It has steep impact angles and a long cruise range, so we could release the bomb several miles from the target. During peace we train to get into precise parameters but during the war you're getting shot at and dodging SAMs and AAA. These hi-tech weapons make the difference.' Slaton and Daughtry were awarded the Silver Star for their actions on the night of 4 February.

Eight AC-130 gunships and Combat Talon Is deployed to Saudi Arabia for *Desert Storm* (one AC-130H was lost on 31 January 1991 with all 14 crew), while Combat Talon Is delivered the 15,000 lb BLU-82/B Big Blue bomb containing a fuel-air explosive, the largest and heaviest conventional bomb in the USAF inventory. On 15 February, Combat Talons began dropping BLU-82s on Iraqi minefields as a prelude to the ground offensive. Leaflet bombs were also dropped with messages telling Iraqi soldiers how to surrender to the ground forces. Other 'psyops' missions dropped leaflets telling Iraqis that more BLU-82s were on the way.

On 24 February, almost 270,000 troops of the Coalition ground forces made an all-out ground assault on the Iraqi border preceded by 900 aircraft sorties. The 101st Air Assault Division carried out the largest helicopter assault in history when some 300 helicopters transported a brigade 50 miles into Iraq. Coalition air forces flew a record 3,159 sorties, of which 1,997 were direct combat support missions. Coalition air strikes turned the road leading out of Kuwait City into a 'Highway of Death' for hundreds of Iraqi vehicles and armour and their occupants.

Although losses were light (the US losses totalled four killed and 21 wounded in the first two days of the operation), on 27 February, a 10th TFW pilot had to witness the death of a comrade on the last day of the war. An OA-10 FAC piloted by 1/Lt Patrick B. Olson was returning to base with battle damage.

The approach looked good when all of a sudden, the aircraft hits the threshold very hard, all the gear collapse and shear out from under him. The aircraft

bounces about 40 to 50 ft into the air. It then rolls into the wind, to the right, The flight lead starts yelling into the radio, and someone on the ground yells for him to punch out. It's too late though, he is probably unconscious from the hard landing. The aircraft rolls into 135° of bank and hits nose first. he didn't have a chance—the aircraft instantly goes up into a ball of flame . . . The next day the war is over, and we have won a big victory. Some have paid a higher price than others.

Also on 27 February, Capt William Andrews of the 1°TFS/363rd TFW(P) was lost over Iraq. Andrews ejected from his F-16C Fighting Falcon and landed in the middle of a Republican Guard infantry unit. Despite a broken leg and imminent capture, he radioed to warn his wingman of a SAM launch.

When they were 10 metres away, I saw an IR [infrared] SAM fired at my wingman. I grabbed my radio off the ground and called for a 'break right with flares.' It was a beautiful sight when the missile bit off the flares and went wide. The soldiers opened fire on me and blew my radio apart as I dropped it like a hot potato.

Andrews would later return safely and receive the AFC for his actions.

The most incredible weapon dropped during the Gulf War was probably the 4,700 lb GBU 28/B 'Deep Throat' 'bunker buster' bomb invented by a Lockheed engineer who hit on the idea of encasing 650 lb of molten Tritonal explosive in lengths of used 8-inch barrels from self-propelled howitzers, and fitted with slightly reprogrammed GBU-27 laser guidance systems. The bombs were delivered to the 48th TFW only 17 days after *Desert Storm* officials requested a more powerful weapon than the 2,000 lb BLU-109 bomb which was being used against Iraqi hardened aircraft shelters. The USAF needed a weapon that would penetrate deeper for use against Iraq's underground command and control facilities built about 100 ft below the surface. During a test at the Tonapah Test Range in Nevada, a GBU-28 penetrated over 100 ft of earth and in a sled test at Holloman AFB, New Mexico one penetrated almost 25 ft of reinforced concrete. The F-111F was chosen as the delivery system after it beat the F-15E in a fly-off compe-

A GBU-28 4,700 lb 'Deep Throat' 'bunker buster' LGB is carried to a waiting F-111F of the 48th TFW at Taif, Saudi Arabia. The weapon was used for the first time on 27 February 1991 to destroy the Iraqi underground command centre at Al Taji, north of Baghdad. (USAFE)

tition. On 27 February, the two GBU-28 bombs were delivered to the 48th TFW base at Taif by a C-141 Starlifter. Within 5 hours of arrival, just before dusk, two F-111Fs took off to destroy the underground command centre at Al Taji airbase, north of Baghdad. Lt Col Ken Combs, the flight leader, recalls:

We were notified about the mission two days before we were supposed to fly. Naturally, we were excited about flying this mission because it was the first time this bomb was to be dropped other than during testing. It was an unknown munition. We didn't have any delivery parameters and didn't know any of it's characteristics. We had to wait to get all the preliminary data from the contractors to even begin planning what we were going to do. The profile we flew was pretty much what we'd been flying all along. We took off just before dusk and flew at high altitude to a tanker for pre-strike refuelling. Then we headed up north, staying at high altitude. The delivery altitude and air speed for this mission were different than what we had used in other missions, so once we got into Iraq, we did a step-climb to get to release altitude.

Maj Jerry Hust, Combs' WSO recalls: 'What we were aiming for was basically a piece of dirt. I thought I had the reticule on the target so we

released the bombs. As we got closer to the target I realised we were off to the left.'

The second F-111F was piloted by Lt Col Dave White, the 492nd TFS operations officer, with Capt Tom Himes as his WSO. White recalls: 'We were concerned about making the target on time because we were delayed on the ground. It was the maintainers who loaded the bombs that made it possible to take off as soon as we did. They only had 45 minutes notice and did an outstanding job getting the bombs loaded so we could meet our target time.' White and Himes were about 45 minutes late taking off, but caught up to the lead aircraft at the refuelling tanker. White continues: 'Col Combs turned the tanker towards us so that we could get on the boom as soon as possible. Actually, we left the tanker at the no-later-than time. So, by turning the tanker when he did, he saved us a lot of time because we just flew behind it and got our fuel.'

The original plans called for White and Himes to hit a second target. However, they were instructed to take the lead and drop on the primary target again. White explains:

Capt Himes was set on hitting another target and when we were instructed to go for the target again, he had to focus back to the other one and make some adjustments. Basically, all I was trying to do was keep the air speed steady and keep the aircraft on course. I think that what made the mission so successful is that Tommy Himes wanted to hit the target. He made it happen.

Below *Iraqi hardened aircraft shelters (HAS) were among the most impenetrable in the world but they stood no chance against direct hits by laser-guided weapons launched from F-111Fs of the 48TH TFW as this photo clearly shows. The 'Liberty Wing' destroyed 245 HASs or two-thirds of the total destroyed during the Gulf War. (USAFE)*

Bottom *An Iraqi tank minus its turret, ripped open by laser-guided bombs delivered by F-111Fs of the 48th TFW, lies rusting in the desert. No less than 920 tanks and armoured vehicles were destroyed in the Gulf War by the 48th TFW. (USAFE)*

The bombs hit the command centre, causing a secondary explosion. It was the final mission of the Gulf War.

When the cease-fire came into effect on 3 March, the Allied air forces had flown 110,000 sorties with devastating effect on the Iraqi military forces. The conflict confirmed the 48th TFW's remarkable reputation for night attack missions, earned over Libya four years before. During the Gulf War, its F-111Fs flew 2,500 sorties and dropped 5,500 bombs, scoring hits on 920 tanks and armoured vehicles, 252

Night aerial refuelling of an F-117A stealth fighter by a SAC KC-135Q from Beale AFB, California in support of Operation Desert Shield. (USAF Photo By T/SGT H. H. Deffner)

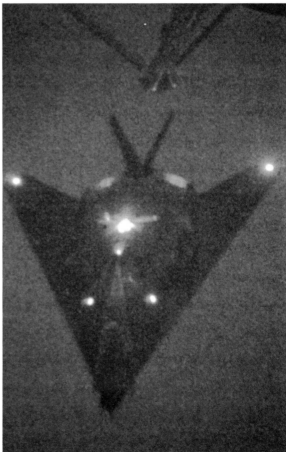

F-117A stealth fighters in Saudi Arabia during Desert Storm. *(Lockheed)*

artillery pieces, 245 HAS's as well as 113 bunkers, 13 runways, 12 bridges (with another 52 seriously damaged) and 158 buildings. In addition, 284 other targets were also hit, including 11 Scud launchers and 25 SAM/AAA sites. Some 321 secondary targets were also knocked out by the hard-hitting 'Liberty Wing' and only one aircraft was damaged by enemy air defences. The F-117A stealth fighters flew almost 1,300 sorties, dropped more than 2,000 tons of bombs, and flew more than 6,900 hours during *Desert Storm*. They were the only aircraft to bomb strategic targets such as aircraft shelters and bunkers in Baghdad and did so using 2,000 lb GBU-27 laser-guided bombs with unprecedented accuracy. Without stealth, a typical strike mission required 32 aircraft with bombs, 16 fighter escorts, eight Wild Weasel aircraft to suppress enemy radar, four aircraft to electronically jam enemy radar, and 15 tankers to refuel the group. With stealth technology the same mission could be accomplished with only eight F-117s and two tankers to refuel them.

The role of the conventional bomber was revalidated in *Desert Storm*. B-52s flew 1,624 missions, dropped 72,000 weapons on targets in Kuwait and southern Iraq, including airfields, industrial targets, and storage areas. Despite being over 30 years old, B-52s turned in higher reliability rates in *Desert Storm* than during operations in Vietnam. In all, they dropped 31 per cent of all US bombs and 41 per cent of all USAF bombs dropped during the war. One B-52G was lost on 3 February in an accident and three of the crew were killed.

The Iraqis lost 43 divisions, 3,700 tanks, 2,400 armoured vehicles and 2,600 artillery pieces, and 112 aircraft, 40 of them in air-to-air combat, including 35 to the USAF. US Air Force F-15Cs accounted for 33 of these using radar-guided AIM-7 Sparrows and heat-seeking AIM-9 Sidewinders, and A-10s destroyed two

Left *B-52G 58-0170, Special Delivery II, of the 416th BW from Griffiss AFB which operated from Moron AB in Spain during the Gulf War. Again, the artwork is inspired by WW2 8th AF bombers. At least three B-17s and B-24s in East Anglia were called* Special Delivery, *while a 489th BG B-24 was named* Special Delivery II. *(Steve Jefferson)*

Below left *B-52G Thunderstruck, 58-0216, of the 42nd BW at Loring AB which completed 22 missions in the Gulf. (Author)*

Bottom left *B-52G Iron Maiden, 58-0193 of the 416th Bomb Wing, which operated from Diego Garcia during the Gulf War. (Author)*

helicopters with their GAU-8 30 mm cannon. In addition, six Iraqi aircraft were lost in accidents and 16 were captured or destroyed by Coalition ground forces. About 375 aircraft shelters were destroyed and it is estimated that 141 aircraft were lost inside these shelters. Another 137 aircraft were flown to Iran. Coalition air forces lost 75 aircraft, including 33 in accidents. Included in these figures are 19 USAF aircraft lost, including three non-combat losses. Eleven US pilots, including eight Air Force pilots, were made prisoners of war.

Much of the success derived from the use of hi-tech laser-guided, TV-guided and infrared-guided bombs and rockets and conventional cruise missiles, the latter launched hundreds of miles away. With these weapons America had finally achieved 'pickle barrel accuracy' a theory first inspired by the 1940s Norden precision bombsight with which it was claimed bombardiers could place a bomb in a pickle barrel from several thousand feet. In 1991, WSOs using Pave Tack finally achieved such accuracy, literally able to aim their weapons through the doors and windows of their objectives. Gen Merrill A. 'Tony' McPeak, USAF Chief of Staff, confirmed that about 90 per cent of all laser-guided bombs released during the war achieved hits. He also said that it was 'the first time in history that a field army had been defeated by air power'.

In any future large-scale war, the technology demonstrated in the Gulf has rendered the costly and long drawn-out battles which were fought in the past, largely redundant. Aircrews will still be needed but will there ever again be the aerial dogfighting on a scale the like of which involved

F-15C 84-0019 flown by 1/Lt Robert W. 'Gigs' Hehemann, 53rd TFS/36th TFW who downed two Su-25 aircraft on 6 February 1991 with AIM-9M Sidewinders. (Steve Jefferson)

Mustang and Fw 190, Sabre and MiG, and Phantom and MiG in the great air battles of the past 48 years? For the US, the Gulf War showed that from a technical and operational standpoint, it could establish air superiority wherever it wished. With the Soviet Union absent as a

McDonnell F-15C Eagles of the 33rd TFW. The nearest aircraft, 85-0099, was used by Capt Lawrence E. 'Cherry' Pitts of the 58th TFS 'Gorillas' on 19 January when he destroyed a MiG-25 with an AIM-7. (McDonnell Aircraft)

Above *BLU-82/B 15,000lb 'Big Blue' free-fall bomb (shown without M904 fuze), the 'Mother of all Bombs' dropped by 7th and 8th SOS teams of the 1st Special Operations Wing MC-130E Combat Talon I to clear Iraqi minefields. Palletised for carriage in the cargo hold, the bomb was simply shoved out of the Hercules onto the target. (Author)*

Below left *AC-130A Spectre gunship 53-3129* The First Lady *from the 919th SOG, 711th SOS based at Eglin AFB, Florida, the oldest aircraft used in the Gulf War, having first flown on 7 April 1955 (it also saw service in Vietnam). An AC-130H Spectre of the 16th SOS, 1st SOW was lost during the Gulf War, on 31 January 1991. (Author)*

Below right *Close up of the twin 40mm Bofors cannon inside the rear hold of AC-130A Spectre 53-3129* The First Lady *sited next to the Motorola AN/AP-Q-133 Beacon Tracking radar. Other armament consisted of two 20mm Vulcan cannon and two 7.62mm miniguns. (Author)*

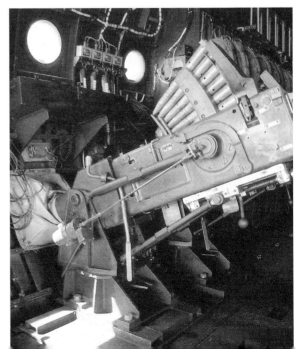

The Highway of Death where thousands of Iraqi armoured fighting vehicles fleeing bumper to bumper from Kuwait were destroyed.

competitor, there was no real challenger to American military aviation. The US, should it choose, could use its air power however it wanted. It has, of course, chosen to use it in the same way it has always done since the outbreak of WW2, when the rallying call from freedom-loving nations has been for military support, and when peace was restored again, for humanitarian aid. During the mid-1990s, when many questions were raised concerning the future military role of the United States in Europe, the 'battle-ground' shifted to Africa and the Balkans. Their role now was peace keeping, or was it peace making?

Chapter Eleven

Providing *Comfort,*
Relief and *Hope*

The Gulf War's aftermath commanded more and more US attention. On 20 and 22 March 1991, USAF F-15s shot down Iraqi fighters for violating the agreement it had made not to fly fixed-wing aircraft. One of the Gulf War's most immediate consequence was the disintegration of Iraq. Civil unrest erupted among Iraq's Shiite and Kurdish minorities. Saddam Hussein used his military ruthlessly, crushing the uprisings with helicopters and what armour his army had left. In the northern part of the country, 500,000 Kurds made their way to the Turkish and Iranian borders. On 5 April, the UN condemned Iraq and President Bush ordered US European Command to assist Kurds and other refugees in the mountains of northern Iraq. The following day, Joint Task Force *Provide Comfort* was formed and deployed to Incirlik to conduct humanitarian air operations in northern Iraq.

On 7 April, USAF aircraft began dropping food, blankets, clothing, tents and other equipment while, at the same time, Iraq was warned not to carry out any kind of activity north of the 36th parallel where Kurdish refugees had gathered. Eventually, 13 countries took part in *Provide Comfort* and another 30 were to provide various types of material assistance. By 8 April, USAF aircraft had dropped approximately 27 tons of relief supplies to the Kurds. On 9 April, the mission expanded to sustaining the refugee population for 30 days. Two days later, *Provide Comfort* took on the additional responsibility of providing temporary settlements for the Kurds. By 6 June, the last mountain gap had closed and the refugee population was in the security zone,

or 'safe haven'. The UN assumed responsibility for relief operations the following day. The last Coalition ground forces left Iraq on 20 July, and *Provide Comfort* ended on 15 July. *Provide Comfort* having been successfully completed, emphasis shifted to preventing a recurrence. Called *Provide Comfort II*, the effort relied primarily on air power. Maj Gen James L. Jamerson assumed command of the operation on 23 July. USAFE aircraft flew over northern Iraq 'to show a presence' and remained 'ready to carry out missions as directed'. The combined task force for *Provide Comfort II* consisted of the 7440th Composite Wing and a Joint Special Operations Task Force at Incirlik, and helicopter and infantry forces based at Silopi and Batman in south-eastern Turkey.

On 15 April, Operation *Provide Hope II* commenced, a long-term effort to aid cities in the former Soviet Union. Sea and land transport were the primary means of shipping excess food stocks from the Gulf War stored in three warehouses in Europe to Rhein-Main AFB 5 miles south of Frankfurt. Rhein-Main was a relatively small base, only 900 acres and 232 buildings, and shared Frankfurt's international airport, the busiest commercial airport in Europe. The 435th Airlift Wing, 17th AF is the host organization and the parent command for the wing is the USAF in Europe, headquartered at Ramstein Air Base. The 435th ALW is organized as an objective wing with three groups and a medical squadron. Its primary mission is airlift within the European theatre and the wing's tactical airlift mission is the responsibility of the 37th

Airlift Squadron. Flying C-130 Hercules, the 37th routinely performs airdrop and airland missions delivering equipment, supplies, and personnel 'on target, on-time'. As host unit, the 435th supports various tenant organizations and operating locations including the 362nd Airlift Support Group, an Air Mobility Command tenant unit, which supports transient Stateside-based strategic aircraft such as the C-5 Galaxy and the C-141 Starlifter.

Airlift missions to the CIS began on 24 April 1992. Supplies were offloaded, palletized, marshalled and loaded onto 65 C-141s and C-5s at Rhein-Main for delivery to areas such as Minsk, and 23 other locations in the former Soviet Union where surface transportation was impractical. The final 'official' *Provide Hope II* airlift mission departed from Rhein-Main on 1 May 1992, delivering medicine to Baku. On 29 July, Operation *Provide Hope II* ended. The US European Command transferred a total of 25,000 short tons of food and medicine from European stockpiles to 33 cities to those in need, the bulk by commercial freight.

On 4–5 May 1992, following a coup on 30 April that overthrew Sierra Leone President Momoh, a US European Command Joint Special Operations Task Force rescued 438 people (including 42 Third World nationals) during non-combatant evacuation operations (NEO) in Sierra Leone. Two C-141 aircraft flew 136 evacuees from Freetown, Sierra Leone to Rhein-Main while nine C-130 sorties carried another 302 to Dakar in Senegal.

From 12 August to 9 October 1992, a 78-person contingent and three 435th Airlift Wing C-130 Hercules deployed from Rhein-Main to Luanda, Angola to be used to relocate government and rebel soldiers during Operation *Provide Transition*, a multi-national UN effort to support democratic elections following 16 years of civil war in Angola. The Hercules flew 326 sorties, carrying 8,805 passengers and 265 tons of cargo during the operation. Although the elections on 29–30 September were generally peaceful, fighting soon broke out again when Jonas Savimbi, leader of the principal rebel group, the National Union for the Total

Local Kenyan workers watch a C-130 of the 314th ALW, Little Rock, Arkansas deliver relief supplies to Wajir, Kenya in September 1992. (Combat Camera Photo by T/SGT Marv Lynchard)

Independence of Angola (UNITA), finished second and refused to accept the results of the election.

On 14 August, the White House, prompted by continuing reports of heavily armed, organized gangs stealing food and famine-relief supplies from humanitarian organizations in the famine-ravaged East African state of Somalia, announced US military transports would support the multi-national UN relief effort. Ten C-130s and 400 personnel deployed to the centuries-old port of Mombasa in Kenya during Operation *Provide Relief*.

War had broken out in Somalia after a former Somali Army officer and diplomat, Mohammed Farrah Aideed, invaded from Ethiopia late in 1990 to fight dictator Mohammed Said Barre. By the time Aideed and his USC (United Somali Congress) supporters had reached Mogadishu in early 1991, Said Barre had fled and Aideed's former ally, Ali Mahdi, had declared himself President. Aideed's resentment of Ali Mahdi led to a clan war which cost an estimated 30,000 lives in four months of heavy fighting. Ten times

that number died in the ensuing famine.

Somalia's problems evoked the pity of the world. Television pictures showing thousands of homeless and bewildered people on the verge of starvation literally brought home the awfulness of the situation in a country that had been rendered virtually ungovernable by civil war. The fighting, largely between two rival factions, began in the summer of 1991, and its intensity quickly made the delivery of relief supplies almost impossible. Within months, the population of seven million, many of whom are nomadic, was in a desperate situation.

In April 1992, the United Nations began to send large shipments of food, medical equipment, medicines and other essential supplies to Somalia under its World Food Programme. It quickly became clear that the continuing civil war was preventing the relief convoys from reaching the people who needed them, so in August of the same year a multi-national air operation known as *Provide Relief* was launched, with participation by the United States, Britain, Germany, France, Italy, Belgium

In the Somalian capital Mogadishu, pallets of water, MREs and other supplies are loaded onto a C-130 of the 463rd Airlift Wing from Dyess AFB, Texas. The Hercules was attached to JTF Provide Relief *in Kenya. (USAF)*

Above *C-130H 74-1675 of the 773rd ALS, 463rd TAW, from Dyess AFB in Abilene, Texas at Moi International Airport for Operation* Provide Relief *in February 1993. Note the retro-fit AN/APN-169A Station Keeping Equipment dome atop the forward fuselage. (Author)*

Right *The map of Mogadishu approach is studied prior to landing. (Author)*

and Canada, under the leadership of the United Nations in Nairobi.

Operation *Provide Relief* began in late August 1992 from a corner of Moi International Airport on the edge of Mombasa as an immediate, short-term response to the sickness and starvation in Somalia. It continued until the end of February 1993, by which time multi-national efforts had restored stability to the refugee locations in the country and it was possible to convey supplies over secure land routes from the Somali ports of Mogadishu and Kismaayu directly to the relief locations.

The operation transformed the refugee camps. At last food and medicine were getting to the people who urgently needed them. The food consisted of powdered milk, bottled water, wheat, beans, rice, maize, various flours, cooking oil, and a corn and soya preparation called Unimix. The supplies arrived by ship in Mombasa—selected by the United Nations because it was the nearest city with a port and airport—and were then trucked to the *Provide Relief* operations centre at Moi. On 8 December, clans fighting for food, territory and ethnic revenge, created a climate of violence in Somalia which prevented *Provide Relief* workers from providing aid in areas of greatest need. In response, President Bush, implemented Operation *Restore Hope*, and sent American troops to protect the relief efforts.

At the peak of the operation in January 1993, Joint Task Force *Provide Relief/Restore Hope* included 1,007 Air Force, Marine, Army and Navy personnel as well as flying units from

Nineteen-year-old Pte Jason Vanburskirk (centre) from Toledo, Ohio, still with Somali desert dust on his black ankle boots, at Moi for R & R in Mombasa, courtesy of the 773rd Squadron after two months in 'Mogue'. (Author)

Germany and the UK. At that time, there were 16 C-130s from the USA and UK, three German C-160 Transalls and five Marine KC-130 tankers sharing the ramp space with occasional C-141s and C-5s. By 25 February 1993, the multi-national unit had flown 1,924 sorties to Somalia and 508 to Kenya, and had carried over 28,000 tonnes of food for international relief organizations who operate feeding centres and clinics for the Somali people in both Kenya and Somalia.

On 28 February, Colonel Thomas Samples, CO of the Air Component at Mombasa, and the Dyess crew of the 463rd TAW made the final US food flight from Mombasa, when they flew three pallets of powdered milk and bottled water to Mandera. The last day of February also saw the departure of two ANG C-130s with their support equipment and personnel. Operation *Provide Relief* really made a big difference. The C-130s operated out of austere dusty runways, sometimes littered with rocks, and as short as 3,000 ft without an accident or with a single mission lost due to a maintenance problem, although several incidents occurred at outlying fields between helicopters and fixed-wing aircraft.

On 1 March, the two RAF Hercules left for home. WOC (Wing Operations Command') Mombasa as it was officially called (for Wing Operations Centre) continued to operate as an air component under the JTF Headquarters in Mogadishu moving support supplies, including food and water for the troops, construction items, equipment and personnel throughout Kenya and Somalia. Scores of US male and female soldiers waited to be taken back to war-torn 'Mogue'. Tired bodies in *Desert Storm*-style camouflaged fatigues, some with their M16 rifles beside them, lay outside the 'passenger terminal' or sat on its wooden benches in the usual military 'hurry up and wait' scenario.

Earlier, incoming troops like 19-year-old Pte Jason Vanburskirk, still with Somali desert dust on his black ankle boots, had arrived at Moi. He and his buddies had been flown to Mombasa for R & R (Rest and Recuperation) courtesy the 773rd Squadron after two months in 'Mogue'. Jason is from Toledo, Ohio where Jamie Farr (Cpl Klinger in M*A*S*H) now runs a place called 'Jamie's Bar'. The parallel with the famous movie and TV series is appropriate, for the military setting at Moi was almost pure '4077th'. With typical ingenuity a 'little America' 10,000 miles from home had been established. Mo's Barber Shop had two customers and in a small outdoor movie tent a Clint Eastwood film was showing. An Army Post Office 'APO 09899' fashioned out of packing crates and with a sign saying '4401 Air Postal Squadron—We Deliver' was doing brisk business in *Restore Hope* tee-shirts. The noticeboard had an announcement by MOGCOM offering 'food at the Military Officers Gourmet Club of Mombasa'; it's subtitle: 'Making Field Conditions Palatable.' On the parade ground nearby, khaki-suited Kenya Air Force squaddies with blue berets marched in the humid high 90s, while white-jacketed Kenyan waiters wearing black trousers waited tables under the shade of the Intercontinental Resort catering facility. The AAEFES BX/PX stores were open for essentials like shampoo and beef jerky.

Jason was joined by two 63rd Engineers of 36 Group normally based at Fort Benning but who since 1 January had been in Somalia and would stay until 10 May. Trouble was brewing again in downtown 'Mogue,' increasing the adrenalin which was already flowing like the sweat on their brows. The 23-year-old *Desert Storm* veteran, David Seay, from Ft Lauderdale, Florida, wearing an 82nd Airborne shoulder patch, and his 31-year-old buddy, John Webb, from Haines City, Florida, both of whom had been picked out of 165 men in their unit for two days' R&R in Mombasa. He told how in Mogue one night 'we went to pick up a water truck at the airport. On the way we turned left and 500 metres down the road we were ambushed. We turned around and 55-gallon drum barricades had been placed in the road. We pulled out after a fire-fight without casualties'. Their unit built the Jailib–Bardera highway in Somalia. A sergeant had his vehicle blown up by a land-mine but was 'OK'. They were hoping to finish their tour of duty and hand over control to the UN but US soldiers could remain—'transferred to the "blue beanies"'. Jason hoped to open his own photographic shop

when he got back to Toledo.

Sombrely, Jason added: 'In Mogue a day or so ago the French blew up a roundabout with a statue with a misdirected bazooka shot.' On 24 February, US troops had killed nine protesters during rioting by USC (SNA) supporters of Warlord Mohammed Farah Aideed, who blockaded and then tried to storm the US Embassy. Rioters threw stones and chanted anti-American slogans in the worst violence since the international force landed in December 1992. Officials of the US Embassy and military officials were all unreachable as reporters could not travel to the besieged building or anywhere else because of the rioting. Apparently, the street battles had flared up again because Aideed's supporters had been angered by alleged US support for rival militia chief Mohammed Said Hersi. For two days, rioting protesters sealed off all roads with flaming car tyres and stoned US troops who repeatedly opened fire. Earlier, US Customs' officer, Bill Rhinebeck, another veteran of the Gulf war, related how he had to sleep in the US Ambassador's house in Mogadishu. However, it was far from palatial because 'the windows and floors were out but at least it had a roof!'

Postcards written to post home speak of: 'Parents of Somali kids won't let you take pictures of them unless you say you're from *National Geographic*! Our RTE [Ready to Eat meals] are also very popular in Somalia.' The postcards describe Somalia as a 'land of contrasts—fancy estates to hotels, barren deserts to lush green vistas—wonder, beauty and friendly people' and of 'monkeys eating French Fries out of my hand' to 'orphaned children begging, "Americain, give me a pen"' and one writer said: 'So much poverty and filth it makes you ill.'

The MAC Transport fleet at Mombasa consisted of four C-130Hs of the 463rd TAW, 773rd ALS from Dyess AFB at Abilene in Texas. The 773rd, which is part of Air Mobility Command, replaced its sister squadron, the 772nd ALS, which redeployed Stateside in the second week of February. It was for an *Absolution* trooping and supply mission to combat units in Kisaamayu and Mogadishu that Captain Paul Britton, check pilot Capt Mike P.

Capt Mike Brignola (right) and Bill Murray (seated), the flight engineer, maintain a watchful eye on things on the first leg of the flight from Mombasa to Kismaayu. (Author)

Brignola from Westchester, Pennsylvania, and the three-man flight crew boarded the sweltering cabin of the C-130 on 1 March. Almost at once, the cabin and massive hold filled with refreshing snorts of steaming icy blasts from the air-conditioning system. Cargomasters sealed the rear ramp door, and soldiers and Red Cross girls on board settled down into the rows of sideways-facing seats for the 510-mile flight up the coast to Mogadishu. Tail number, souls on board and fuel endurance were relayed to Ground Control.

All around the field were aircraft of every size and type. Light aircraft, airliners, Southern Air Transport L-100 Hercules, and a few German and Belgian C-160s and C-130s were parked on the apron. An all-white HS-748 of the Royal New Zealand Air Force, which had flown in from Auckland, looked like a polar bear in the desert. Highly colourful Kenyan Air Force Puma and Tucano aircraft threaded their way to the ramp, adding to the spectacle. A Swiss Air Safaris DC-8 roared noisily into the air.

The C-130 rumbled along the uneven concrete to the threshold. Permission to take off was sought and given. The four massive 4,508 shp Allison T56-A-7 turboprops lifted the C-130H effortlessly into the cloudy sky and the nose-wheel engaged in the well beneath the cockpit with a reassuring thump. Soon the C-130 was on its briefed course at a cruising altitude of 17,000 ft flying at 200–300 knots. Over the Indian Ocean, it flew parallel to the lush green coastline of Kenya, then the Murrum red desert floor of Somalia. It was essential aircrew gave frequent position reports to aid in deconfliction because the E-2C King Control had been withdrawn in December. Prior to entering Somalian airspace all aircraft gave a position report on 127.45 MHz. Loadmasters frequently joined the crew on the flight-deck for a quick look or consultation. Down below, the islands of Jofay and Koyaama appeared. The navigator pointed into the heat haze past the islands. 'Kismaayu!' he said above the thundering clamour of the four engines and rushing slipstream.

Paul Britton checked his map and UHF contact with Kismaayu (call-sign 'Tailpipe Kilo') was established. Bill Murray, the flight engineer, sat like a father confessor immediately behind the two pilots. He smiled then shouted that the C-130 would be going straight in and turning before landing. On 22 February, pitched battles had taken place in Kismaayu between an Aideed backer, warlord Omer Jess, and his rival Hersi known as 'Morgan'—Morgan had taken over the town from the Belgians. At least 11 people had been killed and Jess's USC/SSDF forces had retreated from the city they had controlled since shortly after the 1991 overthrow of Somali dictator Mohammed Said Aarre.

Paul Britton put the C-130H into a 45° descent. It lost altitude rapidly and the altimeter passed through several thousand feet until it read '1'. The young Texan concentrated intensely as he dived for the single paved runway. Up to now, the only threat had been a high-flying stork or crane. Birds such as these had caused the deaths of two light aircraft pilots in 1991. Down and down the C-130 plummeted until Paul levelled off and the Hercules zoomed along above the runway at a very exciting 150 ft doing 260 knots. He was not showing off. This procedure was designed to scatter any cattle, camels and the odd Somali who had decided to cross the runway. None had. The C-130 whizzed past the control tower and assembled multitude of Cobra helicopters. Paul peeled off to the left at the end of the runway in a beautiful 'fighter' turn and circled back for an assault landing. He pulled up within 3,000 ft using the powerful reverse thrust to produce quadraphonic sound all around the flight deck. The Hercules's massive

Above right *The islands of Jofay and Koyaama just off the coast of Somalia in the Indian Ocean come into view just prior to landing at Kismaayu. (Author)*

Right *Capt Paul Britton begins the descent into Kismaayu. (Author)*

Below *The first approach to Kismaayu is a long lo-lo pass to scatter any cattle, camels and the odd Somali who might decide to cross the runway. (Author)*

Paul Britton pulls away to port after buzzing Kismaayu for an assault landing. (Author)

Paul Britton studies the map en route to Mogadishu. (Author)

four-bladed props were still turning as cargo-masters eased the pallet out before the C-130 was off again, trundling down the length of the runway in the other direction this time. The pilot's seat was taken now by Mike Brignola. He pointed out a herd of camels to the left. They were not disturbed by the subsequent take-off. Taking off from rudimentary Somali airstrips in the intense heat with four, let alone two engines, called for strong nerves. Off safely, contact was made with Mogadishu approach at 100 nautical miles, and intention stated. At 60 nautical miles, Mogadishu approach placed the Hercules under positive radar control for a radar service to Mogadishu International. The heart-stopping landing at Kismaayu was dramatic but Mogadishu produced an incredible view for an awestruck observer. Dark grey warships were anchored off shore of the war-torn Somali capital. Large breakers pounded the beaches and sand-coloured Humvees and construction vehicles dotted the landscape inland of the dunes. It looked like a scene from a Normandy beachhead, except that Marines were jogging around the airport perimeter and handball games were in full swing on the beach.

The C-130 taxied to just in front of the tower and the troops and supplies were disembarked. A long file of grunts took their place and flopped wearily into the bucket seats in the cargo hold. A Nigerian C-130 taxied out, returned along the runway at speed, became airborne, and turned sharply onto 270° away from the town as machine-gun fire had been reported in the area.

At 05:35 hrs Paul Britton followed exactly the same pattern and the C-130 was off again and climbing away without incident. The faithful Allison turboprops beat a pulsating rhythm and the tension in the cockpit evaporated with the diminishing heat as the C-130 climbed gradually to 23,000 ft. The crew settled back as the Hercules droned above the coast at a steady 300 knots. Copies of *Stars and Stripes* were being read until the sun went down below the right wing and the orange-red instrument lights and green computer CRTs began to light up the pilots' smiling faces. Darkness descended. The stable Herky Bird headed 'home', the crew relaxed, knowing that in a few hours they would

Mission accomplished! Capt Paul Britton stands on the fuselage of his C-130H at Mogadishu. (Author)

be enjoying 'field conditions' again at their plush hotel in Mombasa after their exertions.

Aid airlifts, of course, cannot end war; sometimes the denouement is further conflict. In June and July 1993, Somalia pushed the war in Bosnia off the world's front pages as American air units fought to prevent General Aideed and his supporters re-taking control of Mogadishu. Aideed's fighters were blamed for the killing of

During operations in Somalia, AC-130 and helicopter gunships were used with deadly effect. Here an AH-1 Cobra helicopter gunship fires two 2.75-inch FFARS (Folding Fin Aerial Rockets) at the weapons cantonment area held by Somali warlord Gen. Aideed on 7 January 1993. (Combat Camera Photo by SGT Daniel R. Hart)

23 Pakistani UN peacekeepers on 5 June. The warlord hoped to control the federal-style parliament due to be set up under UN peace accords late in 1993. Lockheed AC-130H gunships bristling with one 40 mm, two 20 mm Vulcan cannons, one 105 mm howitzer and 7.62 mm machine-guns, and Cobra helicopters of a US Army quick reaction force were used in day and night actions against Aideed and his supporters in Mogadishu. Armed Hercules AC-130A night gunships had seen action towards the end of the Vietnam war. In a 1-hour attack on 11/12 June the Spectre gunships and Cobra helicopters destroyed Aideed's radio station as American soldiers led attacks on his command HQ and weapons caches. Spectres attacked ammunition dumps and garages housing 'technicals' close to Aideed's residence. On Sunday 13 June, Pakistani troops shot dead 34 Somalis during a weekend of rioting. On 11 July, another 16 Somalis were killed in actions by helicopter gunships.

Chapter Twelve

Provide Promise

On 3 July 1992, crews from the 37th Airlift Squadron, 435th Airlift Wing flew the first two C-130s with humanitarian relief supplies from Rhein-Main to the war-torn city of Sarajevo in the first *Provide Promise* mission. On 3 October, an Italian Air Force Alenia G-222 was hit by a missile 21 miles west of Sarajevo and was lost with its four man crew. At least two USAF C-130s received small-arms fire at Sarajevo Airport. Undeterred, C-9 Medevac missions, which operated twice a month, began on 2 February 1993, and in March the operation expanded to include the airdrop of relief supplies in Bosnia-Herzegovina. A USAF Hercules first dropped about a million 3 inch x 5 inch leaflets in less than 40 minutes over eastern Bosnia on 27 February telling residents and refugees that airdropped relief was on its way and cautioned people of the dangers of being too close to the drop zone. Night after night Bosnian refugees stood in the open, and waited, just like the Dutch in 1945, for the 'parcels from God' to drop.

French C-160 Transalls joined in the airlift operations on 27 March and the next day German Transalls became part of the team. All US aircraft used in the operation came from

A stretcher patient is lifted aboard a C-9A Nightingale at Keesler AFB, Missouri in October 1993. C-9 Medevac missions to Bosnia from Rhein-Main began on 2 February 1993 and were soon operating twice a month. (Author)

Rhein-Main where personnel of the 37th ALS and 317th ALW on TDY (temporary duty) from Pope AFB, North Carolina were regularly joined by Stateside-based active duty AFRes and ANG units using C-130E/H Hercules assigned to the 37th ALS, and 40th ALS, 23rd ALW (Pope AFB).

Much of the relief supplies for *Provide Promise* were delivered to the US Army's General Support Centre in Kaiserslautern, Germany where they were stored until delivery to Rhein-Main by the US Army's 37th Transportation Battalion. Other supplies were delivered directly to Rhein-Main by European civilian trucks. Upon receipt, members of the US Army's 5th Quartermasters, Air Delivery Support Branch, as well as French and German soldiers, then broke down the supplies and built the aid bundles. Each bundle was built to certain weight and size standards as part of the accuracy equation, then loaded onto Hercules by loadmasters and 435th Airlift Wing Aerial

Delivery Support Branch personnel.

On 23 March 1994, a typical *Provide Promise* flight to Sarajevo in C-130E *62-1834*, UN Flight 17, was made by an AFRes 'mix and match' crew rather than a 'hard' one. Pilot and aircraft commander 1/Lt Ross Becker, copilot 1/Lt Eric L. Meyers, and navigator Capt Thomas D. Mims are from the 815 Airlift Squadron, 403rd ALW at Keesler AFB, Biloxi, Mississippi. S/Sgt Ronald A. Downer, the Flight engineer, 327th ALS, 403rd ALW, is from Willow Grove Air Reserve Station at Horsham, Pennsylvania. Eric Meyers's father was in submarines and Ron Downer's father was an army combat photographer in Korea and Vietnam. Becker Snr is a farmer in Minnesota but his son has long been hooked on flying. He soloed in a Piper Tomahawk on his sixteenth birthday.

This was Ross Becker's sixteenth mission to Bosnia, Eric Meyers's sixty-seventh, and Tom Mims's twenty-third. S/Sgt Dorothy 'Bobbie' Bach, of the 60th ALW from Travis AFB, the

Pallets containing food, clothing and medical aid for Bosnia stored at Rhein-Main AFB, Germany. Each CDS bundle was fitted with just one 1950s-style G-12D low-velocity parachute which deploys automatically after exiting the aircraft, insuring that the bundle remains upright. The bundle's impact is cushioned by the corrugated honey-comb cardboard base. (Author)

Above left *Capt Ross Becker at the controls of C-130E 62-1834 on the mission to Sarajevo, 23 March 1994.* *(Author)*

Above right *High over the Austrian Alps, Capt Eric Meyers studies data in the* Provide Promise *booklet.* *(Author)*

Sat Comm operator at the 'black box' was flying her 100th airland/airdrop mission to Sarajevo and wore a patch commemorating the event on the sleeve of her flight suit. Brig Gen James E. Sehorn, Director of Operations, 14th AF (AFRes) HQ at Dobbins AFB, Georgia, was also on board. He wore the red triangular 'Flying Jennies' badge on his jacket. Gen Sehorn began his Air Force career in 1963 in primary pilot training. Upon graduation in 1964, he was assigned as an F-100 Super Sabre pilot at RAF Wethersfield, England. He then volunteered for F-105 Thunderchief duty in South-East Asia and was assigned to Korat Royal Thai AFB, Thailand. He received combat crew training for the F-100 in 1965 and for the F-105 in 1967. In December 1967, Gen Sehorn was shot down over South-East Asia while flying a Wild Weasel combat mission and ended up in the 'Hanoi Slammer' as he describes it. He was released in March 1973.

S/Sgt David A. Caldwell was flying his fortieth mission to Bosnia, and assistant loadmaster Senior Airman Eric J. Hebb was on his twenty-fifth mission. Both are from the 758th ALS, 911th ALG, AFRes. Both men come from Pittsburg. A miner for 15 years, Dave Caldwell now works in the construction industry during the summer months between tours of duty. This is his fourth tour in Germany. He did not disguise his delight in being able to make a worthwhile contribution to events in Bosnia by delivering food and medical supplies, his reas-suring no-nonsense approach no doubt handed down from his father who served in Patton's 7th Armoured Division in WW2.

UN 17 lifted off from Frankfurt with a take-off load of 23,000 lb. Vibration and noise was intense. It was like sitting in a tube train running without wheels. Dave and Eric were unseen in the rear of the hold. Brave men. Tied with green webbing, the bundles of food and medical supplies stacked securely behind the raised ramp looked like goods wagons behind railway buffers.

UN 17 over the Alps en route to Sarajevo. (Author)

The C-130E levelled off and headed towards Augsburg then Innsbruck, Vicenza and Ancona. From the flight-deck, the snow covered Alps look stunning, their black jagged peaks protruding menacingly through the high cloud layers below. Radio chatter crackled through the headphones. There was mention of Magic (AWACS) and 'egress' speeds out of Sarajevo in the event of an emergency. Gen Sehorn was in discussion with the engineer. After delivering the load to Sarajevo the C-130E would fly on to Split on the Aegean coast in Croatia and deliver more supplies before returning to Sarajevo with another load. This was to be the pattern throughout the day, finishing in a third flight to Sarajevo when the amount of fuel remaining would determine whether the C-130E would return to Split to refuel or be flown straight home. The General discussed the arrival at Sarajevo with the pilots, querying the predictability of the flight plan— long and slow into the Bosnian enclave. Wouldn't a fast run in be better? Russ explained that the very nature of the mission was its predictability. 'That's the idea and that's what

has been agreed,' he said. The crew had only been together for two weeks but it did not show. They worked well.

Nearing the war zone, camouflaged flak vests were donned. The crew pressed down firmly the front velcro strip. Flying down high valley walls, the C-130 skirted snow-covered mountain peaks. In front, a Hercules toppled over on its left wing and disappeared into the murk for landing as Dave took his turn for Sarajevo Airport. In the distance, the long runway appeared. Behind it there seemed to be a solid mountain wall. The C-130 was a sitting duck for any bored sniper or anti-aircraft gunner. Landing though was without incident. Ears ached with the descent and the pressure squeezed the yellow earplugs until the pain moved to the cheekbones. Some of the white-walled and orange-roofed houses which had looked so picturesque from high altitude were revealed as burned-out hulks, with blackened openings where windows once looked out onto pleasant vistas. UN 17 raced past them and hit the runway perfectly. Dave taxied to the shattered terminal building. Nearby, a white and

blue Ilyushin Il-76 was parked and a French Air
Force Transall taxied in. Evidence of the terrible
war was everywhere. Dave Caldwell said, 'You
should have been here in December—it was like
the Fourth of July!' White UN trucks and carriers milled around and forklift drivers wearing
blue UN helmets unloaded the pallets. In
minutes all the pallets were pushed along the
rollers in the floor and out of the Hercules. Gen
Sehorn clambered over the top and helped two
soldiers push out the pallets too!

Take-off for Split was made in sunshine and
blue sky. Soon the deep blue waters of the
Croatian coast appeared again. Near Split, the
crew was advised to look out for a triple A
emplacement, fortunately friendly. It tracked
every plane in. The C-130 dashed across the

Right *Over Bosnia flak vests are donned for the final
leg into Sarajevo Airport. (Author)*

Below *Final approach to Sarajevo. The runway can be
seen through the pilot's side window to the right of the
photo. (Author)*

built-up area of Split. It was eerie. There were no boats or surfers off shore, and certainly no tourists. On a road in the distance, just two cars were travelling along it. The runway at Split was covered in black tyre marks where a Hercules had burst a tyre but taxied in without problems.

UN 17 was loaded and took off again. Climbing away, the mission seemed almost routine now. But for the flak vests, it could almost have been a training flight. Dave Caldwell said that in the event of an emergency the load could be jettisoned in 10 seconds. The only drama came on the last flight of the day into Split: *62-1834* sprung a hydraulic leak and had to be left at the Croatian airport. The crew hopped aboard C-130H *11231* (the 2,000th Hercules) for the flight 'home' to Rhein-Main. The crew could at last relax. Dave Caldwell got out his hammock and draped it across the width of the Hercules. Soon he was swinging gently to and fro as the Hercules headed back to

Left *Cargo from UN 17 is unloaded at Sarajevo. (Author)*

Right *UN 17 at Split during reloading for the flight to Sarajevo. (Author)*

C-130H 91-1231, the 2,000th C-130 built by Lockheed, pictured at Split being loaded with supplies for Sarajevo. (Author)

Germany. The hangar door welcomed the C-130 with appropriate letters: MISSION SUCCESS.

In addition to the airland missions, as of March 1994, over 2,720 airdrop missions had been flown and over 31,000 bundles had been dropped since 28 February 1993 when the airdrop missions had started. The normal method used was the high-velocity Container Delivery

UN 17 taxies out of Sarajevo for the last flight of the day to Split. (Author)

diameter when open. At first, two parachutes were used per bundle but after well in excess of 25,000 parachutes had been used, and since they were non-recoverable, each CDS bundle was fitted with just one 1950s-style G-12D low-velocity parachute because the manufacturer could only produce 50 parachutes a month—enough for just two night's work. The parachute deploys automatically after exiting the aircraft and insures that the bundle remains upright. The bundle's impact is cushioned by the parachute and the corrugated honeycomb cardboard base.

Air drops have to be made from very low altitudes and as such are prone to small-arms fire and the risk of ground collision in mountainous terrain. In Bosnia, drops have often been thwarted by bad weather conditions and the possibility that the DZ could be immediately overrun by unfriendly forces before food could be offloaded from pallets. Worse, in May 1993, six people were killed and eight injured by aid crates parachuted into Goradze and Srebrenica. At one DZ, five people were killed in the fight around the parachute and at another, a woman and child lay dead beneath a pallet. Other methods had to be tried. The Tri-Wall Aerial Delivery System (TRIADS), a method whereby individual HDR packets packed into 4 ft x 3.5 ft cardboard boxes are 'fluttered' onto DZs, was first used on 20th March 1993 over Srebrenica. The boxes (whose walls are made of three layers of cardboard) self-destruct after leaving the C-130. The ties holding the boxes together are pulled apart and individual HDRs scatter into the air and fall to the ground much like a leaflet drop. On the night of 23/24 August 1993, USAFE C-130s discharged for free fall over Mostar, 13,440 individual packs of MREs (Meals, Ready to Eat) each weighing approximately 20 lb, loaded in boxes designed to open in mid-air to spread the packs over a wide area.

What follows is a typical high-velocity CDS airdrop mission, flown by six Hercules on the night of 24/25 March 1994.

One of them, C-130E Hercules No. 529, UN call-sign '43', belonged to the 23rd Wing from Pope AFB, North Carolina. The day before, a F-16D had collided with a C-130E Hercules of the 2nd ALS at less than 300 ft above Pope as

Dave Caldwell (centre) and some of the rest of the crew of UN 17 take a break during reloading at Split airport, Croatia. (Author)

System (CDS); the delivery of supplies and equipment from an aircraft in flight using a stabilizing parachute approximately 26 ft in

Boxes of MREs are dropped from a C-130 to test the viability of an innovative way to deliver food directly to Bosnia. The Tri-Wall Aerial Delivery System (TRIADS) allows aircrews to drop individual meals directly into cities without the threat of seriously injuring people on the ground. Once the boxes leave the aircraft, they fall apart and the meals 'flutter' to the ground. TRIADS was first used on 20th March 1993 over Srebrenica. (USAF)

both aircraft attempted to land. The F-16 hurtled into 500 members of the Army's 82nd Airborne Division from Fort Bragg, North Carolina and who were preparing to board a C-141 transport for a routine mission. Twenty-three paratroopers were killed and 100 personnel injured. Apparently, the two-seater F-16 had sheared off the right elevator of the C-130 and its two-man crew had ejected. The Hercules crew managed to put down safely. The maintenance crew inside the rear cargo hold of the 23rd Wing Hercules on the CDS airdrop were from Pope.

On a happier note, the aircraft commander of '43' turned out to be Capt Michael P. Brignola again! On this flight, as in Somalia, he was flying as check pilot for the mission pilot who in this case was 27-year-old Capt Darren A. Maturi, an American of Italian extraction from Virginia, Minnesota and who occupied the left seat. Darren graduated in the top 15 per cent at flying school and though this qualified him to fly jet fighters he chose transports. He had no regrets. In the past 18 months he had flown drops in Turkey, the Gulf and Angola, as well as Bosnia, and was the copilot aboard the first Bosnian airdrop mission on 1 March to Cerska when three C-130s dropped supplies in a drop zone 1,138 yards wide and 1,935 yards long.

Mike Brignola gathered the flight crew of nine around him outside the Hercules and went through the AAA fire and SAM avoidance procedures. (Chaff dispensers and inert heat sensitive flares are standard equipment.) Then everyone climbed aboard. Into the rear fuselage went the loadmasters—S/Sgt David T. Marko from Woburn, Massachusetts, T/Sgt Mike Norton from Channel Isles, California, and Sgt Mike T. Hay from Chicago, Illinois. T/Sgt Barney 'Joe' Ivy, an AFRes loadmaster from West Memphis, Arkansas was also along to gain experience.

Capt Mike Brignola (right) goes through the mission briefing with Capt Darren Maturi (to his right) and the crew prior to the night flight in C-130E No. 529 to Bosnia to airdrop humanitarian aid over Bjelimici on 24 March 1994. Navigator, Capt Mark A. Naumann, is far left and Sgt Jim A. Carezas, from Travis AFB, the Satellite Communications operator, is third left. (Author)

On the flight deck, all the crew were from the 37th Airlift 'Blue Tail Flies' Squadron, apart from the Satellite Communications operator Sgt Jim A. Carezas (also in charge of oxygen supply) who was from Travis AFB. During a typical airdrop mission the C-130 travels about 1,500 air miles which takes around 6 hours. On a typical day, four USAF C-130s flew to Sarajevo and 12 made airdrop missions. The French Air Force sent one C-160D Transall and the Germans sent two or three on airdrops.

Darren Maturi donned his red and white cap with its 'Frank Rules' badge (he's a great Frank Sinatra fan). The cap was a present from Col Harry Andersson, a family friend, who flew F4U Corsairs in the US Marine Corps on Guadalcanal in WW2. The navigator was Capt Mark A. Naumann, from Minnesota. Most navigators appear intense and Mark was no exception. His glasses made him look even more studious at his small table as he studied the large green scope,

portable GPS NAVISTAR, maps, and papers marked SECRET. Flight engineer, S/Sgt Robert A. Higginbotham, from Mooresville, Indianapolis, sat pensively studying dials and gauges.

The sun dropped behind the far side of the airport as UN 43 taxied out. In the lead was Capt David A. Peiffer and his all 41st ALS crew. His Hercules was equipped with AWADS (Adverse Weather Aerial Delivery System) and was thus able to navigate to its own release point. There were six Hercules in the 'package': two AWADs and their wingmen. Darren was to have led in order to gain lead experience—what is termed 'spreading the wealth', but an enforced delay aboard Capt Warren H. Hurst's C-130, who was to have been the No. 2, meant Darren flew Hurst's slot. Hurst's copilot was Capt Catherine A. Jacob, one of three female C-130 pilots in the 37th ALS. Hurst would catch up as the mission progressed. To the left, Capt Gallagher nosed out

The sun dips below the horizon as Capt Darren Maturi taxies out at Rhein-Main. Mike Brignola in the right hand seat, checks the details. Note the AN/APN-169A SKE (Station-Keeping Equipment) scope mounted atop the instrument panel. (Author)

to take the third slot, then a fourth with Captains Mike Hampton and Ed Brewer at the controls. Hampton's aircraft was an AWADS equipped Hercules. Capt Jones, who was to have flown the fifth slot, had a malfunction and the spare aircraft, piloted by Maj Douglas D. Delozier, filled in.

Peiffer was soon climbing away into leaden skies. UN 43 followed. Darren Maturi opened the throttles and the C-130 rumbled along the runway. There was a slight judder as it gained height and the wheels were retracted. The orange scope of the AN/APN-169A SKE (Station-Keeping Equipment) atop the instrument panel showed a reassuring line of five red blips with a circle (UN 43—our aircraft) behind the lead blip. To the left of the SKE, the Flight Command Indicator, or 'Fluter Phone', waited to be used to pass commands to the other aircraft. The layer of black cloud grew wider.

On intercom, Darren said, 'We are now entering the "bumpy zone".'

Peiffer's white flashing tail navigation lights disappeared into the cloud. He turned and Maturi turned also. The conga line on the SKE followed a fraction later. At 7,000 ft, the C-130 started to pick up icing. Leading edge de-icers had to be turned on. Only the faithful line of red blips following on the SKE lit up the console. If an artist wanted to paint this scene he would start with a broad black canvas, daub in 15 grey panels for the framed windows, and add a sprinkling of bright yellow, red and green panel lights. A shaft of moonlight entered the cockpit to the left and was then gone again. Both pilots scanned their illuminated notepads on their control columns.

Priorities for drops over Bosnia were provided to US European Command (EUCOM) from the UNHCR office in Geneva. EUCOM passed the information to Joint Task Force at Naples where a targeting board convenes daily to assess information and determine where formations will drop. The information was then passed to planners and schedulers at Rhein-Main who put together the actual mission. At the time, airdrops concentrated mainly on Mostar due to the large concentration of refugees in that area.

West of Munich, Darren Maturi followed Peiffer in the turn. Maturi applied 20° of bank. Intercom conversation was staccato, short and to the point. No BS [bullshit]: '190 knots— That's slow—Yeah, put it back in.'

Maturi eased the throttles slightly. He said, 'I like to fly within my captain's bars. Keep tolerance down.'

Conscious of the C-130s behind, someone said 'Don't want to start an accordion. Fly tight tolerances. You react, guy behind you is going to react. I came from SKE wing. Learned to take it to vis' conditions.'

Maturi and Brignola agreed that it was harder to be element leader, which they were, than formation leader. At this point, Jim Carezas, the Sat Comm operator, reported to Naumann that a fighter pilot had reported triple A in the area. It was made on VHF in the clear so the two pilots agreed that it could not be too sensitive. On intercom someone said, 'On some nights I hear word of 20 sightings—let's press on.'

In really thick cloud now. 'Lost some airspeed coming out of there,' Darren said.

The Engineer leaned forward, flicks switches. 'Got "Red Dog",' he said.

Hurst was still a long way behind, although it did not look it on the SKE scope. Hurst radioed, 'We are 103 miles behind and gaining. Might just catch up.'

The smell of chicken filled the cockpit. Someone asked, 'What's cooking?'

Higginbotham left his chair and took out a dish from one of the small ovens above the stairwell. Soon, Mike Brignola was tucking into his dinner.

'Coming up on Innsbruck,' said Mark Naumann. '198 with new heading.' He checked with drift.

'Roge" someone confirmed.

We saw the lights of the leader again.

'163 on Squawk when you get a chance "Enge".'

'Roge'.'

The moon was high above as the C-130 skimmed the clouds below. Misty gossamer trails scudded past while in front huge clouds loomed like polar ice-caps. Maturi banked away slightly to avoid turbulence. There was a city below. Lights, lots of them. There were no stars visible, only the twinkling of Peiffer's nav' lights. Maturi had got a little high. He banked lightly to the left. The blips followed obediently like carriages being pulled by a locomotive. There was a brief, tantalizing glimpse of the Alps in a rare shaft of moonlight. The pilots were seemingly oblivious to the majestic sight. They were thinking ahead, fully aware of the dangers a full moon presented over the drop zone.

'Full moon out there.'

'Means we'll be visible over Bosnia.'

'Yeah, could do with some cloud.'

On the interphone came a chilling reminder of the recent shooting down by F-16Cs on 28 February of four Serbian SOKO G-4 Super Galeb jets in the first confirmed violation by fixed-wing aircraft since NATO began Operation *Deny Flight* in April 1993.

'Unidentified aircraft land immediately or I will have to take action. You are in violation of UN Resolution 816.'

Nothing further was heard. The pilots showed no more concern in their voices than they did before.

Mark Naumann cut in, 'Twenty minutes off our combat check list.'

The formation headed inexorably into Croatian and then Bosnian airspace. Somewhere out there F-16 escort fighters were patrolling, protecting their 'assets' as the C-130s are termed. Apart from the Hercules there was another, smaller, 'package' of French and German Air Force Transalls heading for their drop zone at Tesanj.

The crew donned their flak vests. Darren discarded his lucky cap, put on his light-blue helmet and clamped his oxygen mask on. Everyone followed suit. Thumbs up showed that everyone's oxygen system was working normally as Jim Carezas turned the controls to depressurize the cabin and the hold. Everyone was now breathing pure oxygen. Navigation and cabin lights were extinguished and the cockpit was bathed in a red hue. Just like on a WW2 bombing mission, Mark Naumann called out the time to the IP (Initial Point). Higginbotham checked the fuel gauges above his head.

WHOOMPF!

Alarmed, Naumann asked, 'What was that?' He didn't wait for an answer. 'Did we take a hit? Did any pieces fly off?'

Fortunately, it was nothing more than an air pocket.

The DZ was Bjelimici, south-west of Sarajevo. Mark Naumann explained the drop procedure.

'AWADS enables us to make airdrops at night or in bad weather when we cannot visually see the drop zone. We have a GPS NAVISTAR navigational computer. We can programme radar targets into the computer, call up the targets and it projects cross-hairs onto the radar scope over the targets. We can then see if the cross-hairs are accurately placed on the target. If not, the navigator can manually move the cross-hair over the target to update the navigational computer. Then we fly off the navigational computer to the release point to make the drop. The rear ramp is lowered. Coming into the drop we slow down a certain distance out, making a series of warning calls, 30 seconds slow-down, 5 seconds slow-down, then the slow-down call itself, slowing down to our drop air speed, which is 140 knots.'

Mark made a 1 minute advisory call and added, 'Confidence high— "Dee Zee" ahead.'

He sent a 'Down Prep' on the SKE system, which our followers received. He made a 10-second call, sent another 'Down Prep' which our wingmen following us received.

Through all of this, he had been evaluating wind speed and altitude and passing on flight directions to Maturi. The biggest variable that occurred after load exits was the wind. For example, a 10 knot crosswind, airdropping at say 10,000 ft, causes the load to drift about 800 yards over the ground. The Hercules was travelling at about 100 yards per second, at a drop airspeed of 140 knots. Mark used his equipment to evaluate the winds, speed of aircraft and other parameters, forecast versus the actual, to come up with the CARP, or computed release point. Darren eased back the control column to reduce his air speed and raised the nose about 8° to allow the CDS to exit from the rear cargo door.

Once Mark Naumann had the DZ in the cross-hairs he informed the pilots.

'Green Light. Green Light, Green light.'

Mike Brignola threw the switch that released the cargo restraining strap and the extraction process was set in motion. Slowly at first, the six pallets of food bundles, medical boxes, clothing, blankets, and Tetanus Serum slid down the rollers towards the black void. The small chemical green pen lights which stayed lit for more than 8 hours to aid recovery, swung pendulously on the webbing straps. It took only about 4 seconds but it seemed longer. Then suddenly, they were gone. Each bundle was attached to a conventional parachute, opened by static line. The 26 ft ring-slot parachutes brought the bundles in at about 60 mph. Special packing techniques ensured the survival of the contents. On one occasion, 4,000 glass vials of penicillin were dropped near a hospital, and not one broke.

Capt Jim Stockmoe had the opportunity to observe an airdrop from the drop zone.

The effort was well organized with strict control measures in place. Prior to the drop, a crew of about 60 local residents under the control of the local police chief, Hurem Sahic, were in place around the drop zone. Most of the crew walked the rugged uphill route from Zepa, a 15 km trek, which takes about three hours on foot. The crew huddled around a small fire, attempting to stay warm in the wind and snow on the high flat drop site.

Prior to the drop, small sorties of NATO aircraft transited the area, an indicator the C-130 Hercules aircraft were not far behind. The window for the drop was passed the day prior through the UNMO CAPSAT communications net, the only link to the outside world. Within the announced time window, the aircraft arrived over the drop zone. An eerie silence fell on the hilltop.

The crew instinctively knew that at any moment the pallets would drop somewhere in the area. The rate of descent (about 50 kph) also meant any one of them could be crushed to death. Experience allowed them to position themselves to minimise the threat. Their silence also expressed their anxiety.

The pallets began to hit with a loud thud. Three pallets struck the south side of the drop zone ahead of the others. Then minutes later, a ripple of impacts, similar to the sound made by dud artillery rounds, echoed across the field. A chorus of cheers emanated from the crew. After waiting about 15 minutes to ensure there were no more drops, the crew rushed to find the pallets. Each pallet was guarded throughout the cold night by a member of Hurem's crew.

The Bosnians expected 56 pallets, based on the information passed through the UNMOs. Altogether, three US planes dropped a total of 41 CDS bundles. By 06:00 hrs, 39 pallets were found. Three of the pallets came down without fully deployed parachutes, without damage to the contents. Hurem's crew inventoried the contents of the pallets, and loaded them on Ukrainian trucks for the trip down the hill to Zepa. On arrival in Zepa, the cargo was once again inventoried, before being warehoused and distributed by the local government. Two persons were arrested for attempting to enter the drop zone and pilfer cargo.

Meanwhile, up in the six C-130s exiting the area, the loadmasters confirmed, 'Load clear.'

The C-130s exited the drop zone and sped off into the night. Down below, Bosnia was illuminated by many hundreds of lights. Aboard UN 43 Mike Brignola remarked on how strange that a country at war had so much electricity. Total flight time was going to be around 6 hours by the time the C-130 touched down at Frankfurt. Upcoming vacations were discussed to help pass the time. Darren favoured Burma but Mike Brignola suggested Peru. Each dismissed the other's choice as too dangerous! And here they were over Bosnia! Someone finally decided that

The pallets of humanitarian supplies exit from the rear of the Hercules. (USAF)

Mission completed over Bosnia, the C-130s wait at Rhein-Main, ready for the next mission. (USAF)

if it was a dangerous vacation they wanted then they should choose Detroit!

Darren spoke of his girlfriend Anna Maria in Venice. Once, she fired off fireworks hoping he would see them as he flew home. There were no fireworks this time, not even sparklers, until the lights of Germany came into view. It was a crystal clear night. Thousands of pearl white and blue gems in large necklaces twinkled majestically on a vast black velvet cloth while clouds whizzed past overhead like a revolving film stage.

Finally, the two parallel runways at Frankfurt appeared, with their green landing bars and red exit bars glowing against the skyline. Minutes later the C-130 was down. One by one the superb Hercules were marshalled into position by ground signallers using illuminated batons. Engines cut, the cabin lights came on. Another six cargoes of supplies had been delivered to Bosnia and for the crews, a day of rest would be taken before it all began again, if not there, then somewhere else in Europe, or the Far East, or Africa: wherever the US Air Forces would be needed next.

American Pilots in the Battle of Britain

Pilot	Unit	Fate
P/O W. M. L. 'Billy' Fiske DFC	601 Squadron	Died of his wounds on 17 August 1940
P/O Arthur G. Donahue DFC	64 Squadron	Killed flying with 71 Eagle Squadron
P/O J. K. Haviland DFC	151 Squadron	
P/O Vernon C. 'Shorty' Keogh	609 Squadron	Killed flying with 71 Eagle Squadron
P/O Philip H. Leckrone	616 Squadron	Killed flying with 71 Eagle Squadron
P/O Andrew 'Andy' B. Mamedoff	609 Squadron	Killed flying with 133 Eagle Squadron
P/O Eugene Q. 'Red' Tobin	609 Squadron	Killed flying with 71 Eagle Squadron

USAF Medal of Honor Recipients

WORLD WAR TWO

Date	Recipient	Where
18 April 1942	Lt Col James H. Doolittle	Tokyo, Japan
7 August 1942	Captain Harl Pease Jr	Rabaul, New Britain 19th 5th AF. Posthumous
8 November 1942	Col Demas T. Craw	Port Lyautey, French Morocco. Posthumous
8 November 1942	Maj Pierpont M. Hamilton	Port Lyautey, French Morocco
5 January 1943	Brig Gen Kenneth N. Walker	Rabaul, New Britain. Posthumous
18 March 1943	1/Lt Jack Mathis 303rd BG 8th AF	Vegasack, Germany. Posthumous
1 May 1943	S/Sgt Maynard H. Smith 306th BG 8th AF	St Nazaire, France
16 June 1943	2/Lt Joseph R. Sarnoski 43rd BG 5th AF	Buka, Solomon Islands. Posthumous
16 June 1943	Major Jay Zeamer Jr 43rd BG 5th AF	Buka, Solomon Islands
26 July 1943	Flt/O John C. Morgan 92nd BG 8th AF	Kiel, Germany
1 August 1943	Lt Col Addison E. Baker 93rd BG	Ploesti, Romania. Posthumous
1 August 1943	2/Lt Lloyd D. Hughes 389th BG	Ploesti, Romania. Posthumous
1 August 1943	Maj John L. Jerstad 93rd BG	Ploesti, Romania. Posthumous
1 August 1943	Col Leon W. Johnson 44th BG	Ploesti, Romania.
1 August 1943	Col John R. Kane 98th BG	Ploesti, Romania
18 August 1943	Maj Ralph Cheli	Wewak, New Guinea. Died as a PoW 6 March 1945
11 October 1943	Col Neel E. Kearby	Wewak, New Guinea. KIA 5 Mar 1944
10 October – 15 November 1943	Maj Richard I. Bong	South-West Pacific. Killed 6 August 1945, Burbank, California
2 November 1943	Maj Raymond H. Wilkins	Rabaul, New Britain. Posthumous
20 December 1943	T/Sgt Forrest L Vosler 303rd BG 8th AF	Bremen, Germany
11 January 1944	Lt Col James H. Howard 9th AF	Oschersleben, Germany
20 February 1944	1/Lt William R. Lawley 305th BG 8th AF	Leipzig, Germany
20 February 1944	Sgt Archibald Mathies 351st BG 8th AF	Leipzig, Germany. Posthumous

20 February 1944	2/Lt Walter E. Truemper 351st BG 8th AF	Leipzig, Germany. Posthumous
11 April 1944	1/Lt Edward S. Michael 305th BG 8th AF	Brunswick, Germany
5 June 1944	Lt Col Leon R. Vance Jr	Wimereaux, France. Killed 26 July nr Iceland
23 June 1944	2/Lt David R. Kingsley 97th BG 15th AF	Ploesti, Romania. Posthumous
9 August 1944	Capt Darrell R. Lindsey	Pontoise, France. Posthumous
9 July 1944	1/Lt Donald D. Puckett	Ploesti, Romania. Posthumous
26 October 1944	Maj Horace S. Carswell Jr	South China Sea. Posthumous
2 November 1944	2/Lt Robert E. Femoyer 447th BG 8th AF	Merseberg, Germany. Posthumous
9 November 1944	1/Lt Donald J. Gott 452nd 8th AF	Saarbrücken, Germany. Posthumous
9 November 1944	2/Lt William E. Metzger 452nd BG 8th AF	Saarbrücken, Germany. Posthumous
24 December 1944	B/Gen Fred W. Castle 4th BW 8th AF	Posthumous
11 January 1945	Maj William A. Shomo	Luzon, Philippine Islands
12 April 1945	S/Sgt Henry E. Erwin	Koriyama, Japan
25 April 1945	1/Lt Raymond L. Knight	Po Valley, Italy. Posthumous
25/26 December 1945	Maj Thomas B. McGuire	Luzon, Philippine Islands. KIA 7 January 1945 Los Negros

KOREA

Date	Recipient	Where
5 August 1950	Maj Louis J. Sebille	Hamch'ang, South Korea. Posthumous
14 September 1951	Capt John S. Walmsley Jr	Yangdok, North Korea. Posthumous
10 February 1952	Maj George A. Davis Jr	Sinuiju – Yalu River, North Korea. Posthumous
22 November 1952	Maj Charles J. Loring Jr	Sniper Ridge, North Korea. Posthumous

VIETNAM

Date	Recipient	Where
10 March 1966	Maj Bernard F. Fisher	A Shau Valley, South Vietnam
24 February 1967	Capt Hilliard A. Wilbanks	Dalat, South Vietnam. Posthumous
10 March 1967	Maj Merlyn H. Dethlefsen	Thai Nguyen, North Vietnam
19 April 1967	Lt Col Leo K. Thorsness	North Vietnam
19 April 1967	Col George E. Day	Conspicuous gallantry while PoW (shot down 1 September 1967)
9 November 1967	Capt Gerald O. Young	Da Nang area South Vietnam
26 November 1968	1/Lt James P. Fleming	Duc Co, South Vietnam
26 November 1968	Capt Lance P. Sijan	Conspicuous gallantry while PoW. Died while PoW January 1968
12 May 1968	Lt Col Joe M. Jackson	Kham Duc, South Vietnam
1 September 1968	Col William A. Jones III	Dong Hoi, North Vietnam. Killed 15 November 1969
24 February 1969	A1C John L. Levitow	Long Binh, South Vietnam
29 June 1972	Capt Steven L. Bennett	Quang Tri, South Vietnam. Posthumous

USAAF Aces of World War Two (Air-Air Victories)

Maj Richard I. Bong	40	Lt Col John C. Herbst	18
Maj Thomas B. McGuire Jr	38	Lt Col Hubert Zemke	17.75
Col Francis S. Gabreski	28	Maj John B. England	17.5
Col Francis S. Johnson	27	Capt Duane W. Beeson	17.33
Col Charles H. MacDonald	27	1/Lt John F. Thornell	17.25
Maj George E. Preddy	26.83	Capt James S. Varnell Jr	17
Col John C. Meyer	24	Maj Gerald W. Johnson	16.5
Col David C. Schilling	22.5	Capt John T. Godfrey	16.33
Lt Col Gerald R. Johnson	22	Capt Lawrence E. Anderson	16.25
Col Neel E. Kearby	22	Lt Col William D. Dunham	16
Maj Jay T. Robbins	22	Lt Col Bill Harris	16
Capt Fred J. Christensen	21.5	Capt George S. Welch	16
Capt Ray S. Wetmore	21.25	Capt Donald M. Beerbower	15.5
Capt John J. Voll	21	Maj Samuel J. Brown	15.5
Col Walker M. Mahurin	20.75	Capt Richard A. Peterson	15.5
Lt Col Thomas J. Lynch	20	Maj William T. Wisner Jr	15.5
Lt Col Robert B. Westbrook	20	Lt Col Jack T. Bradley	15
Capt Donald S. Gentile	19.83	Maj Edward Cragg	15
Col Glenn E. Duncan	19.5	Maj Robert W. Foy	15
Capt Leonard K. Carson	18.5	2/Lt Ralph K. Hofer	15
Col Glenn T. Eagleston	18.5	Capt Cyril F. Homer	15
Maj Walter C. Beckham	18	Lt Col John D. Landers	14.5
Maj Herschel H. Green	18	Capt Joe H. Powers Jr	14.5

USAF Aces of the Korean War 1950–53

Capt Joseph McConnell Jr	16	Maj Donald E. Adams	6.5
Maj James Jabara	15	Col Francis S. Gabreski	6.5
Capt Manuel J. Fernandez	14.5	Lt Col George L. Jones	6.5
Maj George A. Davis Jr	14	Maj Winton W. Marshal	6.5
Col Royal N. Baker	13	1/Lt James H. Kasler	6
Maj Frederick C. Blesse	10	Capt Robert J. Love	6
1/Lt Harold E. Fischer	10	Maj William T. Whisner Jr	5.5
Lt Col Vermont Garrison	10	Col Robert P. Baldwin	5
Col James K. Johnson	10	Maj Stephen L. Bettinger	5
Capt Lonnie R. Moore	10	Capt Richard S. Becker	5
Capt Ralph S. Parr Jr	10	Maj Richard D. Creighton	5
Capt Cecil G. Foster	9	Capt Clyde A. Curtin	5
1/Lt James F. Low	9	Capt Ralph D. Gibson	5
Maj James P. Hagerstrom	8.5	Capt Iven C. Kincheloe Jr	5
Capt Robinson Risner	8	Capt Robert T. Latshaw Jr	5
Lt Col George I. Ruddell	8	Capt Robert H. Moore	5
1/Lt Henry Buttlemann	7	Capt Dolphin D. Overton III	5
Capt Leonard W. Lilley	7	Col Harrison R. Thyng	5
Capt Clifford D. Jolley	7	Maj William H. Westcott	5

Appendix V

USAAF/USAF Aces of World War Two-Vietnam

	WW2	Korea	Vietnam	Total
Maj Richard I. Bong	40			40
Maj Thomas B. McGuire Jr	38			38
Col Francis S. Gabreski	28	6.5		34.5
Col Francis S. Johnson	27			27
Col Charles H. MacDonald	27			27
Maj George E. Preddy	26.83			26.83
Col John C. Meyer	24	2		26
Col Walker M. Mahurin	20.75	3.5		24.25
Col David C. Schilling	22.5			22.5
Lt Col Gerald R. Johnson	22			22
Col Neel E. Kearby	22			22
Maj Jat T. Robbins	22			22
Capt Fred J. Christensen	21.5			21.5
Capt Ray S. Wetmore	21.25			21.25
Maj George A. Davis Jr	7	14		21
Maj William T. Whisner Jr	15.5	5.5		21
Capt John J. Voll	21			21
Col Glenn T. Eagleston	18.5	2		20.5
Lt Col Thomas J. Lynch	20			20
Lt Col Robert B. Westbrook	20			20
Capt Donald S. Gentile	19.83			19.83
Col Glenn E. Duncan	19.5			19.5
Capt Leonard K. Carson	18.5			18.5
Maj Walter C. Beckham	18			18
Maj Herschel H. Green	18			18
Lt Col John C. Herbst	18			18
Lt Col Hubert Zemke	17.75			17.75
Maj John B. England	17.5			17.5

	WW2	Korea	Vietnam	Total
Capt Duane W. Beeson	17.33			17.33
Lt Col Vermont Garrison	7.33	10		17.33
1/Lt John F. Thornell	17.25			17.25
Capt James S. Varnell Jr	17			17
Col Royal N. Baker	3.5	13		16.5
Maj Gerald W. Johnson	16.5			16.5
Maj James Jabara	1.5	15		16.5
Capt John T. Godfrey	16.33			16.33
Capt Lawrence E. Anderson	16.25			16.25
Capt Joseph McConnell Jr		16		16
Col Robin C. Olds	12		4	16
Lt Col William D. Dunham	16			16
Lt Col Bill Harris	16			16
Capt George S. Welch	16			16
Capt Donald M. Beerbower	15.5			15.5
Maj Samuel J. Brown	15.5			15.5
Capt Richard A. Peterson	15.5			15.5
1/Lt John F. Thornell	15.25			15.25
Lt Col Jack T. Bradley	15			15
Maj Edward Cragg	15			15
Maj Robert W. Foy	15			15
2/Lt Ralph K. Hofer	15			15
Capt Cyril F. Homer	15			15
Col John W. Mitchell	11	4		15
Maj Lowell K. Brueland	12.5	2		14.5
Capt Manuel J. Fernandez		14.5		14.5
Maj James P. Hagerstrom	6	8.5		14.5
Lt Col John D. Landers	14.5			14.5
Capt Joe H. Powers Jr	14.5			14.5
Lt Col William J. Hovde	10.5	1		11.5
Col John W. Mitchell	11			11
Col James K. Johnson	1	10		11
Lt Col George I. Ruddell	2.5	8		10.5
Maj Frederick C. Blesse		10		10
1/Lt Harold E. Fischer		10		10
Capt Lonnie R. Moore		10		10
Capt Ralph S. Parr Jr		10		10
Col Harrison R. Thyng	5	5		10
Capt Philip E. Colman	5	4		9
Lt Col Edwin L. Heller	5.5	3.5		9

	WW2	Korea	Vietnam	Total
Capt Cecil G. Foster		9		9
1/Lt James F. Low		9		9
Capt Robinson Risner		8		8
Maj Van E. Chandler	5	3		8
Maj John J. Hockery	7	1		8
1/Lt Henry Buttlemann		7		7
Maj Richard D. Creighton	2	5		7
Lt Col Benjamin H. Emmert Jr	6	1		7
Maj John J. Hockery	7			7
Capt Clifford D. Jolley		7		7
Capt Leonard W. Lilley		7		7
Maj Donald E. Adams		6.5		6.5
Lt Col George L. Jones		6.5		6.5
Maj Winton W. Marshal		6.5		6.5
Maj Stephen L. Bettinger	1	5		6
Capt Charles B. DeBellevue			6	6
Lt Col Benjamin H. Emmert Jr	6			6
1/Lt James H. Kasler		6		6
Capt Robert J. Love		6		6
Maj James P. Hagerstrom	6			6
Maj Herman W. Visscher	5	1		6
Lt Col Edwin L. Heller	5.5			5.5
Capt Richard S. Becker		5		5
Capt Philip E. Colman	5			5
Maj Van E. Chandler	5			5
Col Robert P. Baldwin		5		5
Capt Clyde A. Curtin		5		5
Capt Jeffrey S. Feinstein			5	5
Capt Ralph D. Gibson		5		5
Capt Iven C. Kincheloe Jr		5		5
Capt Robert T. Latshaw Jr		5		5
Capt Brooks J. Liles	1	4		5
Capt Robert H. Moore		5		5
Capt Conrad E. Mattson	1	4		5
Capt Dolphin D. Overton III		5		5
Capt Richard S. Ritchie			5	5
Maj William F. Shaeffer	2	3		5
Col Harrison R. Thyng	5			5
Maj William H. Westcott		5		5

Appendix VI

USAF Air–Air Victories in Operation *Desert Storm*

1991	Aircraft destroyed	Aircraft	Pilot	Unit
17 January	MiG-29	F-15C 85-0125	Capt Jon K. Kelk	58th TFS/33rd TFW§
	MiG-29	F-15C 85-0108	Capt Rhory R. "Hoser' Draeger	58th TFS/33rd TFW
	Mirage F1 EQ (2)	F-15C 85-0105	Capt Robert E. Graeter	58th TFS/33rd TFW
	MiG-29	F-15C 85-0107	Capt Charles J. 'Sly' McGill (USMC)	58th TFS/33rd TFW
	Mirage F1 EQ	F-15C 83-0017	Capt Steven W. 'Tater' Tate	71st TFS/1st TFW
	Mirage F1 EQ†	EF-111A 66-0016	Capt James Denton (Pilot) Capt Brent Brandon (EWO)	42nd ECS/66th ECW
19 January	MiG-25	F-15C 85-0099	Capt Lawrence E. 'Cherry' Pitts	58th TFS/33rd TFW
	Mirage F1 EQ	F-15C 79-0069	Capt David S. Prather	525th TFS/36th TFW
	Mirage F1 EQ	F-15C 79-0021	Lt David S. Sveden	525th TFS/36th TFW
	MiG-29*	F-15C 85-0114	Capt Cesar A. 'Rico' Rodriguez	58th TFS/33rd TFW
	MiG-25	F-15C 85-0101	Capt Richard C. Tollini	58th TFS/33rd TFW
	MiG-29	F-15C 85-0122	Capt Craig W. Underhill	58th TFS/33rd TFW
26 January	MiG-23	F-15C 85-0119	Capt Rhory R. 'Hoser' Draeger	58th TFS/33rd TFW
	MiG-23	F-15C 85-0114	Capt Cesar A. 'Rico' Rodriguez	58th TFS/33rd TFW
	MiG-23	F-15C 85-0104	Capt Anthony E. 'Kimo' Schiavi	58th TFS/33rd TFW
27 January	MiG-23 (2)	F-15C 84-0025	Capt Jay T. Denney	53rd TFS/36th TFW
	MiG-23	F-15C 84-0027	Capt Benjamin D. Powell	53rd TFS/36th TFW
	Mirage F1 EQ	F-15C 84-0027	Capt Benjamin D. Powell	53rd TFS/36th TFW
29 January	MiG-23	F-15C 79-0022	Capt Donald S. Watrous	32nd TFG attached to 53rd TFS/36th TFW

* crashed while chasing a EF-111A Raven
† flew into the ground while manoeuvring during dog-fight
§ 1st victory of the war.

Date	Aircraft destroyed	Aircraft	Pilot	Unit
	MiG-23	F-15C 85-0102	Capt David G. Rose	58th TFS/33rd TFW
2 February	Il-76	F-15C 79-0074	Capt Gregory P. 'Dutch' Masters	525th TFS/36th TFW
6 February	MiG-21 (2)	F-15C 79-0078	Capt Thomas N. 'Vegas' Dietz	53rd TFS/36th TFW
6 February	Su-25 (2)	F-15C 84-0023	1/Lt Robert W. 'Gigs' Hehemann	53rd TFS/36th TFW
	BO-105	A-10A 77-0205 *Chopper One*	Capt Robert R. Swain	706th TFS/926th TFG
7 February	Mil Mi-8	F-15C 80-0003	Maj Randy W. May	53rd TFS/36th TFW
	Su-20/22 (2)	F-15C 85-0102	Capt Anthony R. Murphy	58th TFS/33rd TFW
	Su-20/22	F-15C 85-0124	Col Rick N. Parsons	58th TFS/33rd TFW
11 February	Puma	F-15C 79-0048	Capt Steven B. Dingee	525th TFS/36th TFW
	Mil Mi-8	F-15C 80-0012	Capt Mark T. McKenzie	525th TFS/36th TFW
14 February	Helicopter**	F-15E 89-0487	Capt Richard T. Bennett (Pilot) Capt Daniel B. Bakke (WSO)	335th TFS/4th TFW
15 February	Mil-8 Hip	A-10A 81-0964 *Steal Your Face*	Capt Todd K. Sheehy	511th TFS/10th TFW
20 March	Su-22	F-15C 84-0014	Capt John T. Doneski	53rd TFS/36th TFW
22 March	Su-22	F-15C 84-0010	Capt Thomas N. 'Vegas' Dietz	53rd TFS/36th TFW
	PC-9	F-15C 84-0015	1/Lt Robert W. 'Gigs' Hehemann	53rd TFS/36th TFW

** *downed by laser-guided bomb*

Appendix VII

USAF Losses in Operation *Desert Storm*

Date	Aircraft	Cause	Crew/fate	Unit
18 January	F-15E Strike Eagle		Maj Thomas F. Koritz, pilot KIA Maj Donnie R. Holland, WSO KIA	53rd TFS/36th TFW*
19 January	F-4G Wild Weasel 69-7571	small arms fire	Pilot Capt Tim Burke, safe	81st TFS/52nd TFW
20 January	F-15E Strike Eagle		Col David W. Eberly POW Maj Thomas E. Griffith POW	4th TFW (P)
20 January	F-16C Fighting Falcon	SA-3	Maj Jeffery S. Tice POW	614th TFS/401st TFW
20 January	F-16C Fighting Falcon	missile	Capt Harry M. Roberts POW	614th TFS/401st TFW
24 January	F-16C Fighting Falcon		Pilot recovered at sea	
31 January	AC-130H Spectre 69-6567	missile	14 crew KIA	16th SOS/1st SOW
2 February	A-10A Thunderbolt II	AAA fire	Capt Richard D. Storr POW	
3 February	B-52G Superfortress	lost landing at Diego Garcia	3 crew recovered, 3 perished	4300th PBW (42nd BMW)
14 February	EF-111A Raven 66-0023		crew ejected, Capt Douglas L. Bradt, pilot KIA Capt Paul R. Eichenlaub II, EWO KIA	42nd ECS/66th ECW
14 February	A-10A Thunderbolt II 79-0130		Capt Stephen R. Phillis MIA	353rd TFS/354th TFW
14 February	A-10A Thunderbolt II 78-0722		1/Lt Robert J. Sweet POW	353rd TFS/354th TFW

* attached to the 4th TFW (P)

Date	Aircraft	Cause	Crew/fate	Unit
16 February	F-16C Fighting Falcon	non-combat	Capt Dale T. Cormier killed	17th TFS
17 February	F-16C Fighting Falcon 84-1218		Capt Scott Thomas rescued	17th TFS/363rd TFW (P)
19 February	OA-10 Thunderbolt II 76-0543	missile	Lt Col Jeffrey D. Fox POW	23rd TASS/ 602nd TAW
27 February	F-16C Fighting Falcon	SA-16	Capt William F. Andrews POW	10th TFS/363rd TFW (P)
27 February	OA-10 Thunderbolt II 77-0197 FAC	gunfire	1/Lt Patrick B. Olson KIA	23rd TASS/ 602nd TAW
13 March	F-16C Fighting Falcon	non-combat	pilot rescued	
31 March	RF-4C Alabama ANG	non-combat	Capt John Norman Pilot ejected Capt Jeff Kregel WSO ejected	

FAC *Forward Air Control*
TASS *Tactical Air Support Squadron*

Index